WAR OF THE MINES

WAR OF THE MINES

Cambodia, Landmines and the Impoverishment of a Nation
by Paul Davies with photographs by Nic Dunlop

PLUTO PRESS

First published 1994 by Pluto Press
345 Archway Road, London N6 5AA
and 5500 Central Avenue, Boulder, Colorado 80301, USA

94   95   96   3   2   1

British Library Cataloguing in Publication Data
A record for this book is available from the British Library

ISBN 0 7453 0859 7 hb

Library of Congress Cataloging in Publication Data
Davies, Paul, 1964–
War of the mines: Cambodia, landmines and the impoverishment of a
nation / Paul Davies and Nic Dunlop.
192 p. 30 cm.
Includes index.
ISBN 0–7453–0859–7
1. Political atrocities–Cambodia. 2. Cambodia–History–1975–
3. Mines (Military explosives)–Cambodia.   I. Dunlop, Nic, 1969–
II. Title.
DS554.8.D39   1994
959.604–dc20   94-2724
CIP

Designed and produced for Pluto Press by
Chase Production Services, Chipping Norton, OX7 5QR
Typeset from the author's disks by
Stanford Desktop Publishing Services, Milton Keynes, MK17 9JP
Scans by Data Layout, London, SE1 2TU
Printed in Hong Kong by Dah Hua

Contents

To my wife Helen,
without whose love and support I might never have started this book,
and would most certainly never have finished it.
And to our son, Jack William Samoeun.

Paul

To my mother and father

Nic

Foreword

Ben Kiernan, professor of South East Asian History, Yale University

The Cambodian civil war began in 1967 in a remote, hilly region called Rattanak Mondul. This long-suffering area finally receives the attention it deserves in this book, but not just for historical reasons.

By the time civil war broke out in Cambodia, international military meddling had already begun. Starting in the early 1960s, US special forces teams made secret reconnaissance and mine-laying incursions into Cambodian territory from South Vietnam. In 1967–68 800 such missions were mounted. One Green Beret team 'inadvertently blew up a Cambodian civilian bus, causing heavy casualties'. A total of 1,835 such missions were mounted before the March 1970 coup that overthrew Prince Sihanouk's regime, teams being authorised to lay 'sanitised self-destruct anti-personnel' mines up to 30 kilometres inside Cambodia. An unknown number of people were killed or wounded.[1] Thus, before the Vietnam War's full-scale spill-over into Cambodia in 1970 the country had already had much experience with the silent sentinels that would almost overrun it in 20 years.

After his Khmer Rouge regime came to power in 1975, Pol Pot outlined his strategy of continuing warfare in a secret speech: 'A people's war, and especially a guerrilla war,' he said, 'depends on mines and grenades. This is a strategic problem. We must solve it on a strategic basis.'[2]

He certainly managed to do that. My first understanding of this came ten years later while travelling at the other end of Cambodia from Rattanak Mondul, in the Eastern province of Svay Rieng. Vast areas north of the road looked abandoned. I enquired why. '*Chamcar meen,*' came the reply. It was the first time I had heard the literal Khmer translation of 'minefields'. Of the province's 200,000 hectares of arable land, as many as 10,900 had been sown with mines. Most had been planted in 1977–78 when Pol Pot's regime ordered

military attacks on Vietnam, aggression that eventually provoked a predictable reaction. The regime forcibly evacuated the population from the area (many were later massacred by the Khmer Rouge in Cambodia's north west), but the minefields' deadly harvest was only delayed – as the survivors returned to their homes after the Vietnamese invasion they began to blow themselves up: 1,595 Svay Rieng people were killed or wounded by mines in 1979 alone. Despite the absence of fighting in the province, by 1983 the number of local mine victims had reached 3,200.

Unfortunately, the mines moved west with the Khmer Rouge and Cambodia's internationally revived war. That is the story told in this excellent, horrifying book by Paul Davies and Nic Dunlop. It is the story of wars that overlap in time and of minefields that overlap in the ground. It is the story of a civil war returning to its geographical origins. But it is also the story of multinational involvement in the killing and maiming of civilians. It is also the story of officials behind the mine laying, who first deny having done it and then go private to tender for contracts to clear the mines.[3] Of an international agreement to 'assist with mine clearing' which is quickly shelved by those responsible for carrying it out, who choose to describe the mines as 'a Cambodian problem' and then walk away in triumph.[4]

Cambodians cannot walk away. In the words of Ron Podlaski, Cambodians continue to demine their country 'one limb at a time'. This is a story of terrorism on a world scale, cowardice of historic proportions, suffering on an everyday basis. But this is also a book about people's persistence, with heartening resolve and surprising promise.

Ben Kiernan
New Haven, Connecticut,
December 1993

Glossary and List of Acronyms

ANKI – Acronym for the Sihanoukist (royalist) faction's army during UNTAC period 1991–93

BLDP – Buddhist Liberal Democrat Party. One of the political parties spawned from the non-communist resistance, established to fight the UN supervised 1993 elections. Drawn from former members of the KPNLF (see below).

CGDK – Coalition Government of Democratic Kampuchea. Formed in 1982. An uneasy alliance of Khmer Rouge and the 'non-communist' resistance factions (KPNLF and Sihanoukists) operating out of Thai soil during the 1980s and early 1990s. The CGDK retained Cambodia's UN seat throughout the 1980s.

CMAC – Cambodian Mine Action Centre. The national Cambodian demining agency bequeathed to the new government after the elections, by the United Nations peace keeping operation 1991–93.

CPAF – Cambodian People's Armed Forces. The acronym by which the army of the State of Cambodia (the Phnom Penh regime) was known during the UN operation in Cambodia (1991–93).

CPP – Cambodian People's Party. The political party spawned from the ruling elite of the Vietnamese installed Phnom Penh regime which had ruled Cambodia during the 1980s and early 1990s. The party was formed to fight the UN supervised 1993 elections.

DK – Democratic Kampuchea. The name by which Cambodia was known during the period of Khmer Rouge rule, 1975–78. Re-emerged as the Khmer Rouge's official political title during the UN period (1991–93), during which time they were entitled to participate in the elections. They declined to do so.

EOD – Explosive Ordnance Disposal.

FUNCINPEC – the acronym for the Sihanoukist (royalist) party, formerly part of the non-communist resistance in Thailand, which fought the 1993 elections. Some of its officials had held high rank in the last Sihanoukist government of Cambodia, which was deposed in 1970.

HALO Trust - a British based humanitarian mine clearance agency.

ICRC – the International Committee of the Red Cross.

IDP – Internally Displaced Person. The term referred to those 200,000 or so Cambodians displaced from their home communities by the continuing warfare, even after the signing of the 1991 Peace Accords. They did not however leave Cambodian soil and were thus referred to as 'internally displaced', as opposed to the inhabitants of the Thai border camps who had been living as refugees outside Cambodia for much of the 1980s.

KPNLF – Khmer Peoples' National Liberation Front. The 'non-communist' resistance faction which formed part of the CGDK during the 1980s and controlled many of the border refugees, most notably the large camp of Site 2. It was composed of, in part, former members of the Lon Nol administration which had ruled Cambodia 1970–75.

KPNLAF – the armed forces of the KPNLF.

MAG – Mines Advisory Group. A British based humanitarian mine clearance agency.

MCTU – Mine Clearance Training Unit. The branch of the UN mission to Cambodia (1991–93) responsible for meeting the parts of the mandate which called upon it to 'assist in mine clearance'.

NGO – 'non-governmental organisation'. Humanitarian, non-profit aid agencies specialising in relief and development work in the nations of the South (for example Oxfam).

NCR – non-communist resistance. The two non-communist resistance factions – the KPNLF and the Sihanoukist – who together with the Khmer Rouge composed the CGDK during the 1980s. Together with the Khmer Rouge they operated out of Thai soil, waging war against the Vietnamese and the Cambodian regime they installed in Phnom Penh in 1979. The NCR received both 'lethal' and 'non-lethal' aid from the West, and in particular the USA.

PRK – the Peoples' Republic of Kampuchea. The title of the Vietnamese installed Cambodian regime which ruled Cambodia from 1979–89. Aka the 'Phnom Penh regime'.

SNC – Supreme National Council. The body created by the UN to enshrine Cambodian sovereignty in the interim period between the signing of the Paris Peace Accords (1991) and the elections (1993). It was to be composed of all four Cambodian factions (the former members of the CGDK and the Phnom Penh regime).

SOC – the State of Cambodia. In 1989, with the withdrawal of Vietnamese forces from Cambodia the PRK was renamed the State of Cambodia, and the flag was changed. This was merely a cosmetic change. Aka the Phnom Penh regime, the SOC reformulated itself as the CPP to fight the 1993 elections.

UNAMIC – United Nations Advanced Mission in Cambodia. Preceded UNTAC and started ground work for the peace process in Cambodia from late 1991 until the start of UNTAC activities in March 1993.

UNDP – United Nations Development Programme. The UN agency (multi-lateral) tasked to implement development programmes, usually large scale projects (such as infrastructure).

UNHCR – United Nations High Commissioner for Refugees. The UN agency responsible for refugees. In the Cambodian peace process, UNHCR was tasked to repatriate the 360,000 Cambodian refugees who had been displaced into the border camps in Thailand during the 1980s.

UNICEF – the UN relief and development agency with particular mandate to address the needs of women and children.

UNTAC – United Nations Transitional Authority in Cambodia. The UN body created to oversee the implementation of the peace process as defined in the Paris Peace Accords, signed by all four Cambodia factions in October 1991. The central objective was to create a 'neutral political environment' in which free and fair multi-party elections could be held and a new Cambodian government formed that would be internationally recognised. The mandate period ran for 18 months from March 1992. Elections were held in May 1993.

UN 'Time' – the term by which Cambodians referred to the period of the UNTAC operation in Cambodia.

USAID – the bi-lateral aid agency of the United States government.

World Food Programme – the UN agency responsible in Cambodia for ensuring that food rations were supplied to IDPs, and later returnees from the Thai border.

Author's Note

As this book goes to press attention must be drawn to a renewed wave of fighting in Rattanak Mondul and Banan districts, south western Battambang. In March 1994, government forces succeeded in driving Khmer Rouge units out of Pailin, in western Rattanak Mondul. However, on 18 April, these troops were forced back out of Pailin by a Khmer Rouge counter-offensive which caused a rout on the government side. The following two weeks saw the newly constituted Royal Cambodian Armed Forces (RCAF) pushed back through Treng, Sdao and into Banan district. The entire population of Rattanak Mondul, and much of that of western Banan, district are currently displaced from their homes: 30,000 plus civilians are living as refugees just outside Battambang town. Last week, the RCAF received reinforcements, and the Khmer Rouge have currently been pushed back to Sdao, although it is feared that much of the civilian infrastructure in the area has once again been destroyed, and presumably fresh mines have been laid – possibly in areas which had been slowly cleared during 1993 and early 1994. However, there is also some good news to report: CMAC's short term funding crisis seems now to be resolved and its medium term prospects are looking far brighter than when the last draft of this book was written. Both these updates serve to draw attention to the fact that this book was always going to suffer from a problem of 'timeliness', recording as it does a snapshot of Cambodian life during a fast moving period. Nevertheless, it is felt that the essential themes and structures touched upon here are of enduring importance. Equally, some of the images of people, places and institutions, although even now dated, needed to be recorded as they appeared to those on the ground during the frenetic days of the UN time. As Kundera points out, the struggle of civilisation is the struggle of memory against forgetting. Many of these albeit transitory images, especially those of the UN – viewed from below – need to be remembered.

Paul Davies
8 May 1994
Eaglesfield, Cumbria

MAP 1

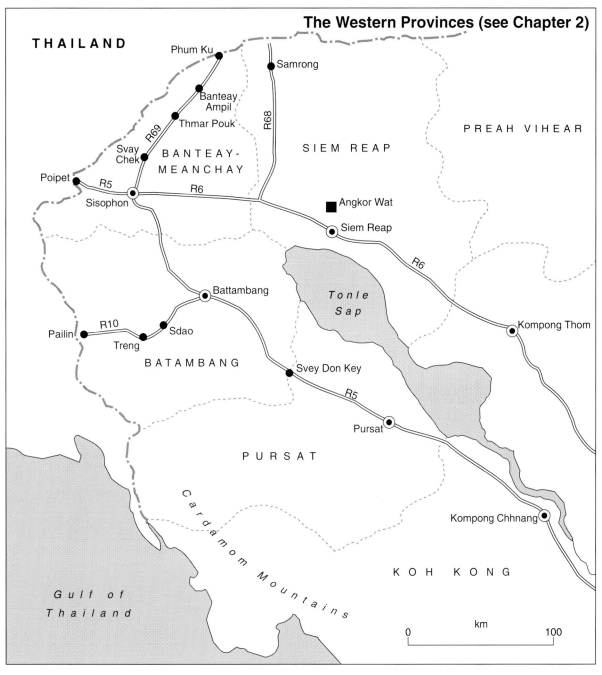

MAP 2

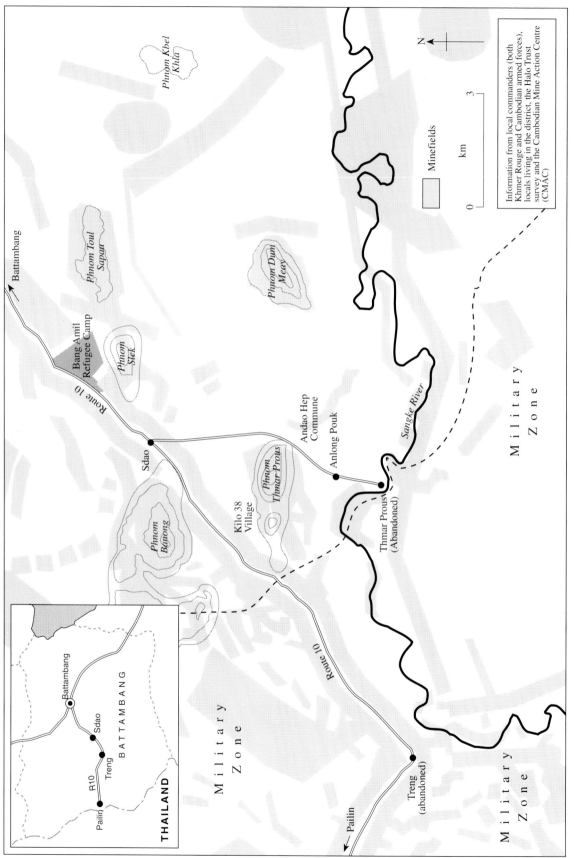

Phnom Kbel Khla

Phnom Toul Sapan

Phnom Dum Meay

Battambang

Bang Amil Refugee Camp

Phnom Siek

Route 10

Sdao

Phnom Banong

Andao Hep Commune

Anlong Pouk

Phnom Thmar Prous

Kilo 38 Village

Sangke River

Thmar Prous (Abandoned)

Military Zone

Route 10

Pailin

Treng (abandoned)

Military Zone

Military Zone

N

km

0   3

Minefields

Information from local commanders (both Khmer Rouge and Cambodian armed forces), locals living in the district, the Halo Trust survey and the Cambodian Mine Action Centre (CMAC)

THAILAND

Battambang

Sdao

Treng

R10

Pailin

BATTAMBANG

MAP 3

Mine producing and mine affected countries

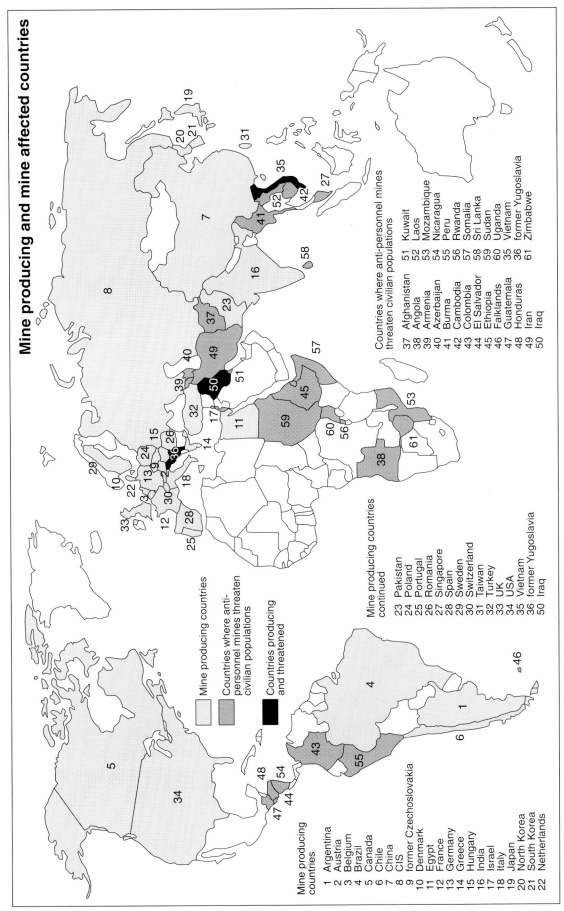

Mine producing
countries

1 Argentina
2 Austria
3 Belgium
4 Brazil
5 Canada
6 Chile
7 China
8 CIS
9 former Czechoslovakia
10 Denmark
11 Egypt
12 France
13 Germany
14 Greece
15 Hungary
16 India
17 Israel
18 Italy
19 Japan
20 North Korea
21 South Korea
22 Netherlands

Mine producing countries
continued

23 Pakistan
24 Poland
25 Portugal
26 Romania
27 Singapore
28 Spain
29 Sweden
30 Switzerland
31 Taiwan
32 Turkey
33 UK
34 USA
35 Vietnam
36 former Yugoslavia
50 Iraq

Countries where anti-personnel mines
threaten civilian populations

37 Afghanistan   51 Kuwait
38 Angola   52 Laos
39 Armenia   53 Mozambique
40 Azerbaijan   54 Nicaragua
41 Burma   55 Peru
42 Cambodia   56 Rwanda
43 Colombia   57 Somalia
44 El Salvador   58 Sri Lanka
45 Ethiopia   59 Sudan
46 Falklands   60 Uganda
47 Guatemala   35 Vietnam
48 Honduras   36 former Yugoslavia
49 Iran   61 Zimbabwe
50 Iraq

☐ Mine producing countries

▨ Countries where anti-
personnel mines threaten
civilian populations

■ Countries producing
and threatened

MAP 4

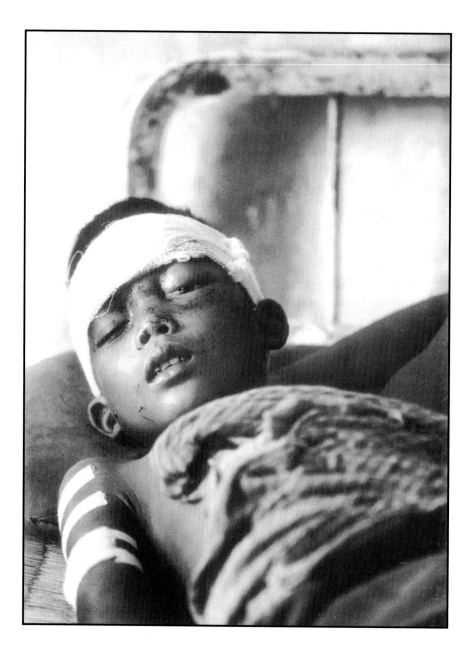

Statement of
Endorsement

War of the Mines is a study of the impact of landmine warfare on communities. Landmines kill and maim their victims, leaving profoundly disabled societies; they impoverish the survivors by denying them access to land and natural resources; the fear generated by their presence creates its own psychological and cultural damage. The lethal and enduring legacy of landmines means that such dangers persist long after direct hostilities are ended, the only remedy being the painstaking and costly removal of mines.

Landmine warfare is therefore a humanitarian issue of the gravest concern.

It is intended that the documentation presented here will focus and enhance support for the worldwide movement seeking to restrict the manufacture, distribution and deployment of these weapons and to ensure they serve only a short-lived, military purpose so that they do not endure to wreak havoc on civilian communities in the long term. It is also intended that the material presented here will give an accurate insight into the nature of the mine problem in Cambodia and the assistance that is most appropriate.

We, the undersigned, endorse these aims having witnessed at first hand, in the course of our humanitarian work, the appalling effects of landmines in Cambodia. We are convinced that a revision of current international regulations is vital if an effective solution is to be found to safeguard future generations from the threats created by landmine warfare. With so many millions of mines, manufactured predominantly by the nations of the north, now at large, predominantly in the nations of the south, this is an issue which needs to be addressed urgently.

The authors acknowledge that all opinions expressed and conclusions reached in this book are theirs alone and that they do not necessarily reflect the individual or collective views of the undersigned.

AAR Cambodia Committee
Action Cambodia
Adventist Development and Relief Agency
American Friends Service Committee
Association of Medical Doctors for Asia
AustCare
Australian Catholic Relief
Australian Third World Health Group
Cambodia Canada Development Programme (CCDP)
Cambodia Development Resource Institute
Cambodia Trust
Campaign to Oppose the Return of the Khmer Rouge (CORKR)
Church World Service
CIDSE
Community Aid Abroad (CAA)
Danish Cambodia Consortium (DCC)
GOAL
Groupe de Recherche et d'Echange Technologiques (GRET)
HALO Trust
Handicap International
Human Rights Watch
International Rescue Committee (IRC)
International Women's Development Agency (Australia)
Japan Overseas Christian Medical Co-operative Service (JOCS)

Japan Sotoshu Relief Committee (JSRC)
Jesuit Refugee Service – Asia/Pacific
Jesuit Refugee Service – Cambodia
Khemara (Cambodian NGO)
Krousar Thmey (Cambodian NGO)
Lutheran World Federation
Mani Tese
Mary Knoll
Mercy Refugee Service, Institute of the Sisters of Mercy
Mines Advisory Group
Overseas Service Bureau
PACT
PADEK
Physicians for Human Rights
Redd Barna
Refugee Council of Australia
SAWA
United Nations Association of Great Britain
United Nations High Commissioner for Refugees (UNHCR)
United Nations Children's Fund (UNICEF)
Vietnam Veterans of America Foundation
Volunteer Services Abroad – New Zealand
World Council of Churches
World Relief
World Vision International – Cambodia

Acknowledgements

The author and photographer would like to thank the following humanitarian agencies without whose generous financial assistance and commitment this book would not have been produced:

Mines Advisory Group (MAG)
World Vision International – Cambodia
UNICEF
UNHCR

… and all those who pledged to buy advance orders of the book, in some cases before it was even written.

As ever, there are innumerable individuals to whom we owe a debt of gratitude for their help, co-operation and support. In particular we would like to thank Rae McGrath of the Mines Advisory Group (MAG) for his unstinting support for, and belief in, the project, especially when it was in its earliest stages and few others were interested. We would also like to thank Justin Byworth, Jaisankar Sarma and Bryan Truman of World Vision International who gave the project initial financial and moral support. A deep debt is also owed to David Appleton, formerly Field Director of the Cambodia Trust Limb Project in Phnom Penh, without whose help, encouragement and sanity, the project might never have been finished. Special thanks should also go to Sandy Koun who painstakingly transcribed the interviews conducted in Cambodia, and to Professor Adam Roberts and Francoise Hampson who spent much time guiding us through the basics of international humanitarian law. We would also like to thank: Ben Kiernan and Peter Carey; Robb Jones, Norman Stewart, Gary Elmer, Chris Horwood and Lou McGrath; Keith Hardy and John Leicester of the Post Publishing Co. Ltd (Bangkok); Helen Davies and Ruth Ashe; Tim Grant and the MATT team; Suzanne Walker, Denise Coghlan; Bobby Muller, Ed Miles, Ron Podlaski and all at the Indo-China Project, Kean Khleang; Darren Wells, Andy Smith and those at the Cambodia Trust; John Ryle; Peter Newman, Woody (for the dems), Mike Croll, Matthew Middlemis, Duncan Gilchrist and all at the HALO Trust – Cambodia; Mieke Bos, Noel Mulliner, George Focsaneanu, Dave McCracken, Jim Vince and Vishw Ambhar Singh; Steve Troester, Fr Jim Noonan, David and Judy Saumwebber, Ven. Maha Ghosananda, Bob Maat, Liz Bernstein, Kevin Malone and Joan Healey; Alf Bjarkoy, Yukio Kanda, Paul Donovan; Heniz Trebbin, Phillippe Steiner and all the staff of the ICRC in Cambodia; Benoit Denise, Alan Nichols, Jiraporn Punchanawat, Pi Noy, Pi Cong, Pi Im, Khun Chat, and all at Chat's studio; Tony Oliver; John and Pat McGraw (for the use of the 'Dungeon'), Julius Pottinger and Robin Bell Printers. Special thanks are also owed to John Pilger and David Munro for much of the inspiration. Thanks to Sio Leang Seang and all the staff at Rattanak Mondul district hospital, Kev Sophal and his staff at the district office in Rattanak Mondul, Drs Paet Vut and Sophi and the staff at the Battambang military hospital, Dr Said and staff at the Phnom Penh military hospital, and the staff of all the provincial hospitals we visited and photographed.

Lastly, we should extend our special thanks to those Cambodian friends who worked with us during the first part of 1993 as we set about researching and photographing this book: Plong Khemara, Bos Sophal, Heng Gao, Darrin and Samouen of the Rural Health Team, Ky Ka and Ky Lok, Senith, Ravi and, during the last stages of our work, Khieu Savann. Without them there would also be no book!

Introduction

Mines have been described as 'perhaps the most toxic and widespread pollution facing mankind'.[1] This book arose as a result of our experiences of Cambodia, just one of at least 35 countries where landmines constitute a humanitarian problem.[2] For Paul the turning point came after he had witnessed the arrival at Rattanak Mondul district hospital of Ches Sary, a 25-year-old mother who was two months' pregnant with her second child. She had been digging bamboo shoots on the banks of the Sang Ke river when a mine detonated, destroying one of her legs. The force and barbarity of the injuries produced by mines is shocking, and to witness such events without acting would seem to amount to complicity with a profoundly unacceptable situation. From such experiences, experiences – which also haunted Nic as he worked in Cambodia – the idea of this book was born.

However, it was not only the horror of the injuries that motivated the book. In agricultural areas where mines deny civilians access to land, they are often the single most significant cause of impoverishment of the entire community. Due to the fact that modern anti-personnel mines endure with lethal capacity for decades, these effects – the maiming and killing of innocent civilians and the impoverishment of the broader community of which they are a part – will continue to bring misery for generations unless they are systematically removed by professionals. With an insidious multiplier effect, mines shatter human potential and drain resources throughout the entire fabric of society, and for these reasons sections of the book address broader issues, such as the medical implications of landmine warfare and the cultural and psychological problems associated with the physical handicaps suffered by the survivors of mine accidents. Lastly, it is argued that landmines as a class of weapon, because of their indiscriminate, enduring and multi-faceted impact, should be considered as distinct from other conventional weapons: their effects place them on a par with chemical and biological weapons, already vilified under international law.

It is argued here that to respond realistically to what should properly be considered one of the worst manmade ecological disasters of modern times, with perhaps as many as 100 million mines already deployed worldwide, nothing short of a complete ban on the manufacture, export and deployment of these weapons will do. Of late, there have been encouraging signs that such a goal, which seemed like so much wishful thinking in the late 1980s, may not be beyond reach. During the autumn of 1993 the US government sponsored a resolution at the United Nations calling for a three-year global moratorium on the export of anti-personnel landmines. Only sustained public pressure can ensure that a complete ban is forthcoming, and it is hoped that everyone who reads this book will wish actively to support the growing international momentum working towards this end.

The global crisis that now exists, however, is a far cry from the origins of the modern anti-personnel landmine in the trench warfare of the the World War One. Anti-personnel landmines were originally conceived of as a means of defending larger landmines that were designed to incapacitate another military innovation of that war, the battle tank. As their 'effectiveness' became apparent, however, they came to be regarded as a weapon in their own right in the period between the two world wars, and were developed to *deny* large tracts of land to the enemy and to *channel* movements on the ground. While such usage of mines in World War Two, for example, was directed at or laid in defence of specific military targets, clean-up operations are still going on today in the affected areas of Europe and Africa. *Mines, unlike other weapons, recognise no ceasefires*. Instead of learning the lessons of these conflicts, weapons manufacturers continued to refine their products, and military strategy came to be led, to some extent, by the technology available. Thus, by the early 1960s strategies of random deployment using aircraft and other systems of 'remote delivery' were introduced; inevitably civilians came to bear the brunt of such military innovations.

While there are numerous legal, technical and military definitions of mines and related weapons, it is important always to consider them in terms of the *impact* they have on civilians, civilian infrastructure and the environment as a whole: such *real* definitions may often be at variance with the *official* definitions given for manufacturing, military or political purposes.[3] Having said this, there are essentially four types of anti-personnel mine, all of which are commonly found in Cambodia.

1. *Blast mines*: laid on the ground, or just below the surface, these mines injure or kill their victims by means of the blast effect of their explosive content. They are usually initiated by the pressure of a footstep applied to the top of the mine. In Cambodia, arguably the commonest mine of this type deployed is the PMN-2. These mines were originally manu-

factured in the former Soviet Union. Blast mines can be 'defended' by a series of strategies such as the incorporation of anti-handling devices. Type 72 mines, produced by China, are also commonly found in Cambodia. The Type-72B variety, while essentially indistinguishable from the 72A when laid, has such an anti-handling device, a tilt-mechanism functioned by a metallic printed electronic circuit. While the low metallic content of the 72A makes it extremely difficult to detect without the most sensitive equipment, the 72B identifies itself more readily, however if it is tilted through ten degrees it will detonate.

2. *Fragmentation mines*: usually laid above the ground, these mines employ either a packing of fragments or a segmented outer casing which, when dispersed by the force of the explosion, is the prime cause of injury of the victim. The Soviet-manufactured POMZ-2 and POMZ-2M are the most commonly found mines of this type in Cambodia. They are usually mounted on stakes which are driven into the ground and initiated by means of a trip wire laid out at leg height. Such trip wires are extremely difficult to spot, especially in areas with a lot of undergrowth. POMZ mines have an effective range of 25–30 metres.

Above left: PMN-2, above right Type 69, below left: POMZ, below right Types 72 A and B

3. *Bounding fragmentational mines*: these mines employ a primary charge to elevate the mine to a predetermined height before the main charge is initiated. They are initiated by means of either a trip wire or pressure. In Cambodia the most common example of this type of mine is the Chinese-made Type 69. Often these are buried with only the tip of the fuse showing, though sometimes they are merely surface-laid, and protected by a belt of blast mines such as the Type 72. The average burst delivers 240 fragments, producing a 360 degree killing zone, with a radius of approximately 11 metres. Unlike both blast and simple fragmentation mines, these mines are generally designed to kill, although when the victim who initiates the mine is travelling in a group, multiple injuries are common due to the mine's large effective radius.

4. *Directional fragmentational mines*: these are either mounted above ground on their own stand or tied in trees, and can be detonated either remotely by means of trip wires or by command. Once activated, such mines have the capacity to kill and injure several people due to their large killing zones. The MON-50 mine, again originally manufactured in the former Soviet Union, has a 50 metre killing zone. While such mines are less common in Cambodia,

at least six varieties of this mine type have been found in the country.

According to information produced by the Cambodian Mine Action Centre[4] at least 28 different varieties of anti-personnel mine are commonly found in the country, the vast majority of which were manufactured in the former Soviet Union, China and Vietnam. However, mines from the USA, Thailand, Bulgaria and Belgium are also included in their listings. There are countless further variations of threats to the civilian population in Cambodia, not only from unexploded ordnance – shells, mortars, grenades, etc, all of which can have mine-type effects since they are all potentially victim-activated – but also from a variety of booby-trapping techniques which employ simple electronic switches and explosives. Also it has been fairly common practice in Cambodia to lay anti-personnel blast mines on top of anti-tank mines, thereby adapting such mines and allowing them to be initiated by a footfall, even that of a child. While it is virtually impossible to produce any definitive list of mines in existence worldwide, records of the Mines Advisory Group document nearly 750 types of landmines and switches, and this listing is far from comprehensive. *Jane's*[5] lists over 30 nations that produce, or have produced, mines, including the United Kingdom, Italy, France, Brazil, the USA, and even nations not renowned for their military pretensions such as Sweden, Switzerland and Japan.

A deadly legacy: mines and ordnance found in Cambodia

1
A Cambodian Chronology

802 AD: Jayavarman II established the Kingdom of Angkor, in the area to the north of the Tonle Sap.

Tenth to thirteenth centuries: height of the power of Angkor. It dominated south east Asia, controlling much of contemporary Thailand and all of 'Cochin-China', or the Mekong Delta area of what is now Vietnam. Cambodian territory extended west into modern-day Burma, south into the Malaysian peninsula and north into Laos. The glories of this period were immortalised in a great temple complex which grew up at Angkor, just to the north of the modern-day town of Siem Reap. Completed in 1150, Angkor Wat has become the enduring symbol of Khmer greatness. Devoted to the Hindu god Vishnu, it remains the largest religious building the world has ever known.

Angkor Wat: heart of the Cambodian Nation

1432: Angkor had to be abandoned under pressure from the Thais, and the empire entered a steady decline.

Eighteenth century: Cambodia had become a pawn in the power games of its powerful and expansionist neighbours, the Thais and the Vietnamese, who by this stage had carved up much of the modern-day country between them. The ruler of what remained of Cambodia was reduced to mere vassal status, seeking protection from whichever of his powerful neighbours offered the best terms. At this time Cambodians were being 'killed and uprooted in a series of ruinous wars carried on inside [their] territory by the Thai, the Vietnamese and local factions'.[1] Such a description could almost directly be applied to 1980s Cambodia, except that both the Vietnamese and the Thai were to some extent vassal states themselves, pawns in a larger game of cold war *real politik*. In the 1990s the course of events in Cambodia will, no doubt, continue to be strongly influenced by the continuing regional rivalry of Thailand and Vietnam.

1863: the very survival of Cambodia was, ironically, ensured by the imposition of a French 'protectorate', and the country became the fifth province of France's Indo-China empire (the empire also included modern-day Laos and Vietnam). Cambodia was 'developed' primarily in order to serve the resource needs of the jewel of France's south east Asian possessions, Chochin China (or southern Vietnam). Cambodia became something of a backwater, and even the formation of the Indo-China Communist Party in 1930 by Ho Chi Minh failed to produce much of a ripple.

But it wasn't only the territorial integrity of Cambodia that was 'rescued', by the French protectorate. Following the discovery of the Angkor Wat temple complex, French scholars were responsible for recreating the national mythology which told of past greatness eroded by the encroachments of scheming neighbours, within which pride of place was reserved for the Vietnamese who for cultural reasons were particularly despised, and continue to be so today.

1941: The French installed 19-year-old Prince Norodom Sihanouk as king. Sihanouk became the most important political personality of the following half-century of Cambodian history.

1954: Cambodia gained its independence from France, and its neutrality was recognised at the Geneva Conference on Indo-China.

1955: not wishing to share power with the emergent political classes, Sihanouk abdicated in favour of his father and entered politics directly. His party won a convincing victory in the elections held that year under the auspices of an International Control Commission established by the Geneva Conference. In Cambodia traditional loyalties to the nation, Buddhism and the throne as personified by Sihanouk were all evocative motivators, and continue to be so today.

The following ten years witnessed a period of relative stability and prosperity as Sihanouk, following his policy of 'extreme neutralism', attempted to keep Cambodia out of the growing conflict in neighbouring Vietnam. During this period he received large amounts of aid from both western and eastern bloc nations. However, as the conflict intensified, walking this tightrope became increasingly difficult. In 1963 Sihanouk cut ties with the US, believing (correctly) that the communists were going to win the struggle in Vietnam.

The US bombing campaign in Cambodia: the destructive equivalent of 25 Hiroshimas

Domestically, through the 1960s, Sihanouk's somewhat autocratic regime struggled, but ultimately failed, to keep control of an internal political environment that was polarising sharply between an emergent urban middle class drifting to the right and republicanism, and intellectuals on the left who believed that only radical policies could overcome the poverty which afflicted the bulk of Cambodia's still rural population, and the all too obvious corruption of the ruling elite.

1963: a small group of radicals fled Phnom Penh for the jungles of the north east, and established the insurgent group that Sihanouk was later to term the 'Khmer Rouge'.

1965: following US intervention in the war in southern Vietnam, the rebel communist forces (National Liberation Front) took refuge in Cambodian territory. Throughout the late 1960s the legendary Ho Chi Minh trail, down which supplies were carried from North Vietnam to the insurgents in the south, was located inside Cambodia.

1969: as his domestic position worsened Sihanouk attempted to re-establish links with the US, but the victory of the 'hawk' republican, Richard Nixon, in the presidential elections of 1968 had to some extent sealed his fate. Without the permission of Congress, the President mounted a massive and secret B-52 bombing campaign of communist 'sanctuaries' inside neutral Cambodia. The bombings failed in their objectives and succeeded only in pushing the Vietnamese deeper into Cambodia, radicalising the peasantry and dislocating social and economic life in many parts of the country. The campaign continued until 1973 when Congress, which had finally learnt to scale of the operation, called a halt. Estimates suggest that at least 150,000 civilians were killed and many more maimed by the bombings (over half a million tonnes of bombs were dropped, estimated to have had the destructive equivalent effect of 25 Hiroshima style nuclear explosions). In May 1973, the CIA reported that Khmer Rouge recruiters were 'using the damage caused by the B-52 strikes as the main theme of their propaganda', and that such propaganda was proving 'effective'. The bombings cost US$7 billion: Cambodians are still being killed and maimed today as a result of left-over unexploded ordnance.

1970: Sihanouk was deposed in a coup by his Prime Minister, Lon Nol, who established the Khmer Republic. Despite protestations that it was not directly involved, the US wasted no time in declaring that, as Sihanouk had been deposed 'legally', the question of recognition 'does not arise'. They were to provide some $1 million a day in aid to prop up the Lon Nol government, which proved to be hopelessly corrupt and ineffectual.

Sihanouk formed a tactical alliance with the Khmer Rouge and, partly as a result, the movement rapidly grew. Cambodia descended into destructive civil war. By 1972 some 2 million Cambodians had been made homeless. Many made their way to Phnom Penh as rural areas progressively came under the control of the communists, whose brutality, even then, was becoming known. Lon Nol fell into a parasitic dependence on American aid for survival, let alone victory.

1975: the 1973 Paris Agreements which ended direct US involvement in the Vietnam War, to some extent, were the writing on the wall for Lon Nol. A little over two years later, the Khmer Rouge were in control of Phnom Penh.

The Khmer Rouge sought totally to transform Cambodia: its society, economy, international standing, borders, beliefs, language, even thoughts. Its revolution was total revolution, obtainable only through total social control, and terror was the mainspring of this control. During the three and a half years of the regime, over 1 million Cambodians died from hunger, overwork, disease and routine executions for the smallest 'offences'. But murder was more than just a by-product of the Khmer Rouge's policies; for some, murder became *the* policy.

Toul Sleng: 20,000 people were detained here for 'questioning' during the Khmer Rouge years; seven survived

Many subgroups were purged almost to extinction: the educated and those 'contaminated' with foreign influences, those connected with former Cambodian regimes, Buddhist monks, the Chinese, Muslim Chams and, especially, the ethnic Vietnamese. As the regime became progressively less stable, internal purges of party cadre, especially those from the eastern zone neighbouring Vietnam, grew in intensity, with many dying at the hands of torturers in the infamous Toul Sleng detention centre in Phnom Penh. Even under the narrowest definitions of the term, what the Khmer Rouge achieved in Cambodia between 1975 and 1978 can only be described as genocide.

An integral part of Pol Pot's (the 'Brother Number One' of the Khmer Rouge movement) vision of the new Cambodia, known as Democratic Kampuchea, was a resurrection of the past glories of the Angkorean empire, and this manifested itself in particular in an obsessive desire to regain territories lost several centuries before to the Vietnamese in the Mekong delta area.

On May 10th (1978) Radio Phnom Penh broadcast the extraordinary call to exterminate the Vietnamese race and 'purify' its own ranks. 'In terms of numbers, one of us must kill thirty Vietnamese ... that is to say, we lose one against thirty. We don't have to engage

8 million people (Cambodia's presumed population). We need only 2 million troops to crush the 50 million Vietnamese, and we would still have 6 million left'.[2]

Border clashes had started just a month after the Khmer Rouge seized power in 1975, and grew in intensity over the following years. In 1978 the Vietnamese attempted, unsuccessfully, to persuade the UN to establish a demilitarised zone along the Cambodian border. By the end of the year they had had enough. On 2 December 1978 Hanoi announced the formation of a 'National Salvation Front', made up mostly of those who had fled or defected from the Khmer Rouge. These forces, together with 120,000 Vietnamese troops, launched an invasion of Cambodia on Christmas Day 1978.

Genocide: the policies and practices of the recent past ...

1979: on 7 January Phnom Penh fell to the Vietnamese, and Khmer Rouge resistance in the vast majority of the country collapsed by the end of the month. However, the success of the 'liberation' did not mean peace for Cambodia. By 14 January, with the Khmer Rouge's leading cadre refugees in Bangkok, and with the rump of its broken and bloodied forces pushed into the Thai border, a secret Thai-Chinese meeting had agreed terms for the support of a guerrilla war by Pol Pot's men

against the Vietnamese in Cambodia. For the Chinese this was viewed as a means of countering what they perceived as encirclement by the Soviet Union (the Vietnamese, having been refused a normalisation of relations with the USA, had forged stronger links with the USSR) and of continuing support for their co-religionists, the Khmer Rouge. For the Thais the proxy war would directly address the need to rebuff their traditional rival, Vietnam, and would stem the ideological threat, represented by the invasion, of a 'domino effect' of the spread of communism through south east Asia. As an added incentive the Chinese promised to cease support

1978: liberation became occupation

for the troublesome Thai communist party. So too in the US the proxy war to be fought against Vietnam using Cambodian guerrilla forces operating out of the Thai border area provided an opportunity to humble the Vietnamese after their victory in 1975, to firm up their recently restored relations with China and to counter what they too perceived as expansionism by the Soviet bloc. The stage was set for the 'civil war' which was to ravage Cambodia throughout the 1980s, the war in which landmines were to play, perhaps for the first time ever, the dominant long-term role.

In September 1979, despite its now internationally known genocidal record in Cambodia, the Khmer Rouge retained its seat in the UN:

> Vietnam's military drive against Democratic Kampuchea, begun on Christmas Day of 1978, was finally checkmated on the green and gold floor of the United Nations. The Pol Pot regime might have been reduced to a band of guerrillas in the hills, but it was voted in as the only legitimate representative of the Cambodian people.[3]

For the next 12 years the United Nations proved to be one battleground where influential friends, following an increasingly anachronistic cold war logic, would ensure that Pol Pot's men were as invincible as his chauvinistic mythology had suggested.

1982: support for the Khmer Rouge was becoming increasingly embarrassing nonetheless. Thus, after much negotiation the 'Coalition Government of Democratic Kampuchea' (CGDK) was formed. This involved a superficial alliance of two 'non-communist' factions – the rump of the Lon Nol regime (known as the Khmer People's National Liberation Front (KPNLF)) and a new Sihanoukist faction. For the West and its allies in the region, the 'non-communist' resistance (NCR) provided a convenient fig leaf for established policy. Somehow they claimed the NCR would emerge as a 'third force' in Cambodian politics, that the Khmer Rouge could be ditched and an accommodation with the Vietnamese reached. However, the primary function of the NCR throughout the 1980s remained the legitimation of continued support for the Khmer Rouge dominated resistance operating out of Thailand, and its role remained one of keeping up the military pressure on the Vietnamese. As Professor Ben Kiernan has noted, the CGDK was neither a coalition nor a government nor democratic nor, even, in Cambodia.

But the war that was fostered in Cambodia during the 1980s was fought with more than just military means: it was also fought with humanitarian aid. Following the defeat of the Khmer Rouge, Cambodia descended into chaos and the population, already weakened by years of brutality under the Khmer Rouge, was faced with starvation. During the emergency phase of the relief operation (1979–82), when UN humanitarian agencies were permitted to work out of Phnom Penh, some $300 million was spent on assisting the 300,000 refugees who had ended up in the resistance-controlled camps along the Thai border; the *same amount* was spent on assisting the remaining 6.5 million Cambodians living inside the country under Vietnamese control. During the 1980s while aid was maintained to the border camps, the rest of Cambodia was to become the only Third World country denied UN development aid – aid that was needed to restore what had been lost both during the war in the early 1970s and under the Khmer Rouge. Infant mortality before the age of five years rose to 20 per cent, and only 5 per cent of the population had access to safe drinking water. Little wonder, then, that Oxfam published a book which argued that international policy on Cambodia came down to Punishing the Poor.[4]

Furthermore, during the 1980s the war ate up some 40 per cent of the meagre resources of the Vietnamese-installed Phnom Penh regime, itself a significant factor in the country's continuing impoverishment.

1989: Vietnamese troops withdraw

1989: as a result of the collapse of the eastern bloc Vietnam finally accepted that it could no longer maintain its forces in Cambodia, and in September the last units were withdrawn. While aid to the newly named State of Cambodia (SOC) government in Phnom Penh collapsed, those who had funded the resistance on the border maintained their support. As a result, as the Vietnamese withdrew the resistance swarmed over the border and the war intensified. The following two years saw a surge in mine-laying.

1991: with the odds stacked against it the State of Cambodia government of Prime Minister Hun Sen had little choice but to accept the terms the international community was offering for a 'comprehensive settlement' of the Cambodian problem – which meant an inclusion of the Khmer Rouge and the dropping of references to its genocidal past in the agreements. (This had now been ambiguously rephrased as the 'policies and practices of the recent past'.) On 23 October, the Paris Peace Accords were signed by the four belligerent Cambodian factions, who agreed to end the war, demobilise their forces and allow to an unprecedented degree the UN (or more precisely the United Nations Transitional Authority in Cambodia (UNTAC)) to run their country during an 18-month interim period, at the end of which multi-party elections would be held and a new constitution drafted. In the meantime Cambodian sovereignty was to be enshrined in a Supreme National Council (SNC) on which representatives of all four factions would sit. Twelve years after the end of its genocidal regime, the Khmer Rouge was set to return to Phnom Penh.

UNTAC, Phnom Penh, 23 October 1992: celebrating the 'peace'

11 March 1992: UNTAC operations got underway in Phnom Penh.

13 June 1992: Phase II of the peace plan was to have commenced. It called for disarmament and the cantonment of 70 per cent of the 250,000 troops of the four factions. Initially, the State of Cambodia and the NCR complied; only the Khmer Rouge refused to honour the agreement. As a result Phase II was essentially abandoned, and the UN's goal of establishing a truly neutral political environment ahead of the elections was made virtually impossible.

12 January 1993: Khmer Rouge guerrillas launched their first attacks against UN peace-keeping forces.

10 March 1993: Khmer Rouge guerrillas were blamed for the massacre of 33 ethnic Vietnamese villagers near the Tonle Sap. As a result of a growing campaign of terror by the Khmer Rouge against the ethnic Vietnamese in Cambodia, up to 20,000 fled the country, often losing everything in the process. The UN appeared powerless to intervene.

Kompong Thom, 1992: refugees flee Khmer Rouge offensive

5 April 1993: UN Secretary General Boutros Ghali launched the election campaign. The Khmer Rouge announced its intention to boycott, and later to disrupt, the elections, set to take place in May.

23 May 1993: voting commenced in heavily fortified polling stations and was successfully completed five days later. The result left no party with the necessary two-thirds majority in the constituent assembly and demanded an enforced compromise between the royalist FUNCINPEC Party and the Cambodian People's Party (CPP), which was composed of the members of the former State of Cambodia government. UNTAC Chief Akashi announced that the elections had been 'free and fair', and thus were acceptable to the UN.

Over the ensuing months Cambodia was finally readmitted to the international community from which it had vanished in 1975. It adopted a new constitution by which it reverted to a kingdom with Sihanouk as head of state, and prepared itself for the challenges ahead. Perhaps the foremost of these remained the Khmer Rouge who continue to lurk in its traditional strongholds of the jungles and mountains of Cambodia, and whose enduring links with Thailand meant that it would remain a threatening force. However, perhaps equally damaging to the prospects for meaningful peace in rural areas remained the landmines, the litter of war, a deadly legacy that continues to reap its harvest of suffering despite the UN's qualified success in bringing peace to Cambodia.

Going home: the UNHCR repatriation operation returned over 350,000 refugees from the camps in Thailand, only to find much of the land taken up by landmines

Cambodia: one of the world's most heavily mined countries

2
Cambodia and the Landmine Burden: A General Overview

Landmines have been described as the 'weapon of choice … in Cambodia'.[1] As a result, conditions described in the following chapters on Rattanak Mondul, widely considered to be one of the most heavily mine-affected districts in Cambodia,[2] are by no means unique. Rather, the reality of 'living with landmines' as described in the Rattanak Mondul chapters is repeated, to lesser or greater degrees, throughout much of Cambodia. In fact, so widespread is the landmine problem in Cambodia that a minefield mapping programme undertaken by the Cambodia Mine Action Centre in Phnom Penh now contains information on minefields in well over 50 per cent of Cambodia's land area.[3] Lt. Col. George Focsaneanu, Assistant Director of the Cambodia Mine Action Centre (CMAC), referred to the scale of the landmines problem in Cambodia during an interview conducted in Phnom Penh in late March 1993 as follows:

> when people talk about mines in Cambodia, they say there are 4–10 million mines … and some people say 'rubbish, there's less than a million'. Well I can assure you, there are more than 4 million mines. All you have to do is look at certain minefields to come to that conclusion. We have one minefield on the south eastern coast … It's 54 km long and contains 360,000 mines. That's a lot of mines.[4]

If these estimates are accurate there may be as many landmines in the country as Cambodians. When were these mines laid? Why were they laid? Why have mines become the 'weapon of choice' in Cambodia? Beyond the obvious human suffering, what is the nature of the burden that mines exert on Cambodian society? These are some of the questions this chapter, a thumbnail sketch at best, will attempt to address. Further detailed studies will have to be made for the true scale of the burden to be made clear. However, the indications are that such a study may not be too long in the making. Over the past five years the issue of landmines has dramatically emerged from the shadows. In 1993 the Phnom Penh NGO Forum pronounced that 'Landmines are the single biggest factor hindering the development of Cambodia'. Finally, the truth of the war waged by landmines in Cambodia is being realised.

Caught in the Crossfire: Mines Arrive in Cambodia

The first anti-personnel mines in Cambodia were laid during the Vietnam War period. In 1967, with Sihanouk's permission, the North Vietnamese army established a series of bases and supply routes along the country's eastern borders. These bases were protected with mines. In response, the United States Airforce, in covert operations which lasted from 1969 to 1973, launched an aerial assault on both the bases and the supply lines, the latter known collectively as the legendary Ho Chi Minh trail.[5] The Americans used not only heavy bombs in these assaults but anti-personnel mines as well, known to the aircrews that delivered them as 'garbage', which were scattered over much of the border area.[6] American Special Forces also responded, fielding units known as Salem House (and later Daniel Boone) teams, who were allowed to delve up to 30 km inside neutral Cambodia in pursuit of the 'enemy' and their Cambodian bases.[7] As they went, the teams were allowed to place anti-personnel landmines.

Following the coup in 1970 the war between the communist forces – the Khmer Rouge and the North Vietnamese (who also fought each other even in the early 1970s) – and the Lon Nol regime, brought conflict to the rest of the nation, and with it came landmines. Even then mines were hardly used in a conventional manner, as Haing Ngor, the doctor, writer and actor (Ngor played Dith Pran in the film *The Killing Fields*) recalls:

> [Lon Nol troops] advancing toward huge, noisy, enthusiastic Khmer Rouge meetings in the country-side, would find only loudspeakers and a tape player – and landmines buried around the tree that the sound equipment hung from.[8]

With the signing of the Paris Peace Accords in 1973, Vietnamese troops withdrew from the Cambodian theatre and the Khmer Rouge were left to fight the war alone. However, by this stage Pol Pot's men controlled large swathes of the country, particularly in the north. In such 'liberated zones' self-contained agricultural co-operatives were established and sealed off from the outside world with booby-traps and guards, creating what Elizabeth Becker describes as 'miles-wide tracts of no-man's-land',[9] a grim warning of the wasting of the land that continued mine warfare produces. No one heeded the warning. As the war neared its conclusion Lon Nol troops increasingly came to rely on mines to beef up defences at key installations and strategic points, such as bridges.

Mines from these earlier periods of conflict were never systematically cleared: 'Many of those mines are now overgrown by vegetation, immersed in water or simply forgotten, but they may be no less lethal as a result'.[10] The contemporary Cambodian mine problem has been growing for nearly 30 years.

During the Khmer Rouge period, and particularly from 1977 as Vietnam was increasingly identified as the movement's number one enemy, mines were once more laid along the eastern borders, again to protect key crossing points and military installations. But mines were also used on the Thai borders to the west. Just as the movement had used booby-traps to seal off agricultural co-operatives in their 'liberated zones' in the early 1970s, they now sought to replicate that policy on a grander scale. They dreamt of fashioning Cambodia into one enormous and hermetically sealed co-operative.

And mines were a perfect ally, ensuring that few would dare to escape from the 'prison without walls', as Cambodians refer to their country during this period. As Haing Ngor's account of his border crossing after the fall of the Khmer Rouge regime indicates, for those who did take their chances the risks were huge:

> We walked cautiously around a bend and came upon the site of a mine explosion. It was a blood-splattered scene, an arm hanging from a tree branch, part of a leg caught in the bamboo. Ten or more dead lay by the side of the path, and many more were wounded. I made a tourniquet, removed some large pieces of shrapnel from wounds, tied makeshift bandages and advised the relatives on preventing infection. With no medical supplies there was little more to do. It was a terrible way to die, or to be maimed, after living through the Khmer Rouge and coming so close to freedom.
>
> The mines appeared on either side of the path, sometimes in the middle. They had coin-size detonator buttons, white or rusted in colour. From the detonator buttons, trip lines made of nearly invisible white nylon thread led to tying-off points such as trees or rocks nearby … All we knew was that we had to keep our eyes on the trail, searching for white threads.[11]

Khmer Rouge times: 'An agrarian utopia'

For the Khmer Rouge, the use of landmines, not only for military purposes but as an instrument of terror for social and economic control over civilian populations, has been a constant element of its thinking and practice for over 20 years. A 1993 Asia Watch report makes this point very clearly. The authors write of a district in south western Battambang:

> The Khmer Rouge in this area used landmines to expropriate land from local villages for their own enrichment. In 1992, the Khmer Rouge claimed control of about 180 hectares of rice paddy belonging to several villages, by planting landmines around it. The guerrillas then planted rice in the fields, or selectively allowed villagers access to their land, demanding two sacks of rice per hectare farmed (a hectare generally yields about 10 sacks of rice). At ploughing season, the Khmer Rouge forced villagers to plough four hectares of land for them before working their own land, a day's work … No one ever refused, out of fear … At the time of the Asia Watch visit, the party (the Khmer Rouge) was continuing to lay mines to expand control of territory in the surrounding villages; it was also charging villagers for safe access through the mines to forests and fields.[12]

Agriculture remains Cambodia's lifeblood

Similarly, during a major offensive in the central province of Kompong Thom, in the first half of 1992, the Khmer Rouge drove villagers from their homes and mined the perimeters of the land it had captured, while at the same time demining the fields inside its newly expanded 'zone'. When the task was complete the Khmer Rouge imported new residents from camps under its control on the border. Unlike UNHCR, whose struggles with the mine problem and land availability for returnees were largely unproductive in heavily mined provinces like Battambang, the Khmer Rouge's brutal integration of landmine warfare into its broader socio-political strategy ironically produced startling results for those under its control.

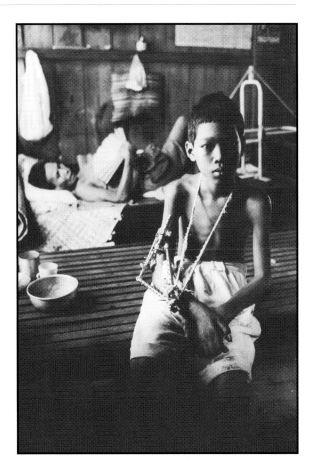

Kompong Thom, 1992: shot by the Khmer Rouge

The Weapon of Choice, 1979 on …

But it isn't just the Khmer Rouge who are to blame for the current burden of mines in Cambodia. Since 1979 the Vietnamese and their clients in Phnom Penh, as well as the two 'non-communist' resistance factions (the NCR), have also relied very heavily on landmines. In part, this was a product of the nature of the war, a guerrilla conflict, where battle lines were extremely fluid and insurgents often penetrated deep into the country, far from their bases, situated on both sides of the Thai border.[13] From 1982 onwards, under what was known as the 'Coalition Government of Democratic Kampuchea' (CGDK),[14] the guerrilla armies of both the NCR and the defeated, but reconstructed, Khmer Rouge movement co-ordinated strikes against the Vietnamese-installed Phnom Penh regime. Mines were laid to protect base areas of factional control and to deny obvious access routes from these areas. They were also deployed to protect key installations and strategic assets (railways, roads, bridges etc.), often tens of kilometres from the 'front lines'. These usage patterns, established early, were maintained for much of the next ten years, and the consequences are all too obvious in the minefield maps drawn up in Cambodia during the UN peace-keeping operation (1991–93). These maps tell the story of the war in its unresolved relics, the uncleared mine fields. They mirror vital communications infrastructures, reveal forested areas and hills (from which the guerrillas might strike and through which they travelled), and display where old forts and frontlines have been. Indeed, it may be the case that never before in the history of archaeology or conflict has so much been told of a war from manmade relics left unwanted in the ground.

In Kampot and the provinces of the south east, CPAF soldiers dared not venture into the minefields laid around the forest-covered hills through which the Khmer Rouge has traditionally moved and from which it launched hit-and-run attacks. In the central province of Pursat minefields shadow the railway and road which traverse the province *en route* from Phnom Penh to the Thai border. Minefields edge the hills, forests and key forts, especially on the roads running south through the lowlands of central Pursat, towards Thailand. These old fields clearly show who controlled what over the years. The same is true in Siem Reap, home of the famous Angkor Wat, which itself has not escaped the scurge of minefields, several of which can be found inside the historic temple complex. Unlike Pursat, mine warfare is not a thing of the past here: in Siem Reap the Khmer Rouge base areas in the north of the province have slowly extended south over the years, through the once thick forests. By 1993 only tongues of CPAF-controlled territory, surrounding key highways, extended precariously north. In April 1993 it was the ability of the Khmer Rouge to engage in 'nuisance mine laying' anywhere in the province which most belied the CPAF's claim to control 40 per cent of Siem Reap. Within the DK areas the minefields showed old fronts and forts, while key towns still under CPAF control were ringed with still tactical minefields – at Samrong, Srey Noi, Angkor Chum. North–south roads, which eerily disappeared into the DK zone, finished their journeys in CPAF lands amid great plugs of minefields and looked like puny stoppers trying ineffectually to stem the holes in the dam wall. But it is the old minefields of Banteay-Meanchay which most graphically tell the tale of changing boundaries between factional zones. Massive swathes run in great straining arcs from either side of Poipet on the Thai border, following the forest fringe east and then north to give protection to the provincial town of Sisophon and its links north along Route 69 from the NCR, and to the south its mirror image, trying to contain the Khmer Rouge and, of late, bandit groups.

However, in terms of the history of the overall conflict, and of mine laying in Cambodia perhaps the key moment came with the 1984 dry season offensive:

Until 1984, the war in Cambodia followed a seasonal pattern. During the rainy season, when heavy military equipment was, for the most part, useless, guerrillas from the border camps were able to infiltrate throughout Cambodia, spreading their propaganda, recruiting new fighters and engaging in sabotage. During the dry season, Vietnamese troops, with help from the fledgling army of the People's Republic of Kampuchea (PRK), would push the guerrillas back to the border.

In late 1984 … the Vietnamese launched a major offensive against the guerrillas and their encampments on the Cambodian side of the border. For five months they pounded the border with artillery fire, sending some 220,000 civilians and combatants fleeing into Thailand … With the guerrillas pushed into Thai territory, the Vietnamese effectively sealed off the border by laying extensive minefields. Similarly, the Thai's and resistance forces, fearing a Vietnamese invasion, heavily mined key positions just over the border … [by late 1985] …. Mines were reportedly placed around the camps to prevent Vietnamese incursions – or to control the movement of refugees.[15]

Of all the minefields laid in Cambodia, perhaps even in the world, the K5 barrier belt is the most notable. Started in 1985, the belt runs from the south western coast of Cambodia, up the Thai border to Laos. It is over 600 km long and contains an estimated 2–3 million mines. The barrier originally consisted of more than just a minefield, however: a complete series of anti-tank ditches and a huge bamboo 'fence' were constructed by the Vietnamese using forced Cambodian labour. Every family in Cambodia was supposed to send one member to contribute to this 'national service'. In reality the privations of the labourers and the danger from both mines and malaria meant that, just like military conscription, the burden fell disproportionately on the poorest in society, and rural communities. Rich families paid the poor to take their places. Many of the 25,000-plus amputees in Cambodia today were injured during the construction of the barrier belt,[16] whose name, K5, is an Anglicised version of the Cambodian *Kor Bram*, the term now used to refer to all forced labour in Cambodia.[17]

The K5 field is extremely densely laid but does not constitute a totally unbroken belt. In some areas it exists only at obvious access points, between the hills. Furthermore, it is a fairly discrete field, varying in width from 1 to 2 km, along the Thai border, while the sections adjacent to Laos are relatively 'thin', and contain only an estimated 92,000 mines.[18] However, in many areas the K5 mines were laid on smaller, patchy fields and put down in previous years by the Thais, Vietnamese, NCR or Khmer Rouge. Further mines have been laid in these areas since the completion of the K5 belt. The result is one of the most heavily mined strips in the world. This is, however, also true of many other areas in Cambodia, particularly in the north west – 'Even the term "minefield" has no real relevance in the border areas because it indicates a formality that does not exist'.[19] Peter Newman of the Halo Trust has cited an example of overlaying minefields along the K5 belt area, in this case just north of the Cambodian border town of Poipet, at the start of one of the thickest sections of border minefields:[20]

> Let me give you a classic … We were looking at the area immediately to the north and east of the town. This area is basically a shanty town. Now it's actually sitting on top of a minefield. We found one of the CPAF officers who was there through a lot of it, and he told us the history. Back in about 1980 the Vietnamese laid a minefield. The ground there is very soft and over the next few years the mines sunk and disappeared. And a few years later when new commanders arrived, he demanded a new minefield thinking there weren't any mines there. So they laid a minefield. And then when the Vietnamese withdrew, the CPAF laid a new minefield, since the previous mines had sunk again. So, there's now three minefields, one on top of the other, all in that one little area. And now they've built a village on top of it. And there have been a lot of casualties there. A lot of it has been demined by the locals, but because these three fields have sunk down so much, no one knows exactly what's in there, what the concentration is, etc. That is a major task.[21]

Not only does this anecdote reveal the problem of overlaying and the historical development of very serious mine problems in certain areas, it also illustrates quite graphically one of the other characteristics of mine laying in Cambodia – the almost total disregard for mapping. Critics of the demining effort in Cambodia contrast the pace with which Kuwait was demined following the Gulf War, and the apparent apathy that has characterised the effort in Cambodia. However, this disregard for the rules of mapping minefields has been one of the key technical differences between the two countries. Not only did the Iraqis lay their minefields 'as per Western textbook patterns', they were scrupulous about their minefield mapping and fencing, which greatly speeded the demining effort. These minefields were planned and laid down with conventional military aims in mind – denying access and channelling enemy movements, thus bringing attackers into the 'killing zone' of defensive fire power.

In Cambodia hardly any minefield records exist. CMAC's Sgt Jansen noted that while the Vietnamese laid mines in orderly patterns which make good military sense, no maps have been passed on to local CPAF

POMZ mine casings, Halo Trust house, Mongkol Berei

commanders whose current division level battle maps will show where old minefields are located, but only in rough terms. But the Vietnamese and CPAF forces were not the only ones to disregard systematic mine mapping. The authors of *The Coward's War* note that 'Several [CGDK] resistance fighters told us that in many parts of the border belt, their own mines were as great a threat to them as those left by the enemy.'[22] They cite a KPNLF soldier, interviewed in Site 2 in Thailand:

> Nobody likes laying mines, but everyone uses them. On my first active duty we had a leader who kept a notebook about where we put mines, all the experienced fighters laughed at that and asked 'Who will read such a book?' I thought it was a good idea, but only if others did the same thing and, of course, they don't. Last year, we were ordered to put mines near a path. As we were doing this I had a feeling – you know – when you think you know a place, that you have been in the place before. Anyway, my attention was distracted because one of the others was blown up, then the man on my right shouted that we were in a minefield and started to walk back to the path and he stood on a mine. I was the only one who got out without being killed or injured. I moved slowly and

carefully, using a stick to check the ground. I knew then why I knew the place, why I remembered it – I had put mines there only three months before. We were putting mines in our own minefield – it was crazy, killing our own fighters.[23]

Similarly, the demining agency the Mines Advisory Group, while working on a series of former military bases, police stations and bridges in the south eastern district of Moung Russey in Battambang province, found that often CPAF soldiers have been the victims of their own minefields. In March 1993 on one site in Phum Krakach where a former CPAF fort existed, a farmer living next to the minefield reported that despite repeated Khmer Rouge attacks in the area, the only person to have died on the minefield had been a CPAF soldier whose unit had taken over the base in 1989 and decided to remine it. The unit had not received maps from the former unit showing where existing mines had been laid. CMAC sources in Phnom Penh confirmed that such incidents were common.

In practice, the quality of minefield record keeping has depended entirely on local personnel on the ground, and on their individual qualities. While most have disregarded mapping rules, some, out of personal initiative or sheer common sense, have made and maintained detailed maps. Warrant Officer McCracken of CMAC came across several engineering officers, like one from the north eastern province of Stung Treng, who had made detailed and accurate maps of the local minefields. McCracken said that the man jealously guards these records and refuses to release them to anyone, even the UN, for fear of them being lost. Back in Banteay-Meanchay, Peter Newman had also discovered occasional individuals, such as the village leader in Anlong Tanang, who had gone against the grain and maintained local records. In general though, accurate knowledge from committed individuals who have witnessed the mine-laying in one area is rare; often those who laid the mines have died or returned to their home communities, sometimes on the other side of the country. Little corporate knowledge remains, but for demining agencies it is vital to identify and link into such local knowledge where it exists.

During the last years of the Vietnamese occupation, with the K5 belt established, the military situation in the interior of Cambodia stabilised slightly. However, particularly in the north western areas of the country, the heavy border minefields did not prevent continued incursions from the resistance. Apart from attempting to secure the borders, Vietnamese mining philosophy in Cambodia sought to protect key military installations and settlements. In troubled areas, key towns were heavily mined and turned into forts, for example Svey Chek north of Sisophon in Banteay-Meanchay, on the tactical highway Route 69 which runs parallel to the border. Despite the protection the K5 belt was supposed to afford, the resistance forces often established effective control of the land in between these strong points and the border. Where Vietnamese defensive minefields ended, NCR or Khmer Rouge fields began, each seeking to protect their enclaves in disputed territory. As front lines moved, so the development of historic but now tactically worthless minefields occurred.

Arguably the most significant episode of mine-laying in Cambodia, however, followed the final withdrawal of Vietnamese troops in September 1989. This precondition of the recent UN peace initiatives for Cambodia, ironically, brought deadly sowing of fresh mines. The power void created by the removal of 200,000 combat-hardened Vietnamese soldiers and their hardware from Cambodia produced two main effects. First, now required to face the combined onslaught of the resistance armies on their own, the fledgling CPAF forces panicked. Jointly strangled by the western-led international embargo on the State of Cambodia, and facing a dramatic reduction of eastern bloc aid, of which the Vietnamese withdrawal was only the most obvious manifestation, CPAF fell heavily on the one major resource they had at their disposal – an enormous quantity of anti-personnel mines. CMAC sources confirmed that CPAF commanders had

engaged in a 'massive' mine laying campaign to beef up their defences at this time. Second, perceiving the weakness of CPAF forces, resistance armies swarmed over the border, launching their biggest offensive of the war to date. The offensive brought conflict, and mine-laying, deeper into Cambodia than had been the case for years. Not only were mines laid in new areas where conflict was ongoing, as the Rattanak Mondul case study reveals, but mines were laid with terrorist intent, demoralising and impoverishing communities that the resistance could not hope to control.

It had long been a characteristic of Vietnamese mine laying that the fields, while following set patterns as in western practice, were of extremely high concentration. Such a high concentration approach was taught to CPAF officers, although their mine-laying was generally less disciplined and ordered. In the minefields of Banteay-Meanchay western demining experts have been shocked by the densities of mines that have been discovered. Sometimes as many as three or four mines per square metre have been found. Such densities are totally unnecessary for standard 'defensive/access denying' military purposes. For example, CMAC sources suggest that if western armies were to lay a 'heavy' minefield, 6 metres deep, they would randomly deploy mines in six rows throughout the depth of that field, so that someone approaching the field would encounter one mine on every metre of minefield frontage. This field, being fenced, would require the enemy to consider every square metre as potentially containing a mine, while in reality only one in six would have a mine in it. The subtlety and economy of such an approach is not evident in Cambodian mine-laying. A diagrammatic comparison is given in Figure 2.1.

In April 1993 Lt. Col. Mulliner, then commanding officer of the UN's Mine Clearance Training Unit (MCTU), noted the different style of mine-laying adopted in Cambodia. During an interview at MCTU HQ in Phnom Penh he said:

> the way the mines were laid by the Afghans is different to the way the mines were laid here. The Cambodians seem to have absolutely no shortage of mines. And I have watched a minefield being demined up in Svey Chek, what they have done is they have put a post in wherever they find a mine, ... in one row ... they are literally about a foot apart and there's just a string of them for about 60 yards, and then there's a double line ... about 2 feet apart. Now that's a hell of a quantity of anti-personnel mines going down, unmarked and designed not to channel (movements), but to maim or to kill.

The Cowards' War confirms that mines have been used in enormous quantities:

> The high density of mines along the border can be inferred from the reported numbers of mines removed in the Thmar Pouk area by clearance teams funded by the US Agency for International Development. They said in an interview with our delegation in April 1991 that teams had dealt with 6,000 anti-personnel devices in a one kilometre stretch of ground close to an old Vietnamese post and 3,800 mines in another two kilometre section.[24]

Lacking the manpower and armaments to defend their country, the CPAF used mines perhaps more exten-

Figure 2.1: Deployment of mines

Standard western field

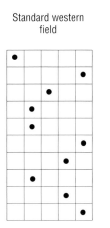

High-density Cambodian field

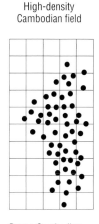

Orderly western pattern – economic, effective and relatively easy to remove if properly mapped

Dense Cambodian field – multiple mines per square metre with little order

NB Such representations are not reproductions of actual fields, but merely intended to give an idea of the different volumes used, and the lack of discipline of Cambodian mine laying.

sively than any other army. As the project manager of the demining NGO, Norwegian Peoples Aid, noted, 'a mine is a soldier standing guard without supplies, night and day'. Mines were used by the CPAF, just as they were by the Vietnamese, to protect key installations against sabotage, to defend strategic areas. Extensive fields were also laid to isolate resistance fighters from local populations by mining forest edges and boundaries between zones of influence, as well as to control roads, which at night are impossible for them to patrol and secure (these mines are then removed at first light). However, mines have also been incorporated in offensives. For example, when CPAF forces lost control of Svey Chek in Banteay-Meanchay during the post-Vietnamese offensive in December 1989, mines formed a key element of their counter-offensive, as *The Cowards' War* notes:

> In February 1990, government troops shelled the village, after surrounding its perimeter with landmines. In the ensuing battle, hundreds of civilians were killed or wounded. By March, Svey Chek was back under government control. Since then government troops have been able to keep their soldiers well supplied ... but the government's greatest deterrence according to KPNLF forces is the wide belt of mines that surrounds the village ....[25]

The report later stresses the key role of mines in the Cambodian conflict:

> A Red Cross worker in Battambang … put it this way: 'The problem with mines here in Cambodia … is that they are the most important weapon … Here there is not a lot of direct confrontation of soldiers in one place … There are no maps because mines are given to soldiers like bullets.'[26]

Also in Battambang, talking with soldiers about how they deployed mines, the authors of *The Cowards' War* heard:

> We put them around the Pol Potist (resistance) positions at night, and they do the same to us. We also use them in the forests and in places where we think the enemy will go. Also, when we find their (resistance) minefields, we sometimes put our mines among them, which gives them problems if they try to pick up their mines to use in other places.[27]

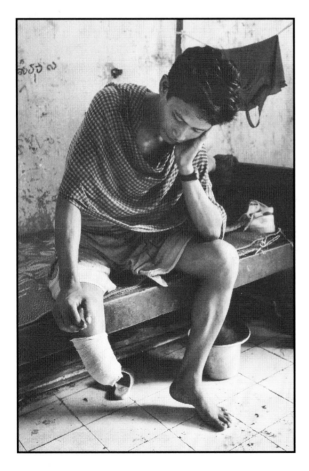

Who is to 'blame' – Cambodian Cowards?

Is this, therefore, a war fought by cowards, or does the blame lie elsewhere than with some 'defect' inherent to Cambodians? Certainly, the extent to which mines have been used, and the intentions with which they have been laid in Cambodia produces a cowardly form of warfare similar in ethos to that denounced in the western media when describing the activities of 'terrorists'. Such intense and irresponsible landmine warfare leads inexorably to enormous long-term problems for civilians populations. As such it is an inexcusable form of warfare. Furthermore, the limited amount of direct contact between the combatants in Cambodia's festering civil war has given rise to accusations of cowardice, and even laziness, as evidenced in these comments by Warrant Officer McCracken of CMAC:

> Landmines are the lazy man's weapon. You show me a check point where the soldiers are awake at any time of the day or night. And how can they afford to sleep? Because they have sown mines around their outposts, even the smallest ones.[28]

The Halo Trust's Peter Newman has also encountered this 'landmine-dependent' attitude in the course of his demining work:

> … not only have you got all the different factions laying the mines, but within the Government forces as well … there's…. the local militia laying them, the official army, the police, and just for good measure the farmers picking them up, moving them and laying them themselves … I cleared a school south of Sisophon … And I had been told categorically 'no mines there'. But it turns out that the local police had put up a little hut … [opposite the school] … and they laid mines. But it wasn't recorded as anything part of the official plan, not that there was much of a plan anyway. This was a local initiative.[29]

However, it has to be stressed that this type of combat has evolved partly out of necessity. Especially since the Vietnamese withdrawal, this has been a 'low budget' war, at least on the CPAF side. Fought between small groups of lightly armed men charged with either attacking or defending huge tracts of land, kilometres of roads, railways and numerous bridges, mines have become the all pervading 'ally'. As much as they are the weapon of the coward, landmines are also the weapon of the poor. Easy and cheap to produce, transport, store and lay, the durability of mines makes them perfect for this type of protracted dispute. CMAC sources cite examples of PMN-2s, one of the most commonly found mines in Cambodia, being unearthed after ten years, and 'once they've had the dirt wiped off they look like new'. Even in harsh environmental conditions such mines remain deadly for decades.

To a lesser extent mines have permeated the strains and stresses of ordinary life, too. As a result of Cambodia's internationalised internal conflict, much of the traditional infrastructure, including law and order, has broken down. Since mines are available and very cheap, Cambodians use them to protect their homes, livestock, fishing ponds and boats and even to settle disputes – a sad but pragmatic response to circumstances. With regard to the village of Kuok Chas in Banteay-Meanchay, the Halo Trust's Peter Newman told me:

There is also an element of anti-banditry mining. At Kuok Chas, the villagers still lay mines on the eastern side of the village at night … and there's no way they are going to let us take them. Every couple of nights someone comes into the village and lifts the livestock. Quite understandably, they don't like it, so they lay a few mines.[30]

This is a dependency into which Cambodians have fallen socially, just as much as they have fallen militarily. The 'militarisation' of Cambodian social and even cultural life has become one of the most alarming traits of recent years.[31] It may be that exposed to similar circumstances those who judge Cambodians might behave in a similar fashion. Indeed, after only a few months in the country some are already aping Cambodian practices: 'One [UN] provincial administrator whose home had recently been robbed told Asia Watch he now placed landmines around his residence every night'.[32]

Like drug addicts, Cambodians have found themselves engaged in self-destructive dependency. And, as in the drugs world, it is the pusher who is really to blame for fostering and enabling the dependency. That mines have been supplied to the Cambodian factions by their backers in enormous quantities is beyond dispute. As recently as March 1992, when the civil war was at one of its lowest ebbs for many years, Warrant Officer McCracken of CMAC visited the CPAF National Army dump on the road to Kompong Speu, south west of Phnom Penh. He found 19 huge bunkers. He entered only one such bunker but found it stacked top to bottom with landmines, from Vietnam and the former Soviet Union. He estimates there may have been as many as 1 million mines in this dump alone. As he pointed out, additional mines will be stored at divisional, regimental, company and platoon levels. There might be as many as 4 million mines still in store on the CPAF side – a grim reminder of what might lie ahead if peace is not genuinely established quickly in the post-election period, and a testament to how Cambodia came to be so afflicted today.

But it is not only the CPAF forces of the Phnom Penh regime who have received vast supplies of foreign-made mines. The resistance forces, both non-communist and Khmer Rouge, also have their backers and sponsors. While Chinese support for their ideologically sympathetic brothers in the Khmer Rouge, delivered via the easy conduit of Thailand, is well known, what has been kept hidden from the public gaze is support from the west for first the Khmer Rouge and, after 1982 for the Coalition Government of Democratic Kampuchea. John Pilger claims that US Congressional 'overt' and 'covert' aid to the 'non-communist resistance' (NCR) may have amounted to at least $24 million during the 1980s.[33] It is not surprising therefore that mines manufactured in the west have been found in Cambodia, or that western-made arms and mines were allegedly observed by an English aid worker inside the Khmer Rouge zone near Pailin, Battambang, during preparations for the major offensive in 1990 which devastated Rattanak Mondul.[34]

However, perhaps the most startling revelation concerning western involvement with, and support for, the non-communist resistance, has involved the role of British forces in training these Cambodian fighters, a fact subsequently admitted in Parliament. *The Cowards' War* has shown that while Khmer Rouge mines strategy 'tends to mirror Chinese doctrine … the strategy of the KPNLF and ANS – the two non-communist resistance factions – reflects British special forces training'.[35] This training, conducted from 1983 until at least 1989, by the Special Air Services (SAS) and the Royal Thai Army, focused on the use of improvised explosive devices and booby-traps, as well as the use of conventional munitions, including mines. The report continues:

Our informants said that the overall objective of the course was to produce effective field commanders who could operate independently in enemy territory, with emphasis on the destruction of military and civilian infrastructure. The students were taught practical command skills … including the use of minefields as a planned and hasty defence.[36]

When publicly challenged about this involvement the British government initially denied it, but was finally forced to admit its involvement.[37]

While the sponsors of the Cambodian factions were prepared to supply and superficially train them in the laying of mines, none seem to have taught them 'responsible usage',[38] according to the rules of war. This includes, for example, knowledge of how to map and fence minefields, an appreciation of the essentially short-term nature of a minefield, and an ability to demine the fields when their usefulness is over. As CMAC sources have rightly observed, to train and supply people to lay mines without ensuring an understanding of their proper usage is almost a criminal act.[39] For example, Cambodians who had attended the SAS courses said that 'British instructors taught their class how to draw a map of a minefield, but explained that "such maps are rarely drawn and it's hardly practical to bother with them".'[40] Without mapping, the task of demining becomes much harder, and locals can determine safe areas and paths only by trial and error involving the loss of life and limb.

Despite the resources invested in the British courses, none of the factions had been taught to demine safely. In the course of one day's attempted demining in Kompong Thom, for example, seven non-communist, Sihanoukist troops died while operating sophisticated metal detectors they had no idea how to use.[41] The eastern bloc suppliers of mines to the Phnom Penh regime have been equally negligent in this area. While, there had been no shortage of resources when it came to providing mines, economies were sought in the 'peripheral' areas. Warrant Officer McCracken noted:

> CPAF have done some demining in Kompong Thom, Siem Reap and in other provinces. Basically, their sappers don't know how to demine – and this comes down to resources, CPAF does not have the finances to properly train its soldiers in demining, nor to provide the equipment. CPAF's demining technique involves using a 3 metres long rake. In Banteay-Meanchay, I talked to a local commander about his success rates in using these techniques. The commander would only admit to one casualty, and he had been 'doing it wrong'. 'What did he mean', I

asked? 'Oh, when you use the rake to demine you are to look away from the minefield. This man was looking at it and was injured in the face. He lost an eye,' the commander replied.

The Demography of Genocide Part II, and the Meaning of the Landmine 'Equation'

> in Cambodia … a third of the population is male and two-thirds are female. Well who are the guys who are getting killed at a rate of 300 a month – they're males … so now you are destroying the male population … adding another burden to the nonexistent infrastructure.
>
> Lt Col. George Focsaneanu, CMAC,
> Phnom Penh, March 1993

During the week of 14–19 March 1993 CMAC had information on 56 separate landmine accidents resulting in over 100 casualties.[42] It is highly unlikely that this was untypical or that it represented the true numbers injured and killed during that week – the reality was probably much worse. As in Rattanak Mondul, those dying in remote areas sometimes never even make it on

Battambang provincial hospital: a 14-year-old boy recovers from a mine injury

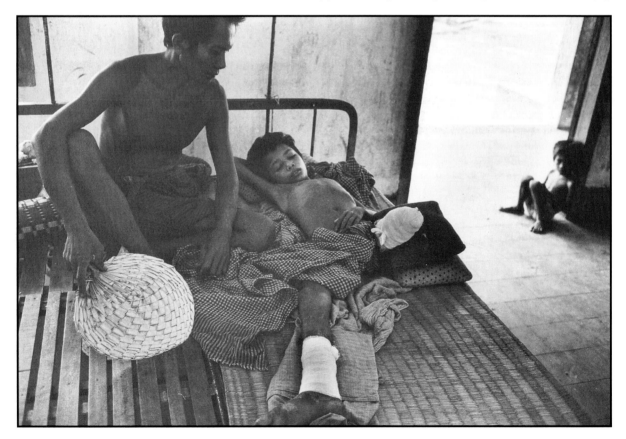

to official Cambodian statistics, let alone statistics held by foreigners. For every mine victim who survives an accident at least one dies, if not two, before reaching hospital. Overall statistics are very hard to come by. However, some impressions can point towards the scale of the problem. Handicap International (HI) estimates that in the latter half of the 1980s and in the early 1990s there were approximately 200 amputations per month, nationwide, the results of mine accidents. Over the last half of 1992 and in early 1993 that rate roughly halved to around 100. However, evidence from several sources seems to suggest that roughly 40 per cent of mine accidents result in amputations.[43] Thus we can estimate that during the first half of 1993 there may have been approximately 250 survivors of mine accidents every month, to which a further 250–500 deaths should be added before the true figure appears.

It is not the raw volume of the casualties that is worrying but rather, as Lt Col. Focsaneanu suggests, the fact that this is happening at a time when Cambodia's population is already out of balance, the result of decades of civil war and the genocidal rule of the Khmer Rouge which claimed the lives of more males than females. This imbalance is now being exaggerated by the highly selective nature of the landmine epidemic affecting Cambodia. Studies have shown that age, sex, location and activity are all key variables in determining who has landmine accidents. The specific nature of the epidemic means that for certain communities – in general poor rural areas such as Rattanak Mondul – the implications of landmine warfare amount almost to a second genocide. In such communities the 'killing fields' have already, literally, returned.

Figures from an ICRC survey of 1,762 registered mine-victim amputees in Phnom Penh revealed that only 5.56 per cent of these people were women. Other studies have confirmed the sex-specific nature of landmine accidents. Data from a survey of the handicapped conducted by World Vision during planning of a skills training programme in Battambang province in 1992 (hereafter referred to as Battambang Handicapped Survey 1992) revealed that of 265 respondents who were mine victims, only 8.7 per cent were women. Similarly, an ICRC database of mine victims, primarily from the western provinces, collected during 1991–93 (known hereafter as the ICRC Database 1991–93) containing information on 585 mine cases at the time of writing has revealed that only 6.84 per cent of mine victims were females. Other studies confirm these proportions.[44]

Is it the case that fewer females than males are having accidents, or is it that, as with children, women are less

Hospital 179, Phnom Penh

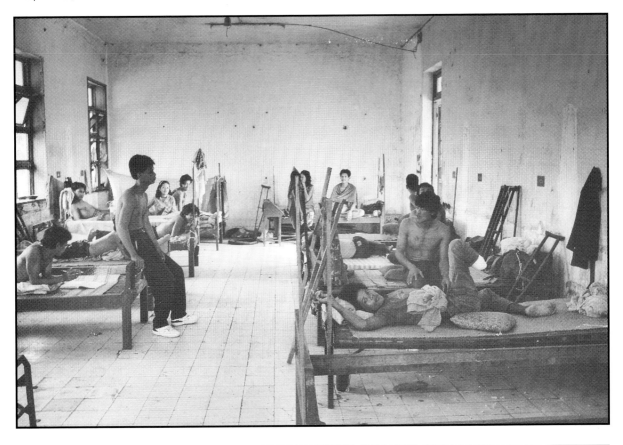

likely to survive their injuries? Some expatriate observers believe the latter to be the case, arguing that women may receive less familial effort, and hence less medical care, following a landmine accident.[45]

While further studies would have to be conducted to confirm this impression the author feels that nothing he has seen in Rattanak Mondul seems to support this notion. As noted in Chapter 3, only 4.98 per cent (14 of 281) of landmine related deaths in the district over the period 1979–93 were women (6.76 per cent were children under the age of 18, of whom 90 per cent were boys). It would seem that women are less likely, at least ten times less likely, to have mine injuries than men. But it is not only the fact that it is males who are getting killed and injured disproportionately by mines which makes those injury rates so demographically significant, it is also the age-specific nature of victims.

Figure 2.2 Age distribution: Battambang Handicapped Survey 1992

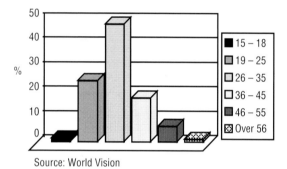

Source: World Vision

As revealed in Figure 2.2, the vast majority of Battambang's handicapped (most of whom are male mine victims) are young males in the prime of their lives. Similar results present themselves from a study of the age and sex distribution of mine victims from the ICRC database (Figure 2.3). Some 74 per cent of all victims are from the male 16–35 age bracket, and 50 per cent of all victims are males in their 20s. David Gould's *Cambodian Landmine Victim Survey* (1993) conducted for CMAC – known hereafter as Gould's Survey – confirms these figures, revealing that of some 1,200 victims, nearly 50 per cent were males in the 21–30 age group. The disproportionate number of Cambodian male victims must be set beside the fact that males constitute only 36 per cent of the population.[46] Since over 50 per cent of the Cambodian population is under 15, the adult male population can only be something in the region of 15 per cent of the whole. The selective impact of mine accidents starts to appear far more threatening in this context than might appear to be the case from the gross figures alone. Again, this becomes yet more alarming

Figure 2.3 Age distribution of male mine victims as percentage of all cases: ICRC Database 1991–93

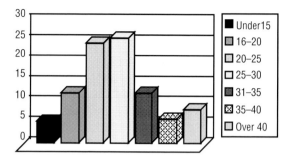

for the communities concerned when one considers the geographical specificity of mine injuries in Cambodia. As shown in Figure 2.4 mine injury rates vary dramatically even within the two most heavily mine-affected provinces, Battambang and Banteay-Meanchay.[47] In districts such as Rattanak Mondul, Thmar Pouk and Srey Sisophon, individuals are hundreds of times more likely to have mine accidents than in other districts of the same provinces (e.g. the comparison between Rattanak Mondul and Ek Phnom districts in Battambang province is quite striking).

Figure 2.4 District comparisons of mine injury rates (ICRC data) per head of population for Banteay-Meanchay and Battambang Provinces, 1992

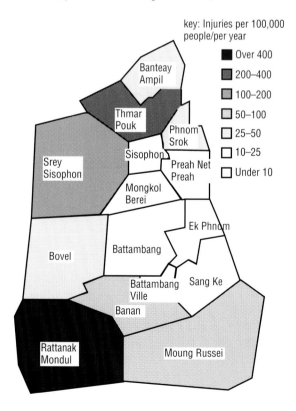

The data from which Figure 2.4 has been created is drawn from injury data contained in the ICRC Database 1991–93 and population information from UN surveys. To assess the true impact of landmines it is important to consider not simply the raw injury data but also the rate of injury per head of population. In Figure 2.4 such considerations are taken into account, and it is tentatively suggested that Rattanak Mondul is the most heavily mine-affected district in the whole of Cambodia. However, as Gould rightly notes, there are serious problems with using the statistics available in Cambodia, due partly to weaknesses in the record-keeping systems of both local authorities, hospitals and even NGOs whose records reflect the needs of their programmes. Data from Cambodian sources is nearly always under-recorded and incomplete. The overall effect of such source data problems, as Gould rightly suggests, is to make estimates of the scale of the problem conservative. Furthermore, it is vital to understand the broader history of the areas from which data is gathered, and any peculiarities of the times during which the data used had been collected. For example, Fiona King's MSc thesis, 'Landmine Injury in Cambodia: A Case Study' (1992) , which contains much of value and to which multiple references here are made, was researched at a time when the civilian population of Rattanak Mondul was greatly reduced due to heavy fighting in the district, as discussed in Chapter 3. Thus, injury rates in the district were negligible according to the data upon which she based her research, and the scale of the district's burden remained completely hidden in her thesis.

It should be noted, however, that mine injury rates may not always reveal the broader economic and social costs of landmines. For example, Gould refers to the Battambang-based demining NGO, the Mines Advisory Group (MAG), who cited that injury rates in 1993 in Banan district, Battambang province,[48] although still high, were dropping off rapidly because people knew where the minefields were located and were able to avoid entering these areas, as this was not absolutely necessary for their survival. Nevertheless, the MAG experts believed that in 1993 some 22 per cent of Banan's fine agricultural land was not being used because of mines, representing a huge economic loss to the farmers and community as a whole. On a larger scale, in Pursat province, which has a similar land area to its neighbour Battambang but only half the population,[49] there is con-siderably less pressure on the land. Thus, while injury rates were extremely high in Pursat during the height of the fighting and the period of active mine-laying (people did not know where the mines were) in the late 1980s and early 1990s, they had reached almost negiligible levels by mid-1993 because local knowledge had developed as to where the mines were, and either alter-native means of finding a livelihood were available or

the amount of mine-free land, although reduced, was still sufficient to enable the population to survive. *It is only when no such mine-free land exists and no alternatives are locally available for income generation that communal tragedies occur, and people are forced to venture into known mined areas.* Such has been the case in places like Rattanak Mondul, as revealed in Chapter 3. Thus, given the fact that the majority of people injured in Cambodia knew they were entering a mined area before they had their accident,[50] the figures reflected in Figure 2.4 should indicate something approaching an index of the pressure that mines are putting on people's ability to survive – assuming a rational population that will only enter known mined areas when it absolutely has to.

Similar localised patterns of communities under extreme pressure from landmines exist in other parts of Cambodia. Clearly such areas will have to be prioritised for mine clearance. Warrant Officer McCracken of CMAC went to many such communities in the course of his survey visits but he recalled one in the Samrong area of northern Siem Reap as being the 'classic' case.

The village was located in a clearing in the forests, and had been an old defensive position, right in the middle of the K5 belt. The ground was marked with former trenches and had 'every type of ordnance lying around', the debris of conflict. The population was made up entirely of former internally displaced people and returnees from Thailand – the only people land-hungry enough to return to the area when the fighting stopped. They had built the basic low-level wood and thatch houses that characterise the less prosperous Cambodian villages, and were mobilising the debris of war in their everyday lives, a question of a 'pragmatic' utilisation of all the 'resources' at their disposal. For example, anti-tank mines had been dug up and the explosives removed and used for fishing and fire starting (the latter is an especially dangerous practice, not least because Russian and Chinese explosives are far more unstable than western ones).

But it was the mines situation in this area which marked it out. Due to its position in the K5 belt the village was entirely surrounded, and people were forced to demine what land they needed to survive. The method involved using long-handled rakes. Miraculously, the village leader claimed that only one person had been injured while demining, and now that people had learnt where the mines were, injuries had declined. Never-theless, a network of footpaths still skirted, and wound through, the minefields around the settlement. One villager showed McCracken 30 MD-82s he had cleared. To get to his store he led them down a small but well-trodden path through the minefield. At the end of the path the villager then 'tiptoed' over a very dense part of the minefield, telling McCracken to stay where he was.

McCracken told the man not to bother, but he was proud of his collection and determined to show them to the UNTAC man. He brought the mines back in a cloth *kroma* – they were all live and armed.

If mine injuries affected the young adult male population disproportionately, does this mean simply that this is a product of the fact that mines were the weapon of choice in the Cambodian conflict, and that young males, conscripted into the army, militia and police – who routinely patrolled in some of the worst mine-affected areas – were bearing the brunt? If this were true, then the demographic effects of mines might be likened to the larger-effects of the war of which they were a key element. Indeed, in the 1980s and early 1990s the majority of victims were from the military. However, as Benoit Denise observed,[51] after mid 1992 while the overall figures for amputations started to fall nationwide the proportion of civilians injured started to rise significantly, indicating that whilst military casualties were an integral part of Cambodia's war of the mines, civilians were going to carry on fighting landmines long after hostilities ended. In places such as Siem Reap and Kompong Thom civilians themselves have in fact become 'military' targets. On 5 April 1993 there were some nine mine-injured civilians – all males in their 20s and 30s – in the surgical unit of Siem Reap hospital, and seven of these thought they had been injured by newly laid mines in areas not previously known to be dangerous. All were now leg amputees; one was a double amputee. Tann Rinn from Svey Leu village had been married for six months. His parents had asked him to build his own house and move out of the parental home. He had gone to the nearby forest, which people from his village routinely used to cut wood. On the road to the forest – a place where no one had been injured before – Rinn stood on a mine. In his village of 200 people there are already ten mine victim amputees, all male. Thus, even though the incidence rates of military mine casualties are directly related to the level of 'hot' conflict, young civilian males continue to suffer disproportionately from mines, both when 'non-confrontational' terror/demoralisation campaigns are being waged, and during periods of peace and ceasefire – as long, that is, as mines affect a community to such an extent as seriously to curtail livelihoods, forcing people to accept the need to enter known mined areas as a matter of routine. Males in both military and civilian life in such areas are occupationally more likely to be maimed or die as a result of landmine accidents.

The debris of war: an unexploded rocket embedded in a tree

Figure 2.5 Activity at time of injury: mine victims from the Battambang Handicapped Survey 1992

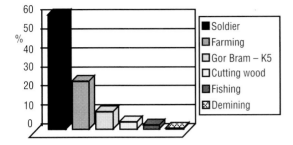

Information from both the Battambang Handicapped Survey (Figure 2.5) and the ICRC Database (Figure 2.6) give what is believed to be a representative picture of occupational activity at the time of injury for landmine victims in Cambodia. The former shows that some 60 per cent of the mine injured in Battambang were soldiers at the time of injury, while the ICRC Database puts the figure at 46 per cent.[52] The different emphasis in the two sets of evidence is a result of the much longer time period from which the Battambang Handicapped Survey data is drawn (injuries from all of the 1980s, plus a handful from the 1970s). However, as shown in Figure 2.6, only 21.4 per cent of those injured were engaged in 'military' activities at the time of accident. Thus, 53.4 per cent of even the military personnel injured were engaged in other, non-military activities at the time of their accident. These activities – wood cutting, food collection, fishing etc – are necessary in an under-resourced conventional army (such as the CPAF) or in a guerrilla force (such as the former resistance) to sustain the army in the field. Similarly, these essentially innocent activities, which have been responsible for the majority of military mine casualties, will be the same as those engaged in by the civilian population when they return to the areas that have been fought over. Only 2 per cent of military casualties described their activity at the time of injury as actually 'fighting'. By far the largest number, 14.8 per cent, were engaged in routine patrols, presumably through territory they considered nominally 'theirs'. This suggests a conscious 'hit and run' use of mines to debilitate and maim the opposition as a strategy of a war of attrition.

A minor point, but significant nonetheless, relates to the issue of 'landmine dependency' noted above. It might seem strange that such a large number of individuals are injured while fishing (3.6 per cent). In part this has to do with the fact that river banks form natural boundaries and thus, as is the case with the Sangke River in Rattanak Mondul, are frequently mined (this is reflected in the 1 per cent of injuries reported as a result of 'bathing in the river').[53] But a greater number of these injuries probably relate to the use of mines, or rather the explosives

and detonators from mines, in fishing. This is an extremely widespread practice. The *Phnom Penh Post* reported one of the more dramatic examples of this practice:

> Six people were killed when an anti-tank mine exploded on Jan 19th [1993] in Ta Khmao – a town in Kandal province, about 10 km from the capital of Phnom Penh. The incident took place in the compound of a military base of the Cambodian People's Armed Forces (CPAF) of the province. The anti-tank mine exploded at around 11.45 am when some of the six were trying to reactivate it so it could be used to catch fish.[54]

Other military equipment, such as the ubiquitous AK-47 assault rifle, are also deployed in fishing and hunting.

Figure 2.6 Activity at time of injury of 500 mine cases: ICRC Database 1991–93

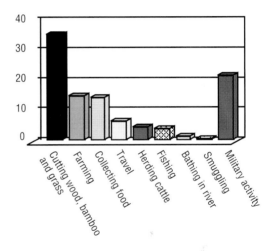

Figure 2.7 Place of injury of 567 mine cases: ICRC Database 1991–93

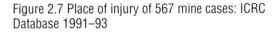

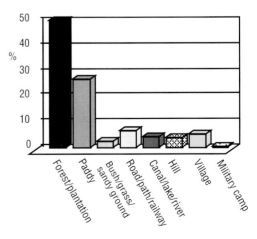

The last key variable which seems to determine mine injuries is location. Again, information from the ICRC database provides graphic illustration. Fifty per cent of all cases occurred in forested regions, the traditional home of the resistance forces and site of factional boundary zones, and well known to be typically some of the most heavily mined terrain in the country. What is significant about this information is that it is men who predominantly conduct the occupational activities that take place in the areas with most mines (predominantly wood cutting, which accounts for 33 per cent of activities at the time of injury from the ICRC Database 1991–93). Fiona King, who based her study on the ICRC Database in mid 1992 when it contained about 150 records fewer than in April 1993 when the author obtained an updated version, writes, 'if military activities are excluded there is a significantly higher proportion of male injuries (in the forests) compared to females ... more males visit the forests than females'.[55] King suggests that such wood cutting/forest visiting is done with a subsistence motive as the primary cause (wood for housing and fuel). However, evidence from Rattanak Mondul would suggest that a commercial motive is sometimes equally important, even when, or perhaps especially when, the mine risks are known. If the forests are mined it may be that the population have also lost too much paddy to support themselves – and are thus forced into commercial reliance on the products of the forests as this may involve less risk than working mined paddy fields.

Other 'most risky' activities are also more likely to be carried out by males, such as food collection (which in the majority of cases probably means hunting) and the riskier aspects of farming – ploughing and fallow land 'recovery' in post-conflict times. King suggests the opposite: 'A significantly higher proportion of women were injured in the rice fields than men.'[56] She suggests the answer to this might lie in the sex-determined division of labour within the ricefield. She writes:

> Given the division of labour (men plough, women plant and harvest) one would expect men to be primarily exposed to any buried mines, disturbing them by ploughing. However the nature of ploughing means that it is actually the buffalo or plough itself which would disturb a mine first. In some cases the farmer may be protected by his position of standing on or behind the plough. Anecdotal evidence suggests that livestock injuries during ploughing are fairly common ...[57]

Rural life: the family economy

Indeed they are. While King's theory on the division of labour in the rice field may have some validity, it should be remembered that in absolute terms a great deal more men than women are injured while farming (14.4 per cent of all the ICRC cases occurred during farming, while women constitute only 6.84 per cent of the total cases). While women do work alongside men in the planting and harvesting stages, men are still exposed to similar risks. More importantly, when villagers first return to fields which have been fought over it will be the men who will attempt to evaluate whether it is safe to work them, and it is in the process of such verification of safe areas that accidents occur. Thus, even if ploughing does afford some protection – which may be true in terms of not standing directly on mines, but may not be the case in terms of shrapnel and other injuries which may prove as damaging in the context – men are still, due to occupation, placing themselves in the areas with the greatest mine risks.

Lastly, King notes that, 'It is perhaps surprising that herding shows a comparatively low proportion of casualties for both sexes. One would expect that an activity involving moving over ground would cause more injuries than reported.' Given the fact that this activity is almost entirely conducted by young children, whose inability to survive mine accidents has already been noted, the mystery becomes understandable. As David Gould comments, 'an explosion designed to tear the leg off a healthy young soldier will often kill a child outright'.[58] Clearly, the herders are dying.

Thus mines are injuring, and by extension killing, a disproportionate number of young male adults in the prime of their lives. This is because the activities in which these male groups engage, both military and civilian, and the places where these activities are carried out, are the most heavily mined areas of the country. The demographic impact of mines is thus significantly greater than the raw injury rates would suggest. Those who survive represent not only a burden on the already extremely weak medical and social infrastructure, but also an enormous social burden in terms of the opportunity cost of their lives as disabled, as opposed to able-bodied, members of the community. This collective opportunity cost is already enormous and is growing yet larger every week. As with the demographic impact, those communities most under pressure from mines will feel this burden disproportionately . Furthermore, it will be these already poor rural communities that are less able to cope. But perhaps this, at the end of the day, was the desired purpose – the landmine as the perfect weapon for a war of total social, economic, cultural and ultimately military attrition. The mine is designed to consume enemy resources, designed not to kill but to maim.

From the moment a man, woman or child stands on a mine three or four others will be involved in the immediate evacuation and in the application of first aid. Many others will be involved in the transfer to hospital, the operation, the post-operative and rehabilitative care, the provision of prostheses, the provision of benefits and pensions, etc. The financial costs of all these resources, and the long-term opportunity cost of the injury, are all parts of the landmine equation. All are elements in the cynical cost-benefit analysis in which designers and manufacturers engage. These calculations cannot be described as anything but criminal.

The Medical Burden of Landmine Injuries

It would be very easy to write about the burden that mines exert in the Cambodian medical system – to quote percentages. But this is one of the areas where words are not as effective as images, and for this reason in this section the following charts will do most of the talking. The weight of the mine burden revealed here is staggering.

Figures 2.8 and 2.9 reveal the situation in recent years in Pursat province. As noted above, Pursat must be considered something of a special case; nevertheless, the resource drain produced by the war is clear to see in Figure 2.8, and within this the predominant role of landmines is obvious in Figure 2.9. A similar picture emerges from records from Siem Reap, a province with a much more active landmine problem during the UN time. Some 18.3 per cent of all surgical admissions are the result of landmine injuries (Figure 2.10), and mines constitute some 36.1 per cent of all trauma cases (Figure 2.11).

In her thesis King explains that once again it is not only the raw volume of mine injuries which is significant, but the fact that mine injuries consume a disproportionate quantity of hospital resources, compared with other war-related injuries, and especially when compared with typical 'non-war' surgical admissions.

However, such findings are not only relevant to third world health infrastructures, like Cambodia's. King writes:

A report from the Royal Thai Army hospital in Bangkok stated that the length of hospitalisation was significantly longer for mine injuries in comparison with other weapons. It reports that the mean length of hospitalisation for the patients with rifle injuries was 83.5 days and for landmine injuries 153 days.[59]

Figures 2.12, 2.13 and 2.14 are taken from data presented in King's thesis. The first two graphically illustrate that while mine injuries accounted for an average of 13 per cent of total surgical admissions in both Mongkol Berei and Battambang hospitals, mine victims consume some 27 per cent of total patient days in each

Figure 2.8 Types of surgical admission: Pursat Hospital 1991 and 92

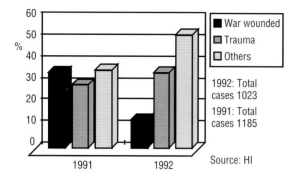

Source: HI

1992: Total cases 1023
1991: Total cases 1185

Figure 2.9 Breakdown of war wounded, injured by 'explosives' (mines, grenades and shells): Pursat Hospital 1990–92

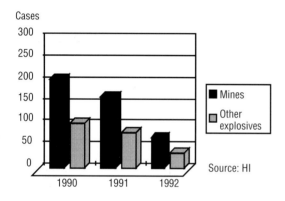

Source: HI

Figure 2.10 Types of surgical admission: Siem Reap Hospital 1992

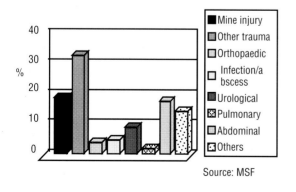

Source: MSF

Figure 2.11 Types of trauma case: Siem Reap Hospital 1992

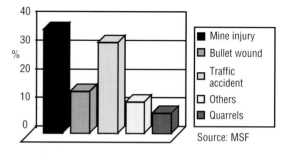

Source: MSF

hospital. As Figure 2.14. further illustrates, mine victims also stay longer than other war-injured patients (an average of 18.2 days for mine victims compared with 13 for other war injuries), and considerably longer than the average non-war surgical admission. Casualties who had stood on mines (35 per cent of the case load in King's study) had far longer stays in hospital than those injured in other ways by mines due to the necessity in most cases to amputate limbs, which requires at least two operations (amputation and then several days later what is known as 'delayed primary closure', when the wound is finally closed – this allows swelling to go down and ensures that the final stump heals properly, leaving good skin and muscle cover of the bone end). In conclusion King writes:

> Landmine injuries take up a disproportionate share of hospital resources in terms of beds and operations.... the patients who use most blood in ICRC hospitals are those injured by antipersonnel mines [using] more than twice the requirement of all patients [sic].... Therefore landmine injuries represent a considerable drain on hospital resources in three main areas – bed occupancy, operating time and blood transfusions. In Cambodia a typical landmine casualty will take up a hospital bed for three weeks and about two operations.[60]

It is also of interest to note the significant differences in lengths of stay for mine victims in Mongkol Berei and Battambang hospitals. The assistance provided by the ICRC in Mongkol Berei hospital means that patients do not need to pay for either drugs or blood. In Battambang during King's study period this was not the case. King writes, 'Mine amputees, because of their high blood and surgical time requirement and long period of immobilisation, can incur huge costs and informal discharge (i.e. patients leaving without doctors' consent or knowledge is common in hospitals where patients have to pay.)'[61]

In Battambang some 43 per cent of mine victims informally discharged themselves during the period of

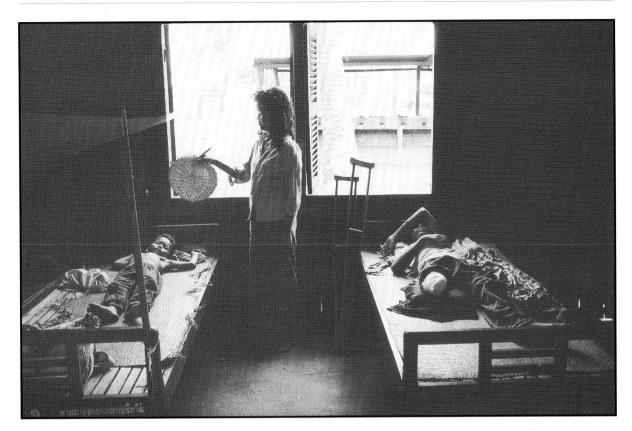

Surgical ward: Kompong Speu hospital

Wat Than, Phnom Penh, 1991: National Rehabilitation Centre

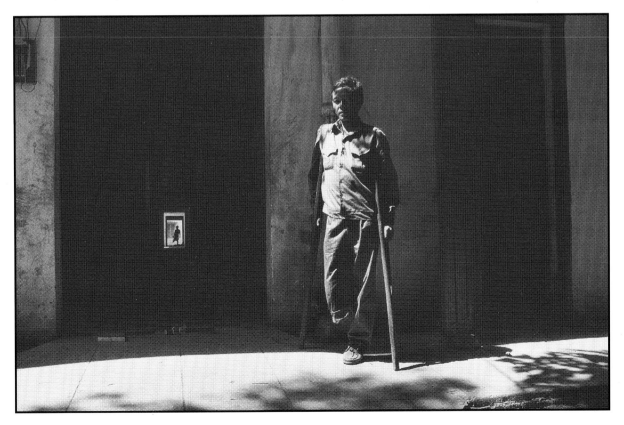

Figure 2.12 Distribution of hospital load, Surgical Unit, Mongkol Berei Hospital, Banteay-Meanchay: January–June 1992

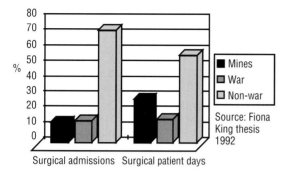

Figure 2.14 Average stay (days) on surgical wards in Mongkol Berei and Battambang hospitals: January–June 1992

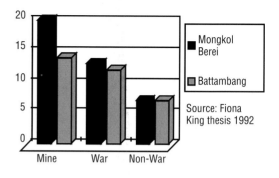

Figure 2.13 Distribution of hospital load, Surgical Unit, Battambang Hospital: January–June 1992

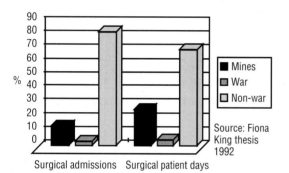

Figure 2.15 Time to hospital, mine victims: ICRC Database 1991–93

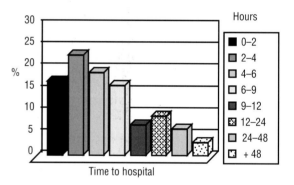

the King study. This is hardly surprising as not only do mine victims in such hospital environments have to pay a disproportionately heavy medical bill because of the protracted nature of their treatment, but the mere fact that they have mine injuries indicates they they are drawn from the poorest sections of the community – conscript soldiers or civilians living under such pressure from mines that they have to take occupational risks with mines.[62] Even before prematurely discharging themselves from hospital, mine victims may have had to make economies in their treatments – in areas such as pain control or antibiotic drugs, and even food. But such economies are so obviously false – poor diet and improper antibiotic treatment in such cases will slow recovery, and in some cases necessitate further operations due to reinfection problems. Cambodian hospitals are not the most hygienic places in which to recover from serious surgery. Mine injuries are a classic example of 'the rich stay healthy and the sick stay poor' – and get poorer still because they are sick.

Further complications in the case histories of Cambodian mine victims occur because of other failings in the health infrastructure – the weakness, and many

cases the total absence, of emergency evacuation facilities. King acknowledges how critical such facilities are. She writes:

> Aside from tissue/organ repair surgical procedure with mine injury is based on the principle of eliminating the dead tissue around the wound as well as any infected material within it. This process is called debridement, and aims to prevent infection occurring. An important feature of fragment wounds is their degree of contamination by foreign bodies. This is especially so with mine injuries where soil and other fragments are blasted into tissue, in particular the leg standing on a mine. An important determinant of infection is the delay between the injury and access to antibiotic treatment (hospital/first aid). An upper limit of 6 hours' delay before antibiotic prophylaxis appears to be 'the safety net'.[63]

As is graphically illustrated in Figure 2.15, in over 40 per cent of the cases recorded in the ICRC database it took the victim more than six hours to get to hospital. In a poverty trap of limited health care resources, mines have a considerable multiplier effect – poor emergency

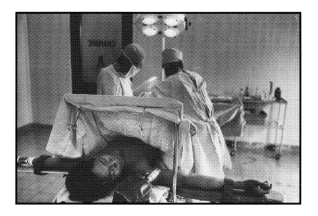

Amputation: Battambang provincial hospital

For much of 1992 there was an effective ceasefire, and yet war-related causes accounted for nearly one in five surgical admissions, of whom 75 per cent were mine patients. In 1992 there were a total of 164 mine cases admitted to the provincial hospital, of whom 95 had leg amputations and another nine hand amputations.[64] In the three surgical wards in Battambang provincial hospital on the 10 March 1993 some 27 per cent of the patients were mine victims (see Figure 2.16).

But the drain on resources does not end at the hospital gate. Perhaps the most startling piece of evidence of the long-term impact of mines in communities such as Battambang comes from the Handicapped Survey 1992, illustrated in Figure 2.17. This reveals that *for 82 per cent of the province's handicapped, the cause of disability is mine injuries.* They have had a profound impact on society as a whole in the province, as well as on those families directly affected. But the 'loss' created by mine warfare can also be calculated in less nebulous terms. In stark contrast to the situation for war-wounded amputees in the non-communist administered border camps, the State of Cambodia government paid pensions to handicapped ex-soldiers despite the fact that this caused a considerable drain on the state's slender resources. As noted above, 60 per cent of the province's mine-injured handicapped people were serving military personnel at the time of their injury. Also eligible for government pensions were the further 9 per cent of the

referral systems lead to greater infection problems, necessitating longer stays in hospital and greater consumption of hospital resources, further removing the possibilities of self-generated improvements in the referral system, to say nothing of the suffering of the patients involved.

In provinces like Battambang, where many communities are under pressure from mines, the drain on hospital resources is not likely to evaporate when the war ends.

Mines may injure only one person, but the whole family suffers

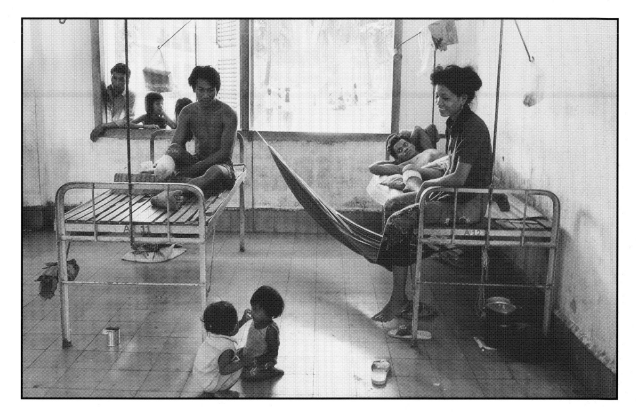

Figure 2.16 Breakdown of surgical load, Wards A, B and C: Battambang provincial hospital, 10 March 1993

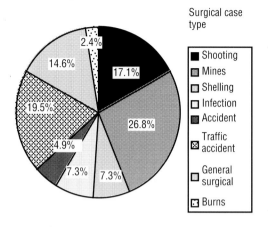

Surgical case type

- ■ Shooting
- ▩ Mines
- ▨ Shelling
- ☐ Infection
- ■ Accident
- ⊠ Traffic accident
- ☐ General surgical
- ☒ Burns

NB Thus *war-related injuries accounted for 51.2 per cent (of which over 25 per cent were from mines) of all in-patients* in the three surgical wards on the day of the survey. Impressions of this ward over 16 months of regular visits suggests to the author that such a burden is typical.

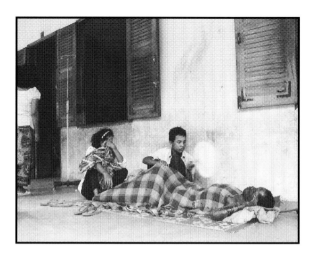

Battambang hospital: full to overflowing

province's mine-injured handicapped, who were maimed, mostly in the mid 1980s, while working as Gor Bram (K5) labourers. Thus, in February 1993, the Ministry of Social Action in Battambang confirmed that it had 4,017 war-injured ex-soldiers and policemen on its books (0.75 per cent of the provincial population in 1992), virtually all of whom had been injured by mines, in addition to a large number of war widows and their families. Although pensions were small, averaging 30,000 riels ($12) a month, the provincial ministry only had sufficient funds allocated from Phnom Penh to support just over 2,000 pensioners, at a total yearly cost of $314,667. Given the then absolute under-funding of

Figure 2.17 Cause of disability: Battambang Handicapped Survey 1992

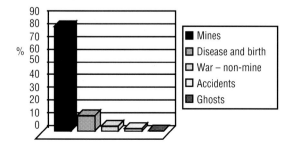

- ■ Mines
- ▨ Disease and birth
- ☐ War – non-mine
- ☐ Accidents
- ▨ Ghosts

all Cambodian government activities, such resources could have been deployed many times over in other vital public spending sectors. Landmines thus continued successfully to wage war years after they struck their victims.

Landmines and Military Health Care

While conditions in provincial hospitals such as Battambang would strike the first-time visitor from the west as shocking (and indeed they are in many cases), it is the conditions prevailing in the military hospital in Battambang throughout the early 1990s that still haunt those who witnessed them. To describe conditions as Crimean would be entirely accurate, and by contrast the civilian hospital looked positively luxurious. It is not the conditions *per se* that are so upsetting about the military health infrastructure but rather the fact that despite the billions of dollars spent in Cambodia during the UN time, none of these resources were even considered for assistance in Cambodia's CPAF-run military hospitals. However 'sound' the arguments for not being seen to fund one faction bilaterally during the UN time, when impartiality was the key word, the logic evaporates when one witnesses the raw human need in such places. In 1992, the Indian Army Medical Corps, responsible for establishing UNTAC's field hospital in Battambang rejected the idea of taking over and renovating the military hospital,[65] the facility being considered simply too unhygienic. They spent considerable resources converting another building to serve as a separate UN hospital.

Militarily, 1992 was a quiet year in Battambang province. Nevertheless, as revealed in Figures 2.18 and 2.19, mines continued to take their toll on the CPAF conscripts. As in the ICRC data presented above, most

Figure 2.18 Admissions to Battambang military hospital 1992, by case type

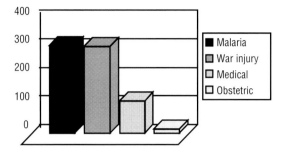

Figure 2.19 Causes of war injuries: admissions to Battambang military hospital 1992

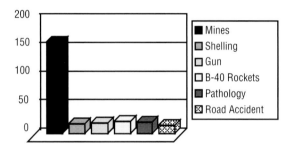

Figure 2.20 Landmine victims in Battambang military hospital 1991–February 93

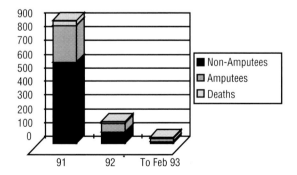

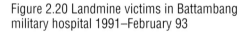

of these soldiers were injured on routine patrols, or while trying to survive in mine-infested frontline areas.[66] The contrast in injury rates from 'hot' years (such as 1991) and those from the uneasy ceasefire conditions

existing the following year are dramatically revealed in Figure 2.20 However, the lack of resources and the conditions under which the military medics are working is perhaps best revealed in notes taken while I spent a day with Capt. Dr Paet Vut, in late February 1993. Dr Vut was the surgeon who tried to save Hearn Boung, the soldier featured in Chapter 4.

24 February 1993: a Morning in the Life of Captain Dr Paet Vut

Captain Dr Paet Vut is one of eight doctors working in the Battambang military hospital. Apart from sharing the surgical duties with one of the other doctors, he has also been deputy director of the hospital since 1992.

Operations tend to take place in the mornings between 6 and 11 a.m. when the hospital is supplied with electricity from the city grid. Despite being able to provide 24-hour electricity to the ever multiplying number of hotels and dancing restaurants catering for the UN and foreign residents, the city power company still lacks the 'resources' to extend such service to the military hospital. The underfunded hospital cannot afford the diesel for the generators that are supposed to provide electricity when the city supply is not connected.

This morning Dr Vut is waiting for the theatre to become free to operate on Captain Kim Reang, who was injured two days before on the front line near Treng, when the tractor he was riding on had driven over an anti-tank mine. Reang's left leg was broken in the accident by a large piece of shrapnel that had entered the top of his left thigh, shattering the bone near the hip. While I chat with Dr Vut an operation is being conducted in theatre to remove the eye of another soldier injured in a mine blast at Komping Poie in Banan.

The military hospital consists of a large compound on the north side of Battambang, with several neglected single-story buildings which serve as wards grouped around the surgical, medical, pharmacy and administrative buildings. The wards were formerly old market buildings in the Lon Nol days. They are subdivided across their width into small rooms, each containing four wooden beds covered with bamboo sleeping mats. They contain little else, apart from the patients and the small bundles of possessions which their comrades, who have accompanied them from the front, bring for them. At either end of these small cells there is a shuttered window and door, both of which customarily stand open to allow for ventilation, but which also bring flies and mosquitoes.

The rooms have concrete floors and the paint on the walls, once a light green, is greyed, dirtied and flaking with age. Patients fresh from the operating room lie on these beds next to others who have almost recovered. There is little order. For some there is extra care from wives who have come to join them. Children run outside, playing in a litter of old dressings and equipment, which is inexcusable, and watch as the daily agonies of wound dressing and cleaning are conducted with antiseptic swabs, applied with stinging directness to raw flesh.

Operating a subconscious 'triage' system the hospital provides a brutal, though quite effective regime of anti-infection care, but economies have been made on the pain control front – there are no painkillers unless one can afford them. Few are in the position to be able to do so. For a married man 40,000 riels ($16) a month is not a living wage, and salaries have only been paid very irregularly for the last year or more.

Even in the surgical block the floor is unevenly paved with the usual yellow and brown tiles, and the walls covered in faded and chipped paint. The general impression is of decay, and it is hard to believe that major surgery is carried out inside these walls. Outside, in an open court-yard, there are the remains of a 'ceremonial garden', whose centrepiece consists of a series of flag poles, wrapped round by a metallic 'banner' proclaiming Vietnamese, Cambodian and Laotian solidarity. A faded hammer and sickle is still visible, a silent testimony to the assistance the Soviets and their Vietnamese allies provided to the hospital in the 1980s – assistance long since removed and greatly missed. The only fresh colours are the blue, red and gold of the flag of the State of Cambodia, which still flew at that time. The hot season is coming on and the tracks in the compound throw up clouds of dust as the small motorbikes drive past.

Dr Vut says that he usually operates once a day, and that about 50 per cent of his cases tend to be soldiers injured in landmine blasts. Originally from an upper middle class Phnom Penh family he had ambitions of becoming an architect in the early 1970s. After the Pol Pot years, during which time his educated father was murdered, he was conscripted but volunteered to become a private in the medical corps. His education quickly singled him out, and in 1980 he had been sent to Vietnam to train as a doctor. He has been posted in Battambang since the completion of his studies in 1986.

Not only has the hospital been desperately short of equipment, drugs and operating finance since the withdrawal of the Vietnamese in 1989 but, as in all Cambodian public employment, resources do not exist to pay the staff adequate salaries. Vut makes do with 40,000 riels a month, and can survive thanks to private practice out of work hours and food sent from his family's farm in Takeo province.

Around 10.30 Dr Vut goes to scrub up. He and his staff work barefoot in an operating theatre remarkable only for its apparent lack of the things associated with its function. The theatre lights are lit with ordinary

household bulbs, the high-powered originals long ago having broken, not to be replaced. In the far wall two air conditioners struggle to bring the temperature in the theatre down to a reasonable level. The daylight shines around the units which haven't been sealed into the walls.

On the old table Reang lies on his side, his right arm outstretched on a support, receiving IV glucose. Although the theatre has a gas anaesthetic unit, it too is broken and the medical assistant in charge of this function tops up Reang's dose with an injected anaesthetic. Vut and his assistants manoeuvre Reang's swollen and bruised thigh into a position where they can access the wound. Vut cuts into the back of the thigh, widening the small entry hole made by the shrapnel. Once located, the main piece the size of a large coin is removed and other affected tissue cut away. The wound is cleaned with swabs, packed with dressings and then bandaged. As Vut is finishing this procedure the power goes off.

Vut stitches a deep gash in the foot of the same leg and then addresses the need to reset the bone. The shrapnel has entered the lower side of the thigh as Reang rode on the tractor, and the break is not clean. It will need an 'external fix' and traction (where a rod is inserted through the bone, and weights applied to pull the bone back into a position from which it can be allowed to heal).

The assistant brings out the drill – an eight-year-old, rusting piece of equipment which is to all intents and purposes broken, and which would in any normal situation would have been scrapped. He struggles to attach the fixing rod which has to be drilled through the thigh and bone, just above the knee. Eventually a technician with pliers is called in to repair the drill. Vut inserts the rod but each time he enters the leg it slips as soon as contact is made with the bone. Once it comes away from the drill completely and is left protruding from Reang's thigh. Eventually Vut succeeds, and the fixing apparatus is attached.

Reang's first operation is complete. The assistants lifts him off the table and on to the metal trolley on which he waited for his operation. He is wheeled out of theatre, past the soldier whose eye has been removed earlier in the morning, and out into the glaring sun. He is bumped over the gravel path that leads to the nearby ward. Vut's assistants set up the traction. They have only an old frame, and the traction cords have to be improvised out of long strips of dressings, twisted for strength. Another nurse turns up with the weights, a few stones in a plastic market bag that approximate to 5 kg. Vut's morning is over, and Reang's leg has been saved.

The Following Day

At mid-morning in the operating theatre ante-room, 20-year-old Gum Jamran lies moaning, shifting his position, and drifting into a fitful sleep. He stepped on a mine the day before, and had his right leg amputated below the knee at 5 p.m. that afternoon. His left thigh has a gaping 3 inch shrapnel gash, which shows around the dressings which pack the wound. An IV drip feeds his right arm, but he has received no painkillers. The flies settle on his bloodied bandages. There is no one to brush them away.

The ante-room would be described in other hospitals as a post-operative trauma unit. But this room is rem-iniscent of images of Scutari conjured by Crimean war reporters. The uneven floor tiles have been washed, but the grime is ingrained. The walls are blackened, and the barred window stands open, the shutters moving gently in the wind.

Later in the day Jamran is gone, moved on to another ward, and 33-year-old Captain Mom An has taken his place. He has stood on a mine at 6.30 a.m., but didn't arrived in hospital until 4 p.m. He has lost a lot of blood Dr Vut tells me, and in theatre he nearly dies. His blood pressure is better now, but his leg is missing.

There are six major CPAF-run military hospitals, corresponding to the six military regions (Siem Reap, Battambang, Bei Chan (near Poechentong Airport, Phnom Penh), Kompong Cham, Stung Treng and Phnom Penh). The hospital at Phnom Penh , situated a stone's throw from Wat Phnom and the then UNTAC head quarters in central Phnom Penh, acts as the last referral stage in the military health hierarchy. If conditions in the Battambang hospital seem extremely poor, things are barely better in Phnom Penh. And in the isolated field dressing stations that conduct amputations in appalling conditions, with equally appalling results, things are even worse. In the Siem Reap military hospital, which lies unvisited, within sight of the towers of the great

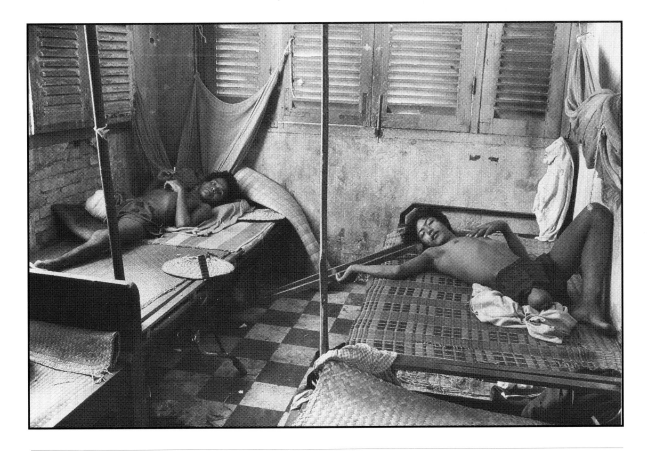

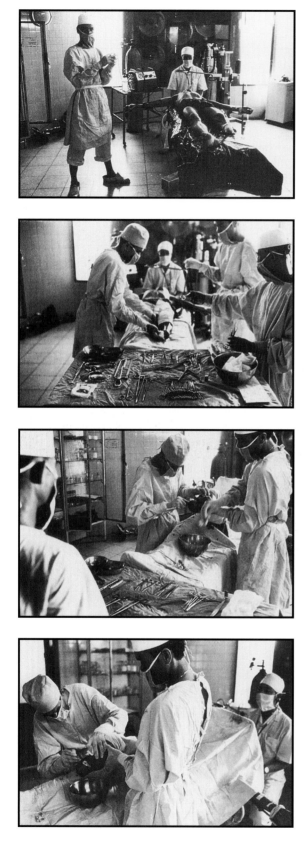

Secondary infection: a reamputation is carried out in Phnom Penh's military hospital

Figure 2.21 Landmine victims, Phnom Penh central military hospital 1987–1992

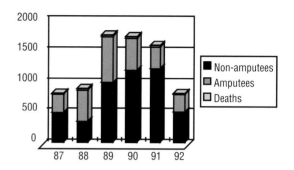

Angkor Wat, I encountered one 18-year-old soldier, a mine victim, whose foot had been half-amputated at a field station in Samrong, in the north of the province. The foot ended in a jagged diagonal line of swollen infected flesh. The boy didn't want to go to Phnom Penh for another operation (he was being 'evacuated' by boat the following day); he didn't want to lose his foot, but it would kill him if he retained it.

Again, the quality of the health care in the Phnom Penh military hospital has been dramatically affected by the withdrawal of Vietnamese assistance – the basics, drugs and equipment, are now missing or in very short supply. Doctors there were angry in a very understated Cambodian sort of way, wondering why the UN were so keen on sweet-talking the Khmer Rouge at a time when they were the ones still fighting and laying mines, while no one from the UN had even visited their hospital, let alone addressed their humanitarian needs. 'When a soldier stands on a mine and loses a leg, he is no longer a soldier,' said Surgeon Dr Said; 'The UN talk a lot about human rights, but what about the rights of these men to proper treatment?' Some idea of the scale of the problem of military mine victims in recent years can be seen from Figure 2.21, which looks only at records from Phnom Penh.

From POMZs to Ploughshares

In Cambodia while researching this book it was the resilience and pragmatism of the people that made visits to even the most appallingly victimised communities and individuals an inspiration. One of the most striking, and hopeful, images I saw was during one of my last days in Battambang. Traders armed with old bicycles and huge bamboo panniers cycle out into areas such as Rattanak Mondul and buy up the metal debris of war from villagers who have been reclaiming their land. In particular, the metal fragmentation casings of the Soviet POMZ mines are favoured. Back in Battambang they are sold on to scrap dealers who supply smelting works in Phnom Penh. However, some of their stock reaches two smelting yards in Battambang. There scrap, including POMZs, is melted down and cast into various pieces of agricultural equipment, including metal cutting teeth for the traditional bullock-drawn wooden Cambodian ploughs that cut through the rich soils of Battambang. Somehow, this simple pragmatism – taking the same metal that has been killing the land, and putting it to use in the process of agricultural life-giving, ploughing – struck me very forcibly as an affirmation, and a rebuttal of those who have fought their wars with the lives, limbs and prosperity of Cambodians.

3
Rattanak Mondul District, Battambang Province: From Prosperity to Poverty

Solitudinem faciunt pacem appellant
They make a wilderness and call it peace

Tacitus, *Agricola*, 30

Rattanak Mondul is one of Cambodia's most heavily mine-affected districts. It very clearly illustrates the impact of indiscriminate mine warfare, both in terms of the toll of injuries and deaths it exacts on civilian populations, and the poverty it induces. The dreadful legacy of mine warfare in the district will not easily be resolved in the foreseeable future. What has happened in Rattanak Mondul is offered here both as a record of what is possible under existing international regulations governing the use of mines in armed conflicts, and as a caution. In some senses Rattanak Mondul is unique, in others it is not, for what happened here could happen anywhere. There are already countless other communities in the many mine-affected nations, where similar burdens are being borne. There are still others where the seeds of such suffering continue to be sown.

The district lies in the south western corner of Battambang province, bordering Thailand. At the time of writing it was divided into four subdistricts, or communes. In the east lay Sdao and Andao Hep, and to the west Treng and Ploumeas. The district consists of rich tree-covered highlands in the west giving way to

Route 10: the road to Rattanak Mondul

fertile lowlands in the eastern areas, interposed with ancient, weather-beaten limestone *phnoms* (this translates rather grandly as 'mountains', although in reality they are only a few hundred feet high at most) which rise from the surrounding fields, interrupting almost unnaturally the geometry of the plains.

Battambang has always been one of Cambodia's most prosperous provinces, and was an important area to reclaim from Thai control when the French asserted their protectorate in 1863. Within the province, Rattanak Mondul has long had pride of place. The name means 'place of the gems',[1] and this reputation was centred on the town of Pailin, which lies in the valleys of the extreme west, very close to the present Thai border. Traditionally the area was known as Pailin district, but was renamed following the Vietnamese invasion of 1979, and its administrative centre was moved to the town of Sdao in the eastern-most commune where the Vietnamese regime's grip was strongest.

The gems of Pailin were only ever one of many sources of prosperity within Rattanak Mondul. The dark soils of the lowlands in the west of the district are some of the country's finest, readily supporting the staple rice crop as well as fruit, cotton, peanuts, and a variety of vegetables and other crops. In the 1960s Battambang

emerged as one of Cambodia's leading centres for commercial agriculture, and Rattanak Mondul was at the heart of these developments, especially with regard to its cotton and orange production. This agricultural potential had been spotted by Sihanouk in the first months following independence, the area having come to his notice after his armed forces had swept through it in 1954 on Operation Samaki.[2] Pailin district was selected as a 'resettlement' area for landless peasants from the south west and for Cambodian refugees from South Vietnam. David Chandler notes:

> The newcomers enjoyed small government subsidies and often incurred the resentment of local people. In the nearby district of Andao Hep, where a cotton cultivation boom (linked to the opening of a textile factory in Battambang) led to a doubling of the population in 1964–66, many local proprietors were driven from the land as it was bought up by merchants and officials.[3]

Despite a degree of concentration of land ownership during the 1960s, the loss of access to the land, while a considerable grievance, was not as absolute as Chandler suggests. Recalling the period, many locals state that while some independent farmers did sell land off and

The fine soils of Rattanak Mondul district made it one of Cambodia's most productive

become wage labourers for the new class of large land owners, most retained substantial garden plots and were able to achieve food self-sufficiency. Certainly the loss of land produced by economic and social change in this period was not of the same scale as that which was to effect the district in the late 1980s as a result of landmine warfare. Furthermore, at that time additional income could always be gained from the forests (the practices of wood and bamboo cutting noted below being traditional to the area), or from prospecting for gems in the west. Trade also offered opportunities for income generation for the people of Rattanak Mondul, since Route 10, a popular trading route to Thailand, cuts through the heart of the district *en route* from the provincial town to Pailin near the border. Partly as a result, the market towns of Treng and Sdao also experienced, and further generated, prosperity in the district.

Today it is tempting to accept the notion gained from talking to local people, that the times before Pol Pot came to power were something of a golden age. For the tribal hill people, the 'black Khmer', of the western reaches of the district, as well as the peasantry of the lowlands, there were considerable economic, social and political grievances in the late 1960s. For example, there were no secondary schools and only a handful of primary schools serving the district's 40,000 or so inhabitants. What social infrastructure there was tended to be concentrated in the lowlands of the east. Partly as a result, the tribal peoples of the west were commonly regarded as 'very ignorant people',[4] who subsisted outside the cash economy of 1960s Cambodia, farming small plots of land in the hills and surviving thanks largely to hunting and gathering activities conducted in the forests. Additional goods, which could not be obtained in this way, were bartered for in the markets. Such people were so cut off from the modern world that when the first cars arrived in the area they offered to 'feed' the vehicles with cut grass. In a society where hierarchy and status are everything, these hill people were well aware that they were a marginalised subclass.

For the peasantry of the lowlands, the increasing hard times and lack of social provisions (schools and a hospital were built in the area only in the late 1960s) compounded the popular view of local officials as a corrupt and self-serving elite in alliance with the province's capitalists. Traditional bonds of respect and obligation broke down under the strains of government-led socio-economic change. The result was the spontaneous upsurge of local anger in the rather grandly named Samlaut rebellion of 1967.[5] Chandler concludes, 'The Samlaut uprising sprang from local grievances against injustice and social change, corruption, and ham-fisted government behaviour.'[6]

Yet, in relative terms – in terms of what the following

two decades have brought Rattanak Mondul – these were golden times. In August 1992 the first Vice-Governor of Battambang province, Tes Heanh, expressed his concept of 'development' for the province as a return to the conditions of 1967. For once his views were probably in line with the vast majority of the people of Battambang, and especially of Rattanak Mondul.

As the 1960s closed, these areas started to produce increasing numbers of Khmer Rouge leaders and fighters. They were drawn to the movement partly as a result of the legitimacy of their unanswered complaints, and partly as a result of the harshness with which the 1967 revolt was put down. These became Pol Pot's 'base people', activists who could be trusted, people who were untarnished by the corruptions of modernity, foreign influences and capitalism: these were 'original Khmers'. As a result, during the years of the Pol Pot regime some of the inhabitants of Rattanak Mondul lived well. Nevertheless, for the majority these years brought the terror and loss, the hunger and hard work which came to characterise Khmer Rouge rule for most Cambodians. In Rattanak Mondul two execution sites were operated, one in Jipang and the other in Chea Montray, both villages of Treng commune. After the overthrow of the Khmer Rouge, a 'killing fields' memorial, a sample of the skulls and bones recovered from nearby mass graves, was established at Wat Treng.

Battambang province under the Khmer Rouge was forcibly populated with 'new people' from Phnom Penh and other major cities, and the population doubled to well over 1 million as the Khmer Rouge brutally tried to construct its agrarian utopia. Many of these were stationed on communes in Rattanak Mondul. In 1979, six days after the capture of Phnom Penh, Vietnamese forces reached Battambang and had 'liberated' most of the western areas of the province by the end of January. Kev Sophal, the SOC district leader for Rattanak Mondul, estimated that some 30 per cent of the population ended up fleeing with, or being forced by, the Khmer Rouge to the Thai border.[7] For those who remained in districts such as Rattanak Mondul, Vietnamese rule brought with it the tensions associated with foreign occupation, and in particular the burden of conscription and occasional periods of forced labour. Nevertheless, the relative stability the occupation afforded in the early 1980s allowed many to return to their former lands and ways of life.

In Rattanak Mondul, even under the austere conditions imposed by the international embargo, an impressive social infrastructure was built up, with schools and health centres being constructed in every commune. The district hospital, constructed in 1965, was repaired

Opposite: Phnom Dum Meay and the shell-scarred fields of Sdao

and extended after the neglect of the Pol Pot years and staffed with newly trained Cambodian medics. As many of the case histories in the next chapter reveal, the 1980–89 period was essentially one of recovery and reconstruction, and is regarded with a certain affection by many in the area.

As the Khmer Rouge-dominated resistance on the Thai border grew progressively stronger, and the international policies which came to characterise the way Cambodia was to be treated in the 1980s took on a sense of refined permanence, the Vietnamese resorted to the old adage that the best form of defence is attack. In December 1984 Vietnamese and fledgling Cambodian forces of the Phnom Penh regime launched a major offensive against the border camps, finally pushing them into Thai territory. Having achieved this goal they attempted to secure it by laying the enormous K5 minefield. These mines, which now form part of Rattanak Mondul's current burden, lie in the western reaches of the district, beyond Pailin, and were the first systematised modern mine-laying that the area had experienced. The Khmer Rouge had laid mines as it retreated towards the Thai border in 1979, but the scale of the Vietnamese operation was unprecedented.

The minefields shown in map 3 were, in the main, laid four years later when the civil war reached new levels of intensity. In September 1989 the Vietnamese started their final withdrawal of armed forces from Cambodia as a precondition of the UN-sponsored peace plan. However, this investment in peace paid strange dividends in Rattanak Mondul. As the Vietnamese withdrew from the province, the Khmer Rouge swarmed over the border from their safe havens in Thailand. Like locusts, they destroyed everything that lay in its path.

In October 1989 the artillery bombardment which accompanied the Khmer Rouge's capture of Pailin was so intense that it could be heard 100 km away in the Thai border town of Aranyaprathet. It was a foretaste of the destruction that was to await the rest of the district. Ever since, the Khmer Rouge has earned incredible wealth from concessions that have allowed Thai contractors to rape the Pailin area for its gem and timber wealth. The ecological damage in this area has been intense. It has turned the Sangke River, which flows through Rattanak Mondul, *en route* to Battambang town and the Tonle Sap beyond, from a crystal-blue, living river into a mud-laden slurry whose sedimentary outpourings are destroying the great lake, the ecological heart of the Cambodian nation. When the Khmer Rouge reached Wat Treng, during the height of the fighting in 1991, it found time methodically to burn the killing fields memorial established by the Vietnamese.

In response to the onslaught the under-resourced CPAF forces responded with the one weapon of which they had seemingly unlimited supplies: mines. They laid defensive fields to try to contain the Khmer Rouge advance and channel its movements, especially along the forest edges and in the valleys which lie between the small hills marking the west and centre of the district. The hills themselves were also heavily mined since they served as infantry bases and artillery emplacements.

In the second half of 1990 the Khmer Rouge closed in on the administrative heart of the district, which lies in the eastern-most commune of Sdao. In November 1990, it set up its artillery pieces on Phnom Dum Meay, a striking mountain which dominates the commune from the southern side of the Sangke River. Over the next three months an artillery bombardment was launched which was utterly to devastate the ancient country towns of Treng, Thmar Prous and Sdao, shattering the district's social infrastructure which had been so painstakingly constructed earlier in the decade. According to local government sources who served there at the time, the district on occasions received between 3,000 and 5,000 artillery shells and mortars a day. As a result the problem of unexploded ordnance is at least as severe as that of mines. Throughout the ordeal, Sio Lean Seang, the medical assistant in charge of the district hospital, dressed the wounds of the injured in a small hand-dug bunker. Over the months of the fighting he watched his hospital literally disintegrate around him.

Before these bombardments Treng and Sdao had been thriving towns of 10,000 inhabitants, with electricity, paved roads and substantial concrete homes. Today Treng is bush country, with only the pock-marked pagoda serving to remind that there once was a town here. Thmar Prous, with its 6,000 inhabitants, boasted proud ancestral homes, built, as tradition demanded, on stilts for ventilation (and to demonstrate social standing – literally, the taller the stilts the more prosperous the family), whose fine *koki* wood had been darkened over the years of use. There is nothing left. In Sdao the only remnants of the former district centre at the close of 1991 were the district office, the hospital and the market building. All bore the scars of the shelling, although by this stage repairs were underway.[8] Today, the cracked and broken pavements, and the rusting metal poles which once carried electricity, bear silent testimony to former times. Those whose task it is now to 'develop' Rattanak Mondul – and by extension Cambodia as a whole – should continually remind themselves that it is not really 'development' that their dollars are buying but, as a first step, a reconstruction of what has been lost.

The Khmer Rouge advance was halted in the last quarter of 1990, as the Phnom Penh regime launched a counter-offensive. As well as mining around its bases and defensive lines during the months of its occupation, the Khmer Rouge also laid anti-personnel mines as they were forced to withdraw with the intent of rendering the land useless for civilian habitation. For example, in Sanang commune of Banan district, that borders Rattanak Mondul, they laid mines around the water gates and along the sides of the Boung Krossar irrigation canal. This reduced the commune's cultivatable area by half. Such a strategy of war making can be disguised in various sanitised military terms, such as 'demoralisation techniques', but in real terms it amounted to nothing less than a declaration of total war: an assault on the means of livelihood of the civilian population in areas which could not possibly be occupied. Such a strategy, which seeks to impoverish and debilitate 'enemy' communities, hoping to undermine the very viability of places where human beings live, can only be described as permanent terrorism by landmine. As will be argued in Chapter 8, such warfare violates one of the most important principles of international humanitarian customary laws governing armed conflict, the concept of non-combatant immunity.

By the summer of 1991, with the UN-brokered peace agreement on the horizon, an uneasy truce and drawing of lines emerged in the district. By this time the Phnom Penh regime had entirely regained control of the two eastern communes of Sdao and Andao Hep. A point 3 km west from Sdao, as one enters Treng commune,

marked the edge of an area administered by the CPAF military commanders and the end of SOC civilian jurisdiction. This 'military zone' at the time of writing (in mid-1993) still consumes all of Treng and Ploumeas communes. The zone extends for a further 20 km to the west before the first Khmer Rouge positions are encountered, a mere 12 km from Pailin, its nominal headquarters.

This 'military zone', whose minefields are not marked on map 3, is far more heavily mined than even Sdao and Andao Hep. Since this area now formed a defensive perimeter, it was extensively remined by the CPAF during the stalemate conditions which emerged after the signing of the Paris Accords in October 1991. Again the aim was to control and channel movements on the low ground between the hills – a task considered impossible without the extensive use of mines given the CPAF's limited manpower and resources.[9] In the south of the district, the Sangke River effectively forms a boundary between Khmer Rouge and SOC zones of influence. However, the boundaries are fluid, and the loyalties of the people in these areas are surprisingly grey – SOC and Khmer Rouge 'supporters' live amicably side by side in the badly war-affected community, where the fighting and its legacies do not discriminate between those they impoverish and maim. Nevertheless, the river has come

Sangke River: Rattanak Mondul's 'frontline'

Previous pages Beng Ampil: 12,000 captives of landmines

to signify a loose boundary, and its banks too have been systematically mined in broad swathes. Some 4 km beyond Treng, Route 10 has been laid with anti-tank mines, some of which have been stacked five deep.[10] The road will never again take this course.

As a result of the fighting virtually the entire population fled the district by early 1990, leaving only a handful of civilians and soldiers' families in Andao Hep and Sdao.[11] They took refuge in and around Battambang city, some staying with relatives, others building themselves makeshift shelters on any free land that was available. Along with another 200,000 civilians nationwide driven from their homes because of the fighting, they became 'internally displaced people', or IDPs as they are referred to in relief worker's jargon.

In August 1991, with the State of Cambodia back in control of part of Rattanak Mondul, the government announced plans for the return of all the district's displaced people. Those from Sdao and Andao Hep could, by and large, return to their homes. The only exception was the devastated Thmar Prous, on the river in Andao Hep, since it was too close to Khmer Rouge positions south of the river and too heavily mined. For those from Treng and Ploumeas, however, a return to Rattanak Mondul did not mean a return to their homes. This was impossible not only because of the continuing uncertainties in the 'military zone' but also because of the intensity of the landmine problem there. When the district authorities tentatively attempted to encourage a few family heads to return to their villages in Ploumeas in May 1992 the endeavour had to be called off due to the appalling casualty rates.[12]

The provincial authorities thus announced plans to build an IDP camp behind the village of Beng Ampil in Sdao commune. This large site, unlike much of the land bordering Route 10, was mine free. However, minefields fenced it round, and in many other senses this was a far from ideal site for such a large 'temporary' settlement. One of the most fundamental criteria for any refugee settlement, water sources, was almost entirely (but necessarily) overridden by the consideration of mine-free land. The site at Beng Ampil has an extremely low water table, at around 90 metres, and in the second quarter of 1993[13] the camp still had only one deep well producing potable water. Nevertheless, from August 1991 the population of the district rose swiftly from 6,000 to around 20,000 by election time in May 1993, with 12,000 of these people, originally from Treng and Ploumeas, now forced to live within the confines of the Beng Ampil settlement.

However, the repopulation of the district was further complicated by the repatriation of the displaced Cambodians from the border camps in Thailand which commenced in March 1992 under the auspices of the UN's High Commissioner for Refugees (UNHCR). In February 1992, it had been revealed that Rattanak Mondul was the most desired district in the entire country for those refugees registering for repatriation: 26,000 people stated an intention to return. Due to the mine and security problems in the district the UNHCR declared Rattanak Mondul a 'no-go area' which was 'closed for returnees'. In no sense could the UNHCR be seen to fulfil its mandate of returning people with 'safety and dignity' when their 'final destination' was a place like this. Nevertheless, by the close of 1992 around 3,000 returnees had arrived in the district, making their way in what were known as 'secondary migrations' from other districts which were declared suitable to receive them. As the repatriation effort entered its final stage in the first quarter of 1993 some 40,000 returnees remained implacable about their desire to return to southern Battambang and a significant percentage of these, despite repeated counselling in the Toul Makak Reception Centre in southern Battambang, made their way to Rattanak Mondul from areas the UNHCR considered safe.

If conditions in the district were so bad, why did these former refugees insist on returning? This is a very involved question, and one which exercised UNHCR and other aid officials working in the district who saw the avoidance of a large-scale spontaneous repatriation into Rattanak Mondul in terms of disaster mitigation. They intensified an information campaign in the second half of 1992, explaining exactly why places like Rattanak Mondul were so eminently unsuitable. While this had some success, for the refugees the desire to return was very deep seated, and confidence in 'official statements' had been undermined by too many years in the border camps. The need to go to Rattanak Mondul in part came down to a desire to 'see it for myself', since the *barang* (foreigner) could not really be trusted. But for many the Rattanak Mondul area was simply home, a place they had left as long ago as 13 years before, and ties of loyalty to ancestral homes, land and family members who had stayed,[14] were so strong that they overrode what western aid officials might consider more rational choices. Thus, even if the illusive 'Option A'[15] repatriation package and its agricultural land had been available in other districts of Battambang, for many Rattanak Mondul returnees, the chances are they would still have made their way there, prepared to wait for an opportunity to return to land with which they felt a sense of belonging, even if it was covered in landmines.

However, vast tracts of suitable agricultural land were not available for the UNHCR or the returnees in Battambang province in 1992, and ironically this provided a further impetus to return to areas like Rattanak Mondul. After an extremely equitable land reform carried out by

Returnees arrive in Beng Ampil camp: back in Cambodia, but still refugees

the SOC authorities at the end of the 1980s, virtually all the productive mine-free land was under cultivation and privately owned by the time the UNHCR arrived at the end of 1991. For the SOC to make land available to returnees in any numbers would have involved taking land from existing owners. The result was that for the former refugees who wanted to return to an agricultural way of life there was extreme land hunger. The only way to acquire farm land was to buy it, and in Rattanak Mondul it was extremely cheap because it was laced with landmines. Furthermore, this now cheap land was also associated with memories of its former productivity and the easy wealth that had accrued to those who had lived in the area in the 1960s. Sio Leang Seang, the hospital director, believed returnees would happily risk the mines to gain access to land of this quality at knockdown prices. He was proved right by the continuing stream of returnees into the district throughout 1993.

For those civilians returning to the district after an extended period on the Thai border, even for those returning from temporary refuge in Battambang in 1991, the district bore little resemblance to the productive place that had been their ancestral home for generations. The district leader estimates that due to the

Chipang Village, Beng Ampil

landmine burden even those able to return to their home villages in Sdao and Andao Hep communes faced, on average, a loss of 50 per cent of the cultivable hectarage that had been available in 1988. In the two western communes of Treng and Ploumeas the situation was even worse. Here some 80 per cent of the cultivable area had been lost to landmines.

This denial of access to land, both in relative terms for the people of Sdao and Andao Hep, and in absolute terms for those from Treng and Ploumeas forced to live in Beng Ampil, was the most bitter legacy of landmine warfare in Rattanak Mondul. For a predominantly agrarian population it amounted to a collective tragedy and is the single most important factor in the current impoverishment of the entire district.

Main street, Beng Ampil

Given these conditions, and in the absence of any large-scale demining effort by the UN or other demining agencies,[16] the civilian population of Rattanak Mondul was left with two stark 'choices' in order to survive, both of which involved taking enormous risks with landmines. The first of these 'choices' was to clear the land of mines – either by themselves, or by employing ex-soldiers with a degree of knowledge to undertake this task for them. Understandably, most were reluctant to take on the role of deminer, and many had reservations about asking others to take these risks, even if they had the resources to buy such services locally. Thus, most resorted to the second 'option', which involved entering known mine-risk areas to cut and gather wood, bamboo and other natural resources. These activities, which had previously been regarded as a useful supplement to incomes gained primarily from agriculture, became for many the only source of livelihood.

The village of Kilo 38, the only part of Treng commune to which civilians had been able to return by the middle of 1993, lies 3 km west of Sdao on Route 10. In January 1992 there were only a handful of civilians living there, their houses tentatively edging on to the much fought-over land either side of the road. By the close of the year

The market gardens of Kilo 38

well over 500 families had settled in the village. At this point on Route 10 dense minefields and UXO litter the land adjacent to the road in a broad band, in places 100 metres wide. These families have cleared their land to free up not only agricultural but also residential land.

The black loamy soils of Kilo 38 had given the village a prosperous reputation as a market gardening centre in the Sihanouk and Lon Nol times. Late in the 1993 dry

Burning off: preparing to clear mines from the field

season the carefully manicured fields, squeezed in between the road to the north and Phnom Thmar Prous and her heavily mined sisters to the south, were once again bursting with vegetables and industrious watering and weeding.

Two of the gardens had been 'cleared' mechanically: local gardeners had paid the CPAF army to drive its tanks around the fields, the going rate for such a favour being 10,000 riels ($4) a hectare. However, such essentially amateur approaches were only storing up trouble for the future, as such clearance would in no way deal with all the mines, and may have complicated matters by burying unexploded mines and ordnance. On the north side, however, only small house plots had been cleared. The minefields there were considered simply too dense and dangerous to tackle in order to free up enough land to make agriculture viable.

The commonest strategy employed by local deminers is direct 'hands-on', manual clearance. First, the fields are burnt, the hope being that the heat of the fire will set off some mines. Although the technique is rightly viewed with scepticism by demining experts,[17] such burning practices do cause some mines to explode. Once the vegetation has been burnt back, so the local logic runs, the deminer will also have a clearer view of any mines that lie close to, or on the surface. The ground is then gently prodded with hoes to reveal the position of mines which, when identified, are lifted or destroyed *in situ*. A French Foreign Legion contingent of UN deminers operating in Rattanak Mondul in April 1993 recorded local deminers stacking the mines and UXO and destroying them *en masse*, often by placing them in the middle of a large pile of wood which was then burnt. However, there is strong evidence that the majority of mines unearthed by locals in this way are not destroyed. Either they are stored for future personal use or they are resold to the military. Other deminers actually dismantle the mines, using the explosives and detonators for hunting and fishing, while the metal casings from UXO and POMZ-2s[18] are sold on to scrap metal dealers from Battambang. In Cambodia, as elsewhere, the refuse of war has been recycled and incorporated into daily life.

Such impromptu local initiatives, conducted without proper detection equipment, training or the necessary site management discipline to ensure that all potentially dangerous land is systematically checked, is hazardous not only to those engaging in it but also to those who subsequently have to use the land. Thus, casualty rates for such deminers have been extremely high. Deap Vuern, one of the civilian deminers from Kilo 38, told me that in January 1992 there had been nine informal deminers operating in the village. During the year four had died, three had had accidents and one had moved away, leaving only him. With so much local demand on his skills it is unlikely that Vuern will cease taking risks with landmines. On one day in January 1993 he removed 28 mines from a site at the far end of the village where a newly arrived family wanted to build their house. In return he received 4,000 riels ($1.6).

Deap Vuern and a Type-72B: the printed circuit is an anti-handling device, tilt the mine more than 10 degrees and it will detonate

Portrait of Deap Vuern, A Local Deminer

In rural areas like Rattanak Mondul, where the land is literally the source of life, deminers derive considerable prestige. This is particularly so in a culture like Cambodia's where the attributes of the warrior – courage, bravery and self-sacrifice for the common good – are highly valued. But if Vuern is a local hero this status does not betray itself in the state of his home. He lives a few yards off the main highway in one of the smaller, more dilapidated shacks that have sprung up in Kilo 38. Its walls and roof are of old grey thatch and contain a space barely big enough for Vuern, his wife and their two small children to sleep in, let alone live. But perhaps Vuern's obvious poverty brings out an important point about landmines: they have a special relationship with the poorest within the societies they plague. It is only the poorest, or those who have lost the most as a result of the mines' arrival, who will be prepared to take risks with them as part of their new daily routines. Vuern is quite candid about this point:

I demine other people's land because I am poor. I have no land of my own, I cannot farm, but I know how to demine.

Vuern learnt his trade during a spell in the army from 1985 to 1990, and claims he would never ask those he helps for money; however, most people are grateful and usually give him something. I asked how he decided where to demine?

I look out for mines myself, when I'm cutting bamboo or harvesting. I want to clear the area. For instance by the mango tree, a cow trod on one so I had to go in to rescue it … the neighbours wanted to sell it but were too frigthened to go in and get it … Or when people have trodden on mines, others come and tell me, and I go and clear there. Some people appreciate it, but others hate me, they're jealous of my skill. But most people trust and like me. They would go into the fields and bamboo groves where I have already demined.

Can you guess how many mines you have taken out?

I've never counted. I sift through the soil with a sickle. When I find the mine, I take it out. I just throw them on a pile. Perhaps 600 PMNs. And hundreds of 69s and POMZ-2s. In all, over the last year or so since I came back here, counting all types of mines, more than 10,000. They use many different types, but I've generally found four – 72s, 69s, POMZ-2s and PMNs. They mix the Type-72s in with the 69s, one 69 to three 72s. Sometimes there were about 100 69s surrounded by the 72s. They want you to see the 69s, so that in trying to go for them you tread on the other mines.

I've sold lots of the POMZs; they are the only ones you can sell for scrap because of the metal. I use the explosive for fishing. I get 300R for each casing. I sell three or four times a month and get 30,000–40,000R on each occasion. I get enough from selling them to live on.

Some of the deminers in the village have had accidents, like the chap over there who copied me, but he wasn't careful. I am always careful to get a feel of the different parts of the mine. And then Hieng and Ouk died but they stumbled on them when they went to harvest. So it wasn't due to demining. Two others were injured. I'm the only one now who demines for people here.

Are you worried about your husband's demining? (to Vuern's wife)

Yes. I am worried and frightened but if there's no demining, we have no way of earning a living. We couldn't harvest.

Vuern added,

My wife does worry for me. But I have demined with my wife. She would stand behind me and I would throw the cases (of the mines) to her. We would clear around 100 mines in a couple of hours. Yes, OK there are risks. But if you're careful you'll be allright. You have to search them out painstakingly and methodically. Really I haven't got much choice; look at this grass I've just cut from out the back here. I had to demine 12 72s to get this. They were laid along the road, the grass was well above my head, nobody's been there for ages, so I bent down to look for mines just in case. After taking out the 12 mines, then I started cutting. I left the cases (of the mines) in the wood, I couldn't be bothered to bring them back ....

So widespread are such informal deminers that by the summer of 1993 the UN-affiliated body the Cambodian Mine Action Centre (CMAC) set up to co-ordinate a sustained long-term response to the mine problem in Cambodia (see Chapter 5), had realised the need to set up a 'village deminers' course'. The idea, still being developed at that stage, was that these individuals would receive some training and equipment, and rather than being encouraged to carry on demining their local areas would work as the eyes and ears of CMAC in the villages. Their tasks might include responding to mine problems and accidents, reporting minefields and marking danger areas. To encourage such local deminers, even if they have received a modicum of training, to attempt to engage in long-term minefield clearance would be to put such individuals, and those that subsequently have to use their 'cleared land', unnecessarily at risk.[19]

Sadly, as the UN's mandate period in Cambodia drifted to an end in mid 1993 expert observers believed that the majority of demining activity in Cambodia was still being conducted by such local deminers. Acting without training, equipment or proper organisational support, they seemed destined to pay with their lives and limbs the price of the shortfall between the needs of ordinary Cambodians for mine-free land and the ability of the UN and others to meet these needs. By the end of 1992 the UN had managed to allocate only one demining team to Rattanak Mondul. However, six months later, when Rattanak Mondul's position as one of the most heavily mine-affected districts in the country had become clear, some 14 UN demining teams had become operational in the district, together with one team supervised by the humanitarian NGO, the Mines Advisory Group. Nevertheless, while this level of organised demining was encouraging, the inability of the Cambodian Mine Action Centre, tasked to employ these UN-trained teams in the long term, to secure funding for demining, seemed to pose a serious question as to the sustainability of this much needed response (see Chapter 5 for further discussion of the role of CMAC, and in particular its funding shortfalls). In the short term these teams in Rattanak Mondul could only start to clear res-

UNTAC base, Treng 1993: while shells fall in the distance …

idential land – land that is being settled by the near constant stream of returnees still finding their way to the district; they can do little in the foreseeable future to tackle the need for the mass restoration of agricultural land.

In the meantime conditions in the district for the majority of its inhabitants remain severe. Due to the long-term lack of access to mine-free agricultural land, the district's entire population continued throughout 1992 and 1993 to be classified as 'Internally Displaced' (IDPs) under the World Food Programme's (WFP)[20] criteria, despite the fact that about 40 per cent of the district's

Food aid: surrounded by some of Cambodia's most fertile, but unusable land, residents of Beng Ampil camp receive assistance from the World Food Programme

population had actually been able to return to their home villages. As IDPs they were eligible for food support. Although, this assistance, consisting of a rice ration, fish, oil and salt, was only ever designed as a supplement – although valuable, it in no way provided a living ration. Thus, despite relief efforts the vast majority of the district's inhabitants, lacking access to enough land to provide even a subsistance income, has been forced to take up the second 'choice' – an almost total reliance on cutting and gathering the products of the surrounding forests and scrublands to survive.

Not only were mines laid in broad bands through fields, and along access routes, rivers and irrigation canals, but they were also heavily laid in the forests which have subsequently become the main source of livelihood for the people of Rattanak Mondul. The deployment of mines in the forests often involved booby-traps, sometimes using trip wires or specially improvised devices. Thus, with a lamentable twist, the people of Rattanak Mondul found themselves totally reliant on their traditional usage of the forests just when the forests had themselves become host to a new and deadly crop.

Previous pages Mine accident survivors, Beng Ampil, 1993

Voices From Kilo 38, Treng Commune, Rattanak Mondul; April 1993

Interview with Ou Ly, 43-year-old widow, Resident of Kilo 38

Ou Ly's house was well known to me when I interviewed her in April 1993. It was the small grass hut on the left as one reached the end of Kilo 38 village which straddles Route 10. I always took visitors there, and turned the car. It presented a dramatic image: the base of the mountain and the red laterite of the pock-marked road bending out of sight, and the lush vegetation closing in on either side. Beyond, the road crossed the wasted military zone, a barren expanse of mine-riddled land and burnt out villages. It was as if Ou Ly's house was perched on the edge of the habitable world. And Ou Ly was a good person to talk to anyway. She had lost her husband in the fighting and, like so many deprived of land by the mines, had to make a risky living cutting grass in areas where mines were known to present a hazard.

How much land do you have?

I've some 2 hectares quite a way from here. I can't work that land because of the mines. I've asked for some land here. I've just got the yard surrounding the house

How do you make money?

I work on what I've got

How many of you are there?

We're a family of four. Three are here. My son is at school in Battambang. Two girls are here.

Do you go to cut grass?

Yes, quite far away where there are no mines. I carry it back on my head. I gather waterlily and other water vegetables.

Are there mines there?

Yes, there are some but I go with deminers and only go into the fields after they've done the demining. I only go to places that have been demined.

How do you know where it's safe to go?

We are told by the soldiers who give out information so people can earn a living. There are both soldiers and Pol Pot men around. Where there are Pol Pot men, people don't touch the mines. They demine areas where there are only our soldiers.

How about you? Would you demine?

I don't know how. Some people are willing but others are too scared to go near the mines.

Are there many accidents during grass cutting?

Yes, some. About 20 people from this village. Halfway through March one person died. Since I came back in 92 about ten people have died and another ten have

lost their limbs. These are only approximate numbers. I haven't counted, I only hear every so often.

How do you feel about not having access to your farmland. Are you angry?

No, I'm not angry with any side. You can say I'm angry, then again you can say I'm not. Even if I was angry, I couldn't do anything against them.

But do you think about it?

Of course I do. I think I can't earn my livelihood as before and that makes me angry. If we're used to living in our own house and we can no longer live in it, then we'd be quite angry.

We've just been talking to Deap Vuern who lives at the other end of the village. Have you ever thought of asking someone like him to demine your land?

I don't know the deminers. I've never been to their houses. It's true that we live close by but we're too busy. I have to go out and cut grass in the morning, carry it back and sell it. I wouldn't dare to ask anyone. If anything happened to them, it would be difficult.

Who does the demining here?

I don't know but I'm told where there are mines and where it's been cleared. There are mines up to 500 metres from the road.

When you go over there to cut grass are you frightened?

Yes I am frightened but I have to go. If I don't cut grass, I have nothing to live on. That's all I can do. The authorities [the World Food Programme working through the local district officials and Cambodia Red Cross] have given us rice once but we have no money for clothes or food.

What about other people who also go grass cutting?

They're just as frightened. We're dealing with the unknown. Sometimes they are well buried and you can't see them. Sometimes they stick out above ground so you can warn others.

How much do you get per thatch?

40 R. I do about 30 bundles a day.

So you do about 200 a week?

Only if I don't cut. If I cut and tie, I can only do 30.

Do the other members of your family help with the thatch?

No, my children are small. They're all at school. I'm on my own.

How much do you make in a month?

I've never calculated. I sell as I go along: 10, 20. I use the money to buy food so I can't tell as I've never kept a record. I spend as I earn. There's never been any money left over so I can't tell because the money comes in and goes out the same day"

What would become of your family if you had a minor accident?

I've no idea. I wouldn't be able to work. Those with savings would be allright. If Angka felt sorry for you, they might help.

Do you get any food from the World Food Programme?

I get rice but have not received any for three months. Before we used to get aid every month or two. It was 15 kg of rice per person. I've not had anything since November or December 92.

Does your family have enough to eat?

No. We live on a day-to-day basis. I get about 300R a day. I have to pay for food, school money for the children and to buy rice. Seven cans of rice is 1,000R. It lasts a day and a half.

Sokhorn: The Returnee's Tale

Forty-eight-year-old Sokhorn, had only just arrived in Kilo 38 when we spoke with her at the end of April 1993. Deprived of her former land in a neighbouring district due to her long absence in the UN-assisted refugee camps in Thailand, she talked to us of her new life in Rattanak Mondul. Sokhorn, a widow with her aged mother to support, has added yet one more 'female-headed household' to those already resident in the district. She has settled close to Ou Ly, and now goes out with her to cut grass and bamboo.

How long have you lived here?

About a fortnight.

Which camp did you come from?

From Site 2, Nong Chan camp.

Why did you leave to go to Thailand in the first place?

When I had escaped from Pol Pot, I didn't know what to do. I was told that if I went over there, the westerners would give me rice. So with my husband and parents we went there in 79. After Pol Pot, I had no land left. Nothing at all.

Did you live in Kilo 38 before?

I don't come from here. I come from Moung Russey district, on the road to Pursat. When I came back from the border camps, I thought that I'd lost all my land in Moung. Those who came back first had claimed it for themselves. I decided to come here and ask for some land.

When you were in the camps did you know that there were a lot of mines in Rattanak Mondul?

No, I didn't. It was only when I got here that people told me the land was heavily mined. They told me not to wander too far out.

How do you plan to make money?

I've got two possibilities: grass cutting and bamboo cutting. I'm scared of mines so I'll only follow the villagers who know the area better.

Do you know that there are lots of mines where the bamboo and grass grow?

I've never seen a mine. A few days before New Year one person died. I only saw the body being carried out. The villagers say that it's dangerous towards the mountains.

Do you ask the neighbours for advice on safe places?

I talk to the neighbour over here and ask to go with her. She's quite willing to take me as she's lived here for a while.

Are you happy living here?

Yes I am. I'm not happy about the mines. But being able to sell the grass and bamboo and to buy some clothes will make me happy to live here.

Did you gather the materials for your house?

I was given money by UNHCR to purchase the materials but the money was insufficient as there are only two of us in the family and we got $50 each. I had to go and cut some grass to cover up the exposed parts.

You can hear the shelling, are you afraid of the Khmer Rouge?

I'm afraid of Khmer Rouge shelling. I don't know who's who. I gather all my belongings together at night.

What do you think will happen when UNTAC goes home?

I'll have to stay here with the villagers but I am scared and sad about UNTAC going because I'm frightened that the Khmer Rouge will attack.

Are you afraid of anyone else other than the Khmer Rouge?

I'm scared of all of them but the Khmer Rouge are the main ones.

Yim Samed: Farming in Rattanak Mondul

Yim Samed lives together with his brothers and sisters and their parents. They pool their land and resources, and are one of the more prosperous families in Kilo 38. Yet even they have lost land to mines.

How long have you lived here in Kilo 38?

Since 82. After the Pol Pot time we came back here. We had been farming in Kandal [near Phnom Penh] but there wasn't enough land, so we came back here. It wasn't easy at first, but the land is good and it was free then. We had to flee to Battambang in 1989, but came back in 1991.

Why did you leave?

Because of the war. It was under heavy attack from Pol Pot. We couldn't live here and had to flee.

What was the fighting like in 89?

It was very heavy. The Khmer Rouge had access on either side of us. They placed their big gun up on the hill to shell into here. The people couldn't remain here. They had to get out to save themselves.

How much land did you have in 88?

A lot of land, over ten hectares. We pooled with my brothers and sisters. Today we are still unable to work the land at the foot of the mountain. We're so frightened of the mines.

So how much land can you use now?

I work on just three hectares near here ... I don't know what the solution is. We rely on the UN deminers but they haven't turned up yet. The people have to do it themselves. If there was an organisation prepared to buy the mines, the people would clear them faster than the deminers. At the moment they get peanuts. About 300R per mine. We need help to demine the agricultural land. In the real forests the mines can stay there. The trees will need some 60 years to mature. The mines will have rotted away.

How is your life for you now then?

If we don't have to flee, we will slowly move forwards. For instance, this year I can buy a pair of cows to plough the fields. So life is a little easier.

Are you angry about the mines?

Of course. I'd be even more angry if they mined my clean land

Are mines good or bad weapons?

Bad. They bring misery.

Should those who supplied the mines pay for the demining Cambodia now?

Yes the right thing to do would be for them to pay for the demining. The major powers who made the explosives available to Cambodians have wrought misery on Cambodian children.

Is the widespread use of mines wrong?

Well, not everywhere is mined. The parties who capture land would tend to mine it to delimit their gains. For instance, there are lots of mines in Thmar Prous, down by the river. There is no way of telling where there are mines even over all the land worked by the people. People find out by stepping on them.

Should mines be banned across the world?

Yes, I think so. I'm very happy to support this good view. If this decision can be taken, the fate of people on this earth would be a happier one.

Surveys by NGOs and international, UN humanitarian agencies[21] have revealed that for the vast majority of the population of Rattanak Mondul wood and bamboo cutting, and the gathering for grasses from which thatches are made (used for roofing and wall covering on simple country shacks), in areas known to the cutters to have landmines, had become an accepted fact of life by 1992, if not before. Studies of mine victims admitted to the district hospital have borne this out: almost all were engaged in cutting and gathering activities in areas where the victim knew there was a risk.

Figure 3.1 Victims of landmines: Rattanak Mondul 1979 to February 93

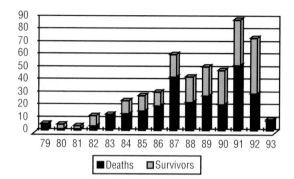

The year ending November 1992 saw some 130 mine victims pass through the district hospital. Yet for every victim who makes it to the hospital perhaps another two perish at the site of injury, most of these never making it on to official injury statistics. Figure 3.1, based on statistics of survivors of mine accidents still living in the district, and statistics of those who have died as a result of mines during 1979–93 (see Appendices 1 and 2 where the statistics are produced in full [22]), reveals the steadily growing nature of the mine problem for the people of Rattanak Mondul. Figure 3.1 not only reflects the increasing contamination of the district with mines, but to some extent it also mirrors the growing intensity of the civil war itself, from the re-emergence as a fighting force of the reconstructed Khmer Rouge movement in 1982, to the escalation of the stakes during 1989.

However, it should be noted that the landmine victim statistics – as appalling as they are – are by no means comprehensive. Due to the weakness of the managerial class in Cambodia, shattered as it was during the Pol Pot time, and governmental austerity imposed by the siege-like conditions of the embargo throughout the 1980s, such local statistics were not meticulously kept. Thus, while all of those named as survivors of mine accidents were located in the villages, typically several more amputee mine victims came forward when we went to check the records. Similarly, it is likely that the death statistics under-record the true size of the problem. Taking even these conservative figures it is sobering to note that in Rattanak Mondul one family in eight has a family member who has either died or been injured by a landmine accident in the last 13 years, over half of these injuries occurring in the last four years.[23] However, given the observations made in Chapter 2 about the sex – and age-specific nature of mine injuries it can be argued that such rates of mine injuries are more threatening than the raw data would suggest. Even accepting these figures as accurate, it can be roughly estimated that one in seven of the adult male population has either died from or been injured by a mine accident in the last decade.[24]

These statistics also indicate both the slowing of the rate of injury and death following the evacuation of the district in 1990 and the renewed surge of injury and death as people returned to the district in 1991, unaware of where the newly laid fields were. Rates in the early part of 1993 looked set to produce another bad year as population pressure buoyed up by the returnees and the last of the internally displaced to leave the Battambang area impacted the district. The surge in injuries in 1987 reveals the effects of another episode of forced labour, *Gor Bram* (K5) on the great barrier minefield in the west of the district. Presumably such repairs to the tank ditches and bamboo wall that complemented the minefields were advance preparations for the eventual withdrawal of Vietnamese troops. In the event these ineffectual efforts cost the people of Rattanak Mondul dear.

However, even these striking figures, taken in isolation, fail to communicate the full effects of mines in impoverishing the entire district. They do not show that mines are the single largest cause of disability in the district, nor that they are one of the district's three most significant causes of death. Mines have produced a medical, social and economic state of emergency in Rattanak Mondul.

For those living in Sdao and Andao Hep, the journey to cut wood, bamboo or grass is typically one of 3–10 km; nevertheless this invariably means either transiting, or entering, a known mined area. Usually this activity is a vital supplement to continued agricultural activity, even if only on a garden-plot scale. However, in Beng Ampil camp, conditions are much harder. While some of the women cut and gather grass in the immediate vicinity of the camp almost all the men are engaged in cutting wood, often at great distances.

Returning from the forests: the daily cycle of risk taking

Loading up: 'entrepreneurs' send their trucks to haul away logs cut by the wood cutters of Beng Ampil

The wood cutting 'industry' run out of Beng Ampil is a formal, organised endeavour controlled by lumber merchants in Battambang who no doubt pay considerable 'fees' to the district authorities to allow them to exploit the pool of under- and unemployed male labour made landless and trapped by war and landmines. These men are contracted to cut wood at piece rates of 700 riels

Wood cutting: in the distant mine-infested forests a mine accident is nearly always fatal

($0.28) per cubic metre while the 'entrepreneurs' merely provide trucks to transport the wood away, either to Beng Ampil itself, where a series of small saw pits sprang into life during 1992, or to Battambang. This is at a time when a family of four requires at least 50,000 riels ($20) a month to exist in addition to the basic support given by the WFP rations.

The wood cutters often travel up to 50 km, deep into the malarial forests which stretch away to the south of Beng Ampil. They will stay in the forest lumber camps for up to three weeks at a time. A mine injury in these remote areas is almost always fatal due to the length of time it takes to evacuate an injured wood cutter. The standard means of transport in such circumstances is a hammock suspended on a pole and carried by two men who might take over 24 hours to reach even a first aid station.

Rates of injury are seasonal, however. During the rice planting, transplanting and harvesting season (the European autumn and winter) rates of injury slump somewhat as people seek paid labour in the rice fields. However, in the dry and hot seasons (spring and summer), when this work is no longer available, people are forced back into a reliance on the forests and scrublands for a source of livelihood.

By the end of 1992 there had developed a keen sense among the people of Rattanak Mondul that they knew where the minefields, and 'safe' paths and areas, were situated. This local knowledge had developed from an awareness of where accidents had occurred over the 18 months since people had returned to the newly mined district. In other words, areas were assumed to be safe until accidents occurred. Such 'confidence' – in part a necessary defence mechanism to enable people to carry on living under such appalling conditions – needs to be severely qualified.

First, having experienced a surge of injuries in 1991 and the early parts of 1992 as 'safe areas' were located, the people of Rattanak Mondul exploited the wood and scrublands in these places. However, as revealed in the case histories in the following chapter, such areas could not provide a sustainable livelihood. 'Safe' woodlands became exhausted, bamboo groves got cut, and so on, and there was a cycle of harvest, exhaustion and the need to find new areas to work. It is in this last phase of the cycle that the injuries occur and that the search for a new copse to cut takes on the characteristics of enforced Russian roulette. During one seven-day period in February 1993, as the dry season gave way to the hot, there were four known mine accidents resulting in as

'Safe path' behind Beng Ampil

Beng Ampil residents provide a pool of cheap labour; middle men take huge profits from local people who take huge risks

many casualties and three deaths. Even the people of Rattanak Mondul were shocked and for a few days people reported that they were too scared to venture among the minefields on their personal searches for safe areas. However, after a few days they were forced back into the daily cycle of risk taking – families needed to be fed and there was no other way of earning an income.

Perhaps it was this protracted torment, the daily fear and grinding necessity without any prospect of speedy resolution, which so shocked those of us who came to know the district at this time. Other wars have rightfully captured the world's attention and sympathy but in Rattanak Mondul it was the slow, routine-like torture and execution of ordinary villagers as they tried to make ends meet in an impossible and poisoned environment which was so shocking.

Secondly, in an area as heavily and as successively mined as Rattanak Mondul there are no truly 'safe' areas until they are verified as such by demining experts and their modern equipment. Even then no absolute guarantees can be given. Some mines remain dormant for years due to a variety of factors, such as the depth at which they are buried, and improper priming of the device. Over time they can become progressively more unstable, especially in hot, humid tropical climates. Thus it must have been for a woman from Beng Ampil, the ninth in a line of 12, who was travelling on a 'safe' path as she and her friends did every day when a mine exploded and destroyed her foot. Similarly, one of the residents of Kilo 38 lost a limb while he was chopping wood from a tree next to his house, an area he had previously 'cleared' and considered safe.

In the context of continuing political and military uncertainties it is not only 'old minefields' which are burdening the people of Rattanak Mondul. In December 1992 a woman stood on a mine a mere 100 metres from where the Dutch-led UN demining team was working, opposite Beng Ampil village. When she had left her rice field the previous Saturday, a field she and her husband had cleared once, the field was probably mine-free (it had been ploughed and planted earlier in the year). As she started back to work on the Monday morning she was injured in a mine blast. Experts believe the mine had been placed there overnight.

There have also been instances of dispute settling in the area using landmines. The laying of mines by locals with the intention of injuring neighbours may be motivated by specific grievances or by a misguided desire to share bad *kama* with others who are more successful, or who have not suffered as much. However, it is possible that some new mine-laying is still directly related to the war. In Rattanak Mondul and many other areas in the western and north central provinces the Khmer Rouge remained committed to a policy of 'nuisance mine-laying' right through the UN time.

Despite the billions of dollars invested by the UN in an attempt to resolve Cambodia's political problems, the people of Rattanak Mondul will never taste the benefits of the 1993 election until they receive substantial and sustained help in their continuing war against mines for control of their land. From the perspective of these rural communities, such an allocation of resources by the UN may seem hollow in the absence of even a fraction of this funding being made available for demining.

Thatch and rattan: the patterns of risk taking

4
Voices From Rattanak Mondul: The Human Costs of Indiscriminate Mine Warfare

I had not thought death had undone so many.
Sighs, short and infrequent, were exhaled,
And each man fixed his eyes before his feet.

T.S. Eliot, *The Wasteland: 1. The Burial of the Dead*

Landmines have robbed Rattanak Mondul district of its prosperity. For a first-time visitor the relationship between landmine warfare and poverty is not so easy to discern. What is obvious, however, as one walks through the small rural villages of Andao Hep, or along the dusty tracks between the sections in Beng Ampil camp, is the large number of amputees, almost every one a survivor of a mine accident. One person in 90 is an amputee in Rattanak Mondul, almost four times the national average.[1]

Below, the stories of just a few of these direct victims are told. Although they represent only a small selection they should be considered as typical. The economic necessity of entering known mined areas to scavenge for a living has led to a production line of death and maimings. A terrorist pollutant has entered this community, and like a cancer it is steadily eating away its living cells.

Researching these personal histories could have been a depressing experience, but it was the opposite – something very positive and inspiring – because these are stories of courageous, spirited individuals carrying on with life under extremely difficult environmental and personal conditions.

Ngeth Bros and Horn Hong

Ngeth Bros and Horn Hong, both young men in their early 20s, were *'por mak slap ruos'* , best friends for 'death and life', sworn to look after one another for ever. They lived in one of the villages of Ploumeas Commune, relocated to Beng Ampil camp in Sdao and, like many, sustained their families by cutting wood in the forests that surround the camp.

On Tuesday 16 February 1993 they set out with Hong's brother, Sophal, to cut wood at Kok Chor, 4 km from Beng Ampil. As usual they travelled to the small settlement in a buffalo cart, and then walked into the forest. The area where they usually cut wood had almost become exhausted, and they knew they would soon have to find a new supply. Thus, when they noticed a fresh track leading off into the forest where other people had clearly been working the day before they were eager to explore its possibilities.

Bros lead the way, followed by Hong, with Sophal trailing behind. They passed the recently cut trees, and decided to go on just a little further up the track where the wood closed in on the path. It was then that Bros trod on a mine, losing his right foot.

Hong, only 4 metres behind, rushed forward to his friend and tied a tourniquet. As he stood back, beckoning Sophal to come and help him carry Bros to safety, he too stood on a mine, which also destroyed his foot. Sophal realised that they had strayed into minefield. Cautiously, he took his axe, and proceeded to prod the ground with the blade to reveal the position of any other mines. It took him half an hour to cover the four metres that separated him from his brother and his brother's best friend. During this time he uncovered 20 small, Chinese-manufactured plastic mines (Type-72As),[2] which are known locally as the 'drum' mine due to their round appearance and the drum-like pressure pad which covers the top of the mine.

Sophal stacked the mines on the side of the path as he slowly advanced towards the two injured friends. Bros had regained consciousness by the time Sophal reached them, and was extremely distressed, not so much by his own injuries but by the fact that his best friend who had risked his life to help him, appeared to be dead. Sophal tried to calm him but he kept saying that if his friend was dead he too should die, such was their commitment to each other.

As Sophal was trying to revive Hong, Bros crawled back down the path and lifted himself over several of the mines Sophal had cleared. He turned his head, and told Sophal to tell everyone what Hong had done for him, and to say goodbye to his family. He then let himself fall on to the mines. He died instantly.

But Hong was not dead, merely unconscious. Sophal managed to carry him back to Kok Chor, and from there take him by buffalo cart to Beng Ampil. From the camp Sophal took his brother by motorcycle taxi[3] to the district hospital. Later that afternoon, he was transferred to the provincial hospital, where his right leg was amputated below the knee. He is now out of danger and should make a good recovery. Although such an injury is a tragedy, as Tith Poue's story below reveals, with a prostheses a reasonable degree of mobility can be regained. The burden of his friend's death may not be so easily overcome.

Bros was cremated that evening at Beng Ampil *Wat* together with a man named Vuern who had died the same afternoon, a result of his misguided attempts to defuse a B-40 rocket which he had found lying near the dam opposite Beng Ampil camp. As Vuern had worked on the rocket, a crowd of children had gathered round to watch the man's expertise, fascinated by his bravery and daring. Fortunately, none of them was seriously injured in the blast. Vuern's brother had died two months before, another of Rattanak Mondul's mine victims.

The following day I arrived at the *Wat*, one of the few buildings to have survived the shelling in the 1989–91 period, at the same time as Bros's relatives. They had come to witness his last rites and, as is customary, collect some fragments of his bones. In the field behind the pagoda smouldering mounds of ash were all that remained of the two men. The ceremony was conducted by an old man who, although not a full-time monk, lived at the *Wat* and understood the traditional burial rites and the correct *Pali* [4] chants, to be used to ensure that the dead men's spirits did not escape the ground. He estimated that in 1992 he had cremated at least 50 mine victims, and he reckoned that perhaps as many people again either had been cremated at home or never recovered from the remote minefields where they had died.[5]

As they were leaving the *Wat*, with Bros's bone fragments tightly wrapped in a white cotton sheet, his family told me that since 1988 they had lost four members of their family to landmines. Bros's bones were taken back to the family home and placed on the spirit table with those of his relatives. Every night extra joss sticks will be lit to the memory of the Ngeth family's latest victim of the war of the mines.

Ches Sary

I first met 25-year-old Ches Sary in July 1992. She was laying on an old bamboo mat spread on a rough iron bed in the surgical ward of Battambang provincial hospital. The long, low building built by the French during the years of their rule, with its tiled floors and glassless shuttered windows, had not been decorated for many a year: its white painted walls, scuffed and worn, now had a grey sheen. It seemed a desolate, painful place, where the only true care a patient might receive was from their relatives and even then, materially, only if they had the money to buy what was needed.

Sary had lost her left leg as a result of a landmine blast on the river bank 3 km from her home in Anlong Pouk village of Andao Hep commune. She had been digging bamboo shoots to sell in Sdao market, as she used to do three or four times a week, hoping to raise the modest sum of 1,000 riels ($0.40) for her day's work. She was two-months' pregnant at the time.

From Anlong Pouk access to the river is very easy, and in more normal times this would be a blessing. However, both banks are now very heavily mined, a product of both the past fighting and the continued presence of the Khmer Rouge south of the river.

Sary was forced to supplement her family's income in this potentially dangerous way since her husband, a soldier, received only 30,000 riels ($12) a month for his role in the defence of the district. Their family needs about 55,000 riels ($22) a month to survive. By 1992 Sary's husband was receiving only half his salary due to the State of Cambodia's lack of resources, a direct product of the deepening bite of the international embargo imposed on the Phnom Penh regime. As she puts it: *sometimes he gets a month's wages every three months. Sometimes two months' wages after a four-month wait. It's not regular. If it were, we might be able to live on it.*

On the day of her accident Sary had set out with two of her aunts and her two younger sisters. Usually they would walk 3 km to the south, cross a small stream, and continue a further 100 metres or so until they reached the Sang Ke River itself. They would wade across and dig their shoots on the south bank of the river. However, the day before, her grandfather had come back from a bamboo cutting outing and suggested that they try digging for shoots along the banks of the small stream, just before one reaches the river. He had seen lots of shoots here – it was clearly an area that few of their neighbours had used yet.

Thus, on the morning of 5 July 1992 the women set off with a new destination in mind. When they reached the stream Sary led the way, her attention drawn by a big clump of bamboo about 3 metres off the path. However, she was looking for small shoots suitable to dig, pot and sell in the market, and there were none here, so she turned and made back for the path, by the shortest route. As she squeezed through the undergrowth that had grown up beside a large tree she triggered a mine. She recalls:

I was out foraging, going to get some bamboo. On the way, I trod on a mine. I couldn't see it from afar. I wanted to be rich, to provide for my child. It was a path I knew well. You never know your fate. I was just walking along when bang! I didn't think I would live. I thought my child would be orphaned ....

*I fell flat on my face. I thought I had been shot from in front. I knew I had lost a leg. As the mine exploded, my aunt rushed to my side to try and pick me up. She couldn't see me through the smoke but called out: 'My niece, my niece.' I said: 'Aunt, aunt, help me. I don't know where my husband is and I'm sure I'll die . I won't pull through.' They carried me down to the water. The smoke from the mine had not yet disappeared. **If there had been two or three more mines, we would all have been killed.** Fortunately they had only laid one mine. My aunt brought me home. The nearest first aid was in Battambang.*

Sary and her relatives knew that the areas they walked through and worked in potentially contained mines, but were forced by their poverty to accept such risk taking as part of the reality of day-to-day life. Since settling in Anlong Pouk in 1991 the family had had access only to a small vegetable garden, most of the prime farming land in the area having been eaten up by known minefields. Lacking sufficient land to grow food to eat and sell, only the forests provided any sort of livelihood. Thus, as with the other stories told here, Sary's injury was less of an 'accident' than an accepted occupational hazard for a community impoverished by landmines. As a result of Sary's accident, however, the people of Anlong Pouk have learnt to stick to the path when they cross the small stream: another piece in the jigsaw geography of 'safe' and 'unsafe' areas has been filled in.[6]

The Rattanak Mondul of Sary's birth was a very different place. Her parents lived in Thmar Prous, on the north bank of the river not far from the site of her accident. Her father was not rich, but she grew up in substantial wooden Cambodian home, a far cry from the small wood pole-and-thatch hut where she and her husband now live. Most people lived in such ancestral homes, she recalls. The family had two hectares of rice paddy and a small fruit garden; the river provided fish, and they kept livestock. Then, as now, the people supplemented their incomes by gathering activities in the surrounding forests, cutting wood, cane, bamboo and thatch.

In 1975 all this changed. The Khmer Rouge took Sary away from her parents and forced her to work in

Ches Sary: despite the fact that she was two-months' pregnant when she stood on a mine, her baby arrived safely

a youth 'mobile' team. Nevertheless, the whole family stayed in the same area, and in 1979 they were quickly reunited and returned to their old village. Although the family suffered no personal tragedy during the Pol Pot years Sary tells the familiar story of hunger and hard work:

We had all sorts of problems under Pol Pot. The rice harvest was plentiful, but they took the rice, and all our belongings, away. We were only fed on rice gruel. They treated the people very badly. Those who protested were shot. Whether you produced six or 100 bags of rice per hectare, it didn't matter, they would take it all away in lorries. I don't know where they were taking the rice.

In 1984, aged 17,[7] she completed primary school and started to work full time with her family, their lives dominated by the natural cycles of the land. However, the relative tranquillity of the 1980s and the opportunity it afforded for putting lives back together again after the shattering experiences of the Pol Pot time was swiftly interrupted following the withdrawal of the Vietnamese. Sary and her family were again driven from Thmar Prous by the Khmer Rouge. Sary remembers:

There was fighting. For over a month ... we were shelled from the other side of the river. There were three or four of them at a time ... the village was destroyed and we moved here, to be further away from the river. About ten people died – five from the mines and five from the shells – and five others were injured

Despite the war Sary and her husband found the time to marry, as they had been planning to do for some time:

I remember the fighting was intense, but my husband was given a week's leave to get married. He was then called back. We could not live together as husband and wife. It was bad. I could not rely on my husband to support me as he was away at the front. I had no one else to turn to, so I stayed with my parents, as before. There was fighting every two to three days.

Despite these difficulties Sary and her husband tried to make their new life as normal as the circumstances would allow, and a year later their first child was born.

When the fighting died down in 1991 they were able to set up home in Anlong Pouk. Due to its proximity to the Khmer Rouge area south of the river, and the intensity of the mine problem there, her old village of Thmar Prous was no longer a viable place to raise a family: Anlong Pouk was the nearest inhabitable village. For rural Cambodians such as these their sense of tradition and relationship with the land is strong, and in part perhaps this is the reason why they are reluctant to give up their

mine polluted birthrights. On a more practical level, their property being wasted and denied them, they do not have the resources to move elsewhere.

On the day of her accident Sary's brother went to her husband's army unit to tell him the news. He recalls being terrified, not knowing the extent of her injuries, and he deserted to be with her in the provincial hospital the following day. The speed and success with which people recover in Cambodian hospitals depends largely on having relatives available to supplement the care they receive, as well as the economic ability of the family to purchase the necessary drugs, especially those that relate to infection control. Starved of resources, staffed by 'corrupt'[8] medics, Cambodian hospitals in the 1980s and throughout the UN time and beyond were a harsh environment within which to recover from horrible wounds.[9] Sary remembers a surprising amount of her first hours as a mine victim, although her idea of what constituted a 'reasonable' emergency evacuation to hospital reveals a very humble level of expectation.

It didn't take long really, to get to Battambang. Not long at all. The explosion happened at 8. At 9 my brother and sisters, and my sister in law, started to carry me to Sdao hospital. We got there about 10. We then left Sdao hospital and got to Battambang at about 3. We hired a moto-taxi for 5000 riels. The driver was reluctant to take me. He was worried that we wouldn't be able to pay. It was a Sunday and no one was at work at Sdao hospital; the hospital car wasn't there.

When I got to Battambang they put my leg in a bag. They tied it very tightly and I was given an injection. The pain was very bad. I thought I'd die. After the injection, the physical pain diminished but I felt a lot of anguish. I didn't expect to live. Blood was flowing like water. I could only think of my child. Perhaps I would live because the doctors would save my life. I would see my husband, my child, my mother, my father, my brother and sister, again.

Sary stayed in hospital for two months, returning to her village in early August 1992 where she stayed with her mother. She says that friends and neighbours were happy to see her home. Perhaps because landmine accidents are so common in this close-knit rural community those who suffer them do not seem to experience the social problems or rejection observed in other contexts. Despite the traumatic injuries Sary sustained, her second child was born safely in January 1993.

Two weeks after the accident Sary's husband, Ian Goy, was given extended leave from the army to care for his wife and young family. He started cutting bamboo full time to support them. Working on piece rates, Goy is able to earn twice what Sary had managed, his risk taking with landmines bringing home the princely sum of 12,500 riels ($5.00) per week. But Goy realised that unless he could get his family some land they would never regain even the tenuous independence they had enjoyed from Sary's earnings. He responded as many in his village have done, by clearing mines from a piece of free land, although he has no real training or equipment to undertake such a dangerous task. Furthermore, it is possible that what he now considers 'clear' is in fact far from safe. Nevertheless, the family now has access to 2 hectares, some of which Goy planted with corn. His recall to poorly paid, full-time military duty has since left his young wife in an almost impossible situation.

I have nothing to plough this land with. I have to hire the cows. They want 15,000 riels ($6) in baht.[10] That's about 150 baht. Where can I find that sort of money? I don't want him (Goy) to be a soldier. I want him to work on the land. As he is a soldier, there is no one to look after the fields. I had a word with someone in authority that I didn't want my husband to be in the army as I have lost a leg. Who would work to feed my child? Yesterday, I told him to come back. I don't want him to be in the army. I won't let him go to war. After all I am disabled and there is no one to provide for my child. He used to work with rockets. He used to earn 26,000 riels a month and that's not enough for even half a sack of rice.

During the interview my translator was obviously surprised by Sary's courage in speaking out, especially to high-placed local leaders whose authoritarian style was well known. But she said that they made allowances for her since they knew she was disabled, and she remains confident that Goy will be discharged and that maybe life will improve.

She laughed when I asked her if she and her husband were planning to have more children – *We'll have many, many* – she said. Despite the fact that she still obviously has the love and support of her husband, Sary continually 'grieves' the loss of her leg. Her biggest problem is her lack of mobility and the implications for her ability to make money.

When I was able bodied I wanted to work for our future. I wanted to be rich, to be able to look after my child, my brother and sister. After my accident I had no idea how I would earn a living. I couldn't walk. I was totally dependent on my husband. If he earned enough, we would eat. If not, not …. When I was able bodied people knew I worked hard and earned a reasonable living. My aunt now says she doesn't know how I can make a living since I can't go anywhere. She says my life must be wretched. I feel miserable not being able to earn a living.

In an attempt to overcome these mobility difficulties Sary was keen to have a prosthesis made and so in November 1992 she went back to Battambang to visit the ICRC workshop. However, she was advised that it would be better to wait until after the baby was born before making the final adjustments to the limb. In April 1993 she returned and had her prosthesis finished, completing the necessary work with the physiotherapists to enable her to walk with her new limb. I asked her if she was planning to rejoin her friends and neighbours when she becomes more proficient with it, cutting wood and digging for bamboo shoots in areas where mines might strike at any time:

I could go but I want to stay at home …. I've had enough … I could use the leg to go out but I don't want to. I want to get into agriculture and not into cutting wood or bamboo. I used to go to the mountains, but I've lost my nerve. … But the leg works well, it's comfortable and well made and I can go to this house and to that house in the village …. I can cook and cope with domestic chores, go to the market.

Understandably Sary has had enough of the forests and their risks, but without the cash to hire the oxen to plough their newly cleared land, even if Sary's husband is released from the army, it is unlikely that the family will be entirely free from this deadly dependency. Now, however, the stakes are higher. If anything happened to Goy, Sary's life would depend entirely on the continued generosity of her family.

Sonn Thi

Thirty-nine-year-old Sonn Thi is another of Anlong Pouk's 13 amputees,[11] survivors of landmine accidents. With a total population of only 560 people this dubious distinction makes the village one of the worst affected in the district.[12] No longer married herself, she lives with her older sister, who was widowed in 1987, and her sister's four children.

Their family originally came from the western-most parts of Rattanak Mondul, then known as Pailin district. When the Khmer Rouge took over they emptied these areas to prevent people from slipping over the border to neighbouring Thailand. Thi and her family were moved to Sdao, where she worked in a warehouse. Given the fact that she was selected for non-agricultural employment it is likely that she was regarded by the Khmer Rouge regime as at least 'reliable', if not an actual member of the movement itself. This trusted status was confirmed by her officially sanctioned marriage, in 1978, to a local soldier. However, in 1979 when the Vietnamese arrived in Battambang her husband fled to the Thai border fearing, as Sonn Thi put it, that local people would kill him if he stayed. In the confusion,

Sonn Thi was left behind. She has not seen her husband since, nor has she remarried. Despite what are regarded locally as his crimes, she says she still loves him. Local people know full well her past associations but as she noted, 'nobody blames me, they say I was just a simple woman'. In village life there is a great deal of toleration and acceptance.

After the Pol Pot time Sonn Thi settled in Anlong Pouk with her sister's family. They farmed a small rice field and grew some vegetables; however, they always had to go into the forests to cut thatch, wood and bamboo to supplement their incomes. Before the district was fought over and extensively mined in 1989 this provided a hard but stable living. After the death of her brother-in-law, Sonn Thi and her sister relied on the eldest son, Mon, to do the heavy work in their rice field. However, two years ago, when he was 18, he was conscripted into the CPAF, and was posted to old Thmar Prous, on the river. The other son, at 13, was too young to help out, and thus for two years they have grown no rice. Although mines have not been laid in Sonn Thi's sister's field, as they have in those of so many of their neighbours, the strains of the war have nevertheless taken a toll on their family economy.

At the same time that relying on the forests to provide a source of livelihood became so critically dangerous because of the landmine problem, it also became the family's sole source of income. Mon does sometimes send money back to his aunt and mother, but it is only a token contribution.

On 19 May 1992 Sonn Thi headed south from her village with her friends and neighbours to cut cane. They crossed the river, as they did about three times a week, and headed south along a 'safe path' through the forests to a place they knew had good cane, and no mines. She estimates that these trips provided an income of 4,000 riels ($1.60) a week, and they were in addition to grass-cutting expeditions to make thatches, for which Thi and her sister used to stay on the north bank of the river closer to their home.

The cane was brought back to the village and sold on to middle men who took it to Beng Ampil camp, where contract labour split the cane and made it into mats. Wage rates for these labourers were lower than out in the villages of Andao Hep and Sdao, reflecting the relative poverty of the Beng Ampil people and their lack of alternative sources of employment. Even amidst the acute mine-induced poverty of 'communist'-led, SOC-controlled Cambodia, the capitalist instinct of some 'entrepreneurs' was all too evident: minimising labour costs, maximising returns, exploiting natural resources and seeking out the best terms of manufacture and

Sonn Thi: weaving thatches has become the family's only source of livelihood

markets. Yet in Rattanak Mondul, the entrepreneurs, the true risk takers, were those like Sonn Thi who were, and at the time of writing still are, daily prepared to enter minefields to gather the products of the forests to make this 'free market' function.

As they crossed the river Sonn Thi met a friend from Beng Ampil. They fell away from the main group, and he offered to show her a short cut to the cane cutting area which he said would knock 3 km off the journey. Sonn Thi asked him if it was safe, and he told her not to worry.

Three kilometres down their usual path, he led Sonn Thi off to the right down a small track through the forest. He walked in front of her. They had gone 100 metres when they came across three large stones lying on the path. She followed her guide's steps, but as she trod on the first stone she slipped to her right, pushing one of the other stones off the path. In doing so she set off a mine which shattered her right leg below the knee. The guide fled. She has never seen him again.

Sonn Thi was rescued by her friends who, hearing the blast, came to find her. She was carried back to Anlong Pouk in a hammock suspended on a pole, and from there by ox cart for the remaining 5 km to the district hospital where her wounds were dressed before she was transferred to the provincial hospital.

Sonn Thi's sister left her children with friends in the village and went to Battambang to care for her. Although she spent their last cash reserves on drugs , they could in no way afford the full cost of the antibiotics course necessary to fight off infection and allow her wounds to heal. Consequently, her stump became infected and the infection produced swelling which meant that although her amputated leg had been 'closed' a few days after the initial amputation it refused to heal properly.[13] Sonn Thi's suffering, like Ches Sary's, was compounded by the totally inadequate health infrastructure.

Instead of leaving hospital with a well-healed stump, with good skin and muscle cover of the bone end, Sonn Thi ran out of money and left the hospital with her leg still infected and the bone protruding from the stump end. As noted in Chapter 2, such informal discharge of mine victims is a common phenomenon at Battambang.

Once at home, Thi resorted to traditional Cambodian medicine, and dressed the wound herself. Given the lack of sterility of these traditional remedies, her infection problems worsened. It was only the intervention of World Vision's rural health team, who had been funded in part by UNDP specifically to handle such emergency health needs in the district, which saved her life. Once they realised she had discharged herself they followed her up at home and made the necessary arrangements for her to return to the provincial hospital and undergo the further amputation which had become necessary.

Once back on the wards they carefully monitored her care to ensure that she received the necessary drugs to prevent a recurrence of the infection problems.[14] After a successful recovery from her second operation Sonn Thi returned to Anlong Pouk in October.

As I chatted with her in February 1993, Sonn Thi was weaving thatches outside her home. Her sister now assumes sole responsibility for gathering the grass from which the thatch is made. She usually travels 2–3 km, to the foot of Phnom Thmar Prous, an area with mines.[15] She claims to feels relatively safe there, as she believes that local people now have a good idea of where the mines are. In reality, however, during the opening months of 1993 local knowledge had not checked the injury of either people or animals around the base of the hill.

Sonn Thi takes about 20 minutes to make one piece of thatch from this grass. On average she makes between 20 and 30 a day. One thatch fetches 45 riels, giving the family a total income of around 32,000 riels a month ($12.8).

Sor Bun Tuern

Sor Bun Tuern lived in Chipang village, in the Ploumeas section of Beng Ampil camp, with his wife, her sister, and their two children. On 29 May 1992 he set out with some friends to walk the 10 km to Kompong Kul, where they had been three times before to cut the natural twine used in the mat-making process. They had only recently been tipped off that the place was a good site, and were pleased with the amount of twine that could be cut there. Since they were paid by the kilo, such considerations were vital. Their usual place, 15 km behind Beng Ampil camp, which was thought to be mine-free, had almost become exhausted, and yields were down to such an extent that it had ceased to be economic to cut there. Some days Tuern had managed to cut only 3 kg, which at 600 riels a kilo did not represent a living wage for his family.

Tuern

In Komping Kul they had managed 10 kg each. Although Tuern and his friends did not know the area well, they were reassured by the fact that many others had used it safely on a regular basis.

That day Tuern failed to make his quota. He was climbing a large tree when he missed his footing and fell. As he hit the ground a mine went off, causing severe injuries to his face, especially around his eyes. The mine also cost him his right hand. His friends carried him home and put him in a motorcycle taxi to the district hospital where, after having his wounds dressed, he was transferred to the provincial hospital. He lost his right eye, and his right arm had to be amputated mid forearm.

Lacking resources, Tuern discharged himself from the hospital in early July and went home to recuperate in his small shack in Beng Ampil. By October he was suicidal. The blast had caused a traumatic cataract to form on his left eye, and he was unable to see. Dal Huang, his wife, was starting to reject him as is sometimes the case when mine injuries hit families living so close to destitution. She told him that since he had ceased to be able to provide for his family he was no longer a man – he had died as a man in the accident, and since he had died, the whole family was dying.

Since Tuern's accident Huang's 20-year-old sister had been too scared to venture into the forests to cut twine or thatch and her brother, at 14, was too young to be able to support the family. Huang was five months pregnant at the time of Tuern's accident, and as their other child was only three, she could not make a significant contribution to the family's income. In the harsh economic light of Beng Ampil life Huang was right to see Tuern's accident as an economic as well as a personal tragedy for the entire family.

However, Tuern was referred to an eye specialist in the provincial hospital, and in November a successful operation was performed on his left eye, partially restoring his sight. In January he received spectacles and could see almost normally again. However, due to the loss of his right hand, it was difficult for him to perform his usual work, and he maintained that when he became fit enough to return to the cutting areas he would have to rely on his friends to help him. On the morning in mid January when I interviewed him he had just returned from his first trip out to the paddy fields opposite Beng Ampil, looking for frogs to eat and sell. Clearly, as a result of his accident, even with the 'lucky break' of access to the eye surgeon, Tuern's ability to provide for his family had been shattered.

Most of Tuern's adult life had been extremely difficult. During the Lon Nol time he had lived in Kieng Svay district of Kandal province, close to Phnom Penh, where his father served as a policeman. When the Khmer Rouge came to power some of his family's relatives 'denounced' his family to the Khmer Rouge village guards. As a result the Khmer Rouge took his mother and father away for a 'meeting'.[16] He never saw them again.

In 1979, when the Vietnamese invaded Cambodia, he was forced into the army and sent to Battambang to fight the retreating Khmer Rouge. He remained a soldier for ten years, and met Huang in Chipang village of Ploumeas commune, which was her family home. In 1989 they married and Tuern, newly discharged from the army, went to seek his fortune digging for gems in Pailin. After four fruitless months he gave up. During the entire time he had been terrified of the Khmer Rouge who were preparing for their big offensive into Battambang as the Vietnamese withdrew. When the attack started he returned to Chipang and for a few brief months supported the family by cutting wood and cane in the nearby forests. However, when the shelling closed in on Chipang they fled, eventually settling on a small piece of land in Takreum commune, Banan district, 14 km from Battambang which the government had set aside for displaced people. Tuern found a job as a wage labourer, and the family tried to establish a degree of stability.

When the government announced plans for the return of all the displaced people from Ploumeas and Treng communes to Beng Ampil camp in August 1991 Tuern and his family stayed away for as long as possible, knowing that it would be harder to make a living in Beng Ampil. However, in January 1992 they gave in and went to the camp.

Despite the hardships they were experiencing, Tuern and his family talked keenly about the larger problems facing Cambodia. In particular, they were very aware of the threat posed by the Khmer Rouge and were fearful of their return. As I left, Tuern expressed his hope that finally Cambodia might be allowed to 'bleed no more'. 'We need peace,' he said.

At that point I thought I had enough material to tell Tuern's story. However, the 'bad fate' he blamed for his first accident had not finished with him. On the morning of Wednesday 17 February 1993 Tuern and two friends left Beng Ampil to go fishing in the Sangke River. Because his eyesight was less than perfect, Tuern walked in between his two friends. The one who led the way had brought his dog with him. As they approached the river and turned east to walk up the bank the dog took off back up the track, and its owner gave chase. Instead of waiting for his friend to come back Tuern continued on up the path. As he rounded a corner he walked into a fine trip-wire, spread at chest height across the path and attached to a booby-trap device, possibly a bounding mine. He died instantly. His friends fled without recovering his body.

In early April Huang was still deep in mourning. Her head shaved, she rocked back and forth on her haunches as she squatted in their tiny hut, one of the poorest even by Beng Ampil standards. She was extremely distressed and had been so since Tuern's second, fatal accident. As if to confirm her vision of the death of the family, where before there had been a certain sense of order among their absolute poverty, now there was only chaos and the hard air of hopelessness.

We talked about the accident and how she and her family were now coping. She was clearly greatly troubled that Tuern's body had not been recovered and that a proper funeral ceremony had not been conducted to prevent his spirit from roaming endlessly:

How have you all managed since Tuern died?
I don't. I am still breastfeeding. I get a bit of money weaving for people. I can't go far because of my child. I know how to weave mats.
How much are you paid a day?
2,000–3,000 riels ($ 0.8–1.2) for a mat. I get one done every two to three days. Then I can buy cakes and other things for my children.
Do you earn enough from weaving the mats to feed your family?
No. I can scarcely feed my children … My younger sister chops wood now and goes into the forest. But she's scared and I don't like to venture out so I'd rather go without.
Did Tuern know there were mines where he was going?
No, not at all. His body was not brought back. I didn't have the money to pay for someone to go and collect it. I asked people to fetch his body but they couldn't get there because they were too few and they were scared as I didn't have enough money to pay them.
How much money do you need to bring the body back?
I don't know how much. I don't know how much I've spent so far. They're too frightened to go in a small group. With lots of people, it adds up into the tens of thousands. I thought it would be 4,000–5,000 riels but I still don't have the money. They can name their price. You can hire them just to take you to the place but you'd have to take the body out yourself.
Why did the people who were with him not bring him back?
I don't know … They said he caught the full impact of the explosion. He fell over on his face. They prodded him but he didn't move. They said he was dead. They didn't even turn him over … He died on his own.
Why was he in such a dangerous place again?
We were sick and without food. We needed the money. He went to cut cane. He came back on the next day and I told him that people had gone to catch fish. So he decided to go along as well.

Sdeng Phal

Sdeng Phal was 12 years old when he had his accident. On 25 July 1992 the family's two cows that he was tending only half a kilometre from their home village of Beng Ampil panicked and ran into the trees that edge the field. Phal knew very well that this area was heavily mined.

I was very scared, he said, *but I had to get them back.* He walked into the tree line and stood on a mine. He lost his right foot, and suffered severe lacerations to both legs.

The loss of a cow is an economic disaster for most Cambodian families. Phal was well aware that over the previous year perhaps as many as 60 out of the total of 500 cows kept in his village had perished after stepping on landmines. His father estimated that a cow that has been killed or maimed in a mine accident fetches only 150,000 riels (about $60). The cost of a new animal depends on breed and quality, but at the time of writing even an average animal cost 500,000 riels ($200). The difference, $140, represents a small fortune for most Cambodian farmers eeking out a marginal living from their land.

In November 1992 Phal received an artificial leg from the ICRC workshop in Battambang. When he had been rescued from the minefield his uncle had tied a tourniquet around his thigh to prevent the blood loss. In a common mistake, he had failed to release this every 15 minutes or so to allow oxygen through to the lower leg. Consequently, when Phal reached Battambang his lower thigh, knee and the remains of his calf had been starved of oxygen to such an extent that the limb had to be amputated above the knee. The mine had originally claimed 'only' his foot.

Since children are still growing, after amputation their stumps do not stabilise in the same way that an adult's does.[17] For the prosthetists this creates additional challenges, and they would expect to have to change a child's artificial leg every six months or so, to allow not only for stump stabilisation but also for growth. However, Phal was already having problems with his new prosthesis when I visited him in January 1993; he was capable of walking only a short distance with the limb, and even then he found it painful. Initially, he was hopeful that once he had his new leg he could take up where he had left off, but this was not to be the case. For example, although he had managed to walked to school a couple of times he found it too uncomfortable to sit on the hard wooden benches with the limb still attached. I referred him to the World Vision health team who worked in the area and they in turn facilitated his referral back to the ICRC workshop for the prosthesis to be revised. An appointment was made for February.

When I returned to the district in early April he had developed a painful infection in his stump. Without correct treatment an infection can easily become life threatening. The revised prosthesis had proven even less successful than the first, and had rubbed his stump raw. In general, ICRC's work is technically excellent but problems of access to their facilities for poor amputees, especially in such circumstances where repeated adjustments and long-term supervision are required, can lead to serious problems as was clearly the case in this instance.[18] This is not to condemn the work of agencies who are attempting to meet the enormous prosthetics needs of Cambodians, merely to point out that in Cambodia today there are, unfortunately, few easy answers.

Phal's mother, Chea, was very distressed and at last openly angry. In one revealing outburst she told me more of what had happened, and of her feelings, than in all my previous visits:

I haven't even ground the rice yet this morning to make flour for the cakes. I have to sell cakes every day. I have had nothing but accidents this year. First, the girl gets blood fever. A week after she comes out of hospital, one of the cows steps on a mine by Wat Beng Ampil. Barely a week later the boy treads on a mine. The father is also ill. I can't find the wherewithal to pay the debts I've accumulated over the last couple of years.

[On the day of the accident] ... After he had finished eating, he went out to tend the cow. I told him to mind the cow and went out to sell cakes. When I came back I heard an explosion at about 1 o'clock. People called out to me: 'Phal has trodden on a mine.' I couldn't believe it. The cow wanted to mate so it went into the woods. He decided to chase it out because he didn't want it to die and not be able to mate. He went into the woods and trod on the mine.

I feel so sad, so sorry for him. I couldn't believe it was my child who had trodden on the mine. It had to be someone else's. His uncle carried him back in his arms. I was crying. I've no money. I'm working so hard selling cakes to feed my children and now he's been hit by a mine. Oh, it's hard ...

All my relatives gathered round. I wasn't looking after my children. I was just sobbing. I said to my son, 'I don't know what we can count on because you need money to go to hospital.' All the relatives contributed a little each and we raised 9,500 riels. A trishaw was called to take us to Sdao ...

In the hospital in Battambang they didn't give away a single tablet. We had to pay for everything. When we first got there. I had no money ... we just waited... He was screaming with pain and he would shout 'Mother, I want some water'. So the nephew went out to buy a coconut. I said to the doctor 'Please take pity on my son, he's desperate for a drink and he's so badly injured.' He said: 'If you're going to feed him coconut water, why did you bother to bring him here? You should have left him at home. Are you the mother? Have you come from

Phal at home

far? Have you any money?' 'No, I haven't any,' I said. So he walked away from me ...

The doctor came back after about half an hour and said 'So you've got some money now.' I said I didn't have any. He got quite cross, 'If you don't have any money, how can we amputate his leg? He'll need some blood transfusion, and some other medicines.'

I asked my uncle who was with me to go to the pawnbrokers where I was able to exchange 60,000 riels ($ 24). I bought 0.5 litres of serum, and the transfusion cost 10,500 riels. I also bought the other medical requisites. I stood there cradling my child. It was now 5 o'clock. Others who came with money were seen to immediately. At 10 o'clock I was still holding my son. The other child, who had come with his brother to hospital, just sat forlornly on his own. I hadn't eaten for a week .... The father was away .... It was really hard.

At midnight he went in. I followed as my son was crying out for me. My other son was peeping through the window. They asked me 'Are you the mother of this lame boy?' 'Yes', I said. They told me, 'Go away.' They did the amputation in two hours. The three of us sat on the floor waiting. They asked again, 'Are you the mother of this lame boy?' 'Yes', I said. 'Who's going to look after him?' 'I am.' We took it in turns through the night.

When day came the cleaner asked me if I was the mother of the amputee. I was told to go and bury his soiled clothes along with the amputated part of the leg. I said I couldn't as I had my children to look after. So I paid him 1500 riels to clear it away. In the morning they told me to pack up to go to Ward 7 or 8 where they keep people injured by the mines. When we got there, I gave them the doctor's papers and had to buy another lot of medicine. We had to pay for everything. This was in the big hospital in Battambang. Eventually, the Europeans there took pity on me and gave 30,000 riels. It was really tough in months 7 and 8 of 1992.

He's now had this new artificial leg for about three months. He walked on it to school and now his leg has got infected. I give up. I took him to Sdao Hospital and they wanted to keep him in. They washed and cut into the wound as it was infected ... he screamed and was told off like a dog. I was upset that he was so badly treated, which wouldn't have happened if he was at home. They shouted at him, 'Well you (derogatory form), do you want your leg washed or not? If you don't want to, you can die here.'

But he stayed there and I looked after him, but again there was no money to buy him food. The doctors only know about looking after diseases, they don't know about my financial needs. When he was injured it was the same. I had to get into debt. When it was better they gave him ten boxes of medicines to take home, but it's worse again now and he keeps on asking to go back to the hospital. I would be prepared to let him go. I would go and visit him, but I'm scared they'll amputate again. I feel so sad for my son. He's the hardest working of them all.

Phal's family have always lived in Beng Ampil village. Before the area was fought over in 1989 they farmed a hectare of rice paddy and had two hectares of commercial fruit farm. Since their return to Beng Ampil in May 1991 they have been unable to use their fruit farm as it is heavily mined. This has cut their income in half, Phal's father told me. He took an old piece of paper and rolled a cigarette, and continued:

We fled to Battambang because of the war. When we came back we found a serious problem with the mines. Since most people live off agriculture, their livelihood is threatened due to fear of accidents to their animals and to themselves. And accidents do occur. What I really want is for international organisations to solve the mine problem. Whether it's UNTAC or any other organisation, I want all mines to be cleared from Cambodia so people can live in peace and safety. And until they are, you know, fear dominates. Fear of death, of being maimed, fear for the animals. We have no competence as far as demining is concerned. That's why we have to ask international organisations to help us.

Tith Poue

Tith Poue and his friends knew they would have to find a new place to cut wood. By early May 1992 the western part of Phnom Lien Por, 5 km from Beng Ampil, had been heavily cut, and they needed to explore fresh territory. On the morning of Poue's accident they had headed into the south eastern corner of the small wood that covers the hill. They knew there had been a Khmer Rouge base in this part of the wood in 1990, and no one from Beng Ampil had yet started cutting in the area. Poue says they didn't think that there were mines there.

They turned right off the small track that led to the base, and had gone about 30 metres. Poue was trying to decide where to start when he stood on a small, plastic Chinese mine that destroyed his left foot (probably a Type-72). He says he remembers thinking he was going to die.

His two friends tied a tourniquet low on his left calf and stemmed the flow of bleeding. They carried Poue 2 km, and then, finding an ox cart, brought him back to the main road. Once there they hired a moto-taxi to take him to the district hospital, where his wounds were dressed. In Battambang hospital he had an amputation just above the ankle.

Poue recovered quickly and returned to his village after only a month. In October 1992 he went to ICRC's workshop in Battambang and had an artificial limb fitted (since three of his friends had had mine accidents, the services on offer there were common knowledge in the village). As a result, by February 1993 he was up and about again, able to walk easily for a couple of kilometres, with only a minimal limp detectable.

On arrival at Rattanak Mondul district hospital Poue received basic dressings before transfer to Battambang provincial hospital. After a gruelling journey his foot was amputated. As he recovered, the daily ordeal of changing his dressings eased. Nine months later, with a prosthetic limb, he is able to return to family life in Beng Ampil

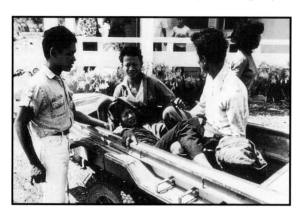

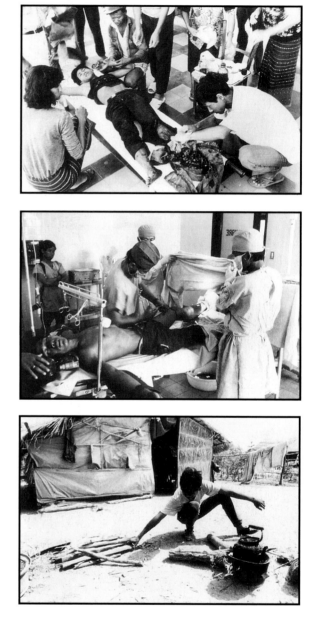

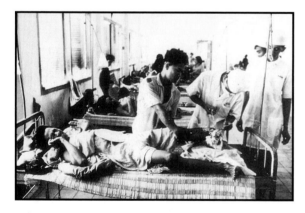

In the future Poue wants to learn a good trade which does not require him to walk and stand a great deal, for example motor mechanics. Consequently, he has applied to be considered for the World Vision Skills Training Centre for the Handicapped which started operations in Battambang in 1993. As a motivated high school graduate, Poue stands a good chance.

His large extended family, whose support was perhaps the key element in his successful rehabilitation, earned its living as others did in the camp cutting wood, bamboo and grass, which the women made into thatch and matting. They still owned a cow, a reminder of the fact that before 1989, when they lived in Chea-Montray village of Treng commune, they farmed several hectares and made a reasonable living. When I asked what had happened to Poue's father, he said that he didn't know. However, his mother recalled very clearly the morning in 1975 when fellow villagers 'denounced' him as being a member of the village militia under the Lon Nol regime. He was called to a meeting from which he was never to return. Poue was three years old at the time.

Pal Joern

In early 1989 Pal Joern's husband went out for a smoke before going to bed. He strolled slowly behind their house as he did every night. This time, however, he set off a mine. He died the following afternoon in Battambang hospital. Joern said that she did not believe the mine which claimed her husband's life was newly laid, rather it was more likely to have been an old Khmer Rouge mine that had remained dormant in the ground for several years and had at last, for whatever reason, become lethal.

They had married in 1966 and made their home in the western area of Pailin district, farming 3 hectares of rice paddy and 1 hectare of fruit. In 1975 they were moved by the Khmer Rouge into what is today Ploumeas commune where they remained after the Vietnamese invaded, eventually settling in Watt village since their original land was still on the front line between Vietnamese and Khmer Rouge troops. Here they farmed a smaller amount of land and supplemented their incomes with wood cutting and thatch making.

In 1984, with the Vietnamese planning a big offensive against the Khmer Rouge, Joern's husband was conscripted into the army. Although life was hard during those years, since her husband's death Joern has fallen into absolute poverty even by the modest standards of her neighbours in Beng Ampil. Her latest 'home' is a small, rickety shack no bigger than 8 ft by 4 ft, which provides shelter for Joern and her five children.

Because of the strains of war, and the steady slaughter wrought by mines female-headed households are common in Rattanak Mondul, and especially in Beng Ampil. They form a subclass, invariably living in extreme poverty. Those with large extended families in the vicinity often fair better than those without; Joern is in the latter group, for although her brother and his family live in the same village, he has many children and cannot help her.

During the rice growing season it is sometimes possible for Joern and her eldest two children to get day-labourers' work, making 2,500 riels ($1) a day. However, when this work ceases they, along with the others in the camp, have to rely solely on wood cutting. Joern says that she can cut only enough wood to earn 500 riels ($ 0.2) a day in such times, and life for the family becomes nearly impossible. They are forced to rely on their neighbours for help and extra employment, for example sometimes carrying water to earn a meal from those who can still afford to pay others to help them out.

Pal Joern and family

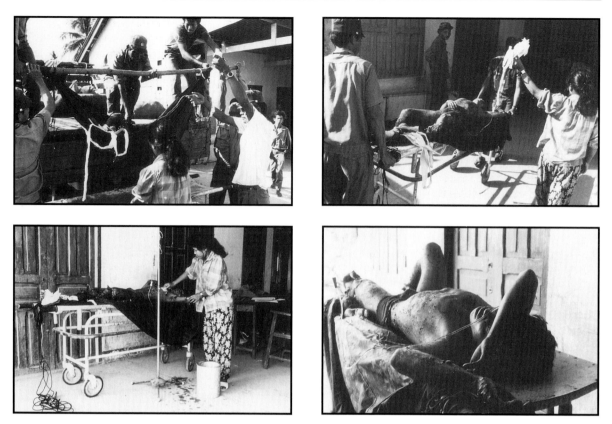

Hearn Boung's arrival, Battambang military hospital

Hearn Boung was to endure a further amputation. Within a week he was dead

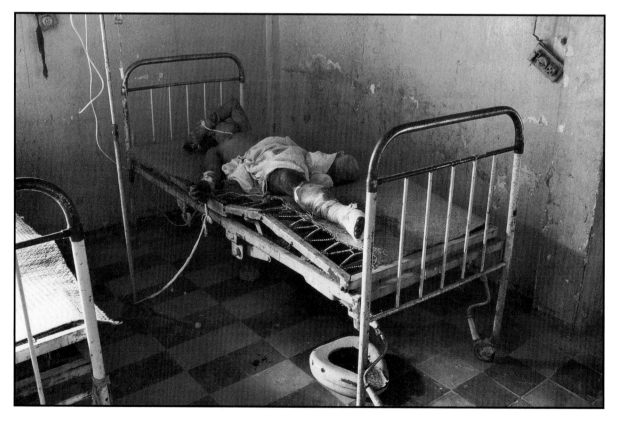

Hearn Boung

On Sunday 1 December 1991 Hearn Boung was on a routine patrol with his CPAF unit in Treng commune, in the west of Rattanak Mondul. He stood on a mine at midday, and three hours later arrived at Battambang's military hospital. Along with a wounded colleague he had been transported in the back of an old Soviet truck, his blood-stained hammock suspended between the frame over which the truck's canvas hood should have been spread. Boung was lifted out of the truck and on to a hard metal trolley. His left shin had disintegrated, but strangely his foot had been perfectly preserved, although it now lay protruding unnaturally from underneath his left thigh, connected to the leg by the thinnest strands of tissue.

It took half an hour for a doctor to arrive, but Boung's amputation could not start for another five hours due to the lack of drugs, oxygen, blood for transfusion and fuel for the generator. Boung continued to lay outside the theatre on his trolley, under the lean-to roofing that provided some relief from the sun. Ironically he was complaining of a stomach ache that he had had before the mine blast.

As we waited for the materials necessary for the operation to be bought, borrowed or stolen, Dr Vut, the surgeon, told me how the absolute lack of resources in the military hospital seriously impeded the ability to deliver even the most basic of surgical and medical services to the CPAF soldiers serving in Battambang. For example, due to the lack of a blood bank at the hospital, all transfusions have to come from live donors. There are no measures taken to guard against HIV or hepatitis transmission. At the time of researching this chapter the same was true of the civilian hospital in Battambang. In the military hospital 'live donors' usually means other patients who themselves are struggling along the road to recovery, a journey made additionally hard by the inadequate diet provided in the hospital. On occasions the staff themselves give blood, Dr Vut told me. Judging by his anaemic, washed-out appearance, it seemed that this was a practice he was resorting to more often than he should.

Hearn Boung died five days later. The surgeon had tried to save his right leg, which had been badly damaged in the blast, but this had resulted in massive infection. 'It would have been better', he said in retrospect, 'to have amputated both legs. But what sort of life would he have had like that? Maybe it was better this way.'

5
Demining Cambodia

You can't develop a country, you cannot set up an infrastructure … until you resolve the demining issue. And that's the key word that everybody's got to damn well understand, because if you don't resolve that issue, you're not going to resolve anything else.

Lt Col. George Focsaneanu, Assistant Director, Cambodian Mine Action Centre, March 1993, CMAC HQ, Phnom Penh

… places just die because of landmines; the land is dying, the villages are dying. You can send millions of dollars, you can send NGO workers to train people to grow more rice, but if they cannot go into their fields, if they cannot transport their rice from one point to another, nothing can happen, absolutely nothing ….

Benoit Denise, Handicap International, CMAC Governing Council Member, April 1993, HI Office, Phnom Penh

If you were from the Overseas Development Administration[1] (ODA) do you think I would have convinced you that you need to spend money on demining in this country? The point is that the ODA and other donors will turn round and say, 'Well, what is our involvement in Cambodia? Do we want a long-term commitment to fund Cambodia?' If they say we're not interested, then let them sit back and watch the number of casualties carry on at these levels ….

The ODA will sit there and say, 'Fine, Cambodia. But tomorrow I'm going to Mozambique. And there I'll hear the same story. And I've been to Afghanistan and I've heard the same story there. And then Somalia. And then Angola. Now what are you asking me? Are you asking me to fund on a long-term basis, demining in all these countries?' We come to an immense problem.

Lt Col. N. F. Mulliner, C/O Mine Clearance Training Unit (MCTU), UNTAC, April 1993, MCTU HQ, Phnom Penh.

Demining Cambodia is of vital importance. There is little difference of opinion about that simple fact in Cambodia – among the military men who made up the parts of UNTAC mandated to address the problem, among the ex-military men now working for demining NGOs, among the relief and development personnel of the NGO community, and among those working for inter-national organisations such as the UNDP, UNHCR and UNICEF. In fact, Benoit Denise[2] believes that the experience of the 'UN time' in Cambodia has been for many expatriate NGO and UN workers an immensely important learning experience, where the linkages between mines and development, mines and civilian losses, mines and lasting peace have finally been understood. Those who needed no convincing were, of course, ordinary Cambodians. Even today the majority of Cambodians who regularly engage in demining activities are not those employed by the demining NGOs or the Cambodian Mine Action Centre, the agency bequeathed to Cambodia by the UN to employ and sustain the deminers it trained during the mandate period. Rather, they are the untrained, ill-equipped local deminers – like Dith Vuern from Kilo 38 in Rattanak Mondul – trying to attempt to reclaim their land and forced to accept the consequences of their amateur initiatives. Cambodians understand why demining is important.

But being important may not be enough. As Lt. Col. Mulliner suggests, above, because of the immense costs of demining, its slow and painstaking nature, and the enormity of the worldwide landmines problem (predominantly in the nations of the south), funding agencies may be tempted to ignore nations such as Cambodia unless there are good strategic or economic reasons to undertake demining, as in Kuwait. Furthermore, some of those most intimately involved in the demining process during the UN time[3] came to question both the commitment and the methods of the UN. It will be argued here that it was perhaps only the strength of the 'learning experience' within Cambodia itself, referred to by Benoit Denise, which forced the UN into demining live minefields and planning for the long-term support of the deminers they were training. As the chronology below reveals, these two vital activities – live demining and long-term planning – only occurred well into the UNTAC time in Cambodia. Despite the success of these belated responses the key question remains: was and, perhaps more importantly, is the international community serious about demining Cambodia? Perhaps the mess was considered just too big, and Cambodia of too little strategic importance.

By March 1993, CMAC had completed some estimations of how many man-hours it would take to demine certain minefields. One, in the north western province of Banteay-Meanchay, was estimated to have 50 years of work in it for one 32-man demining platoon using manual methods. Banteay-Meanchay has many similar fields. It has been estimated that there might be as much as 250 years' manual clearance work to be done in Cambodia.

Such gloomy estimates are, however, a little misleading. Manual demining can be greatly enhanced by the use of dogs trained to locate mines, and the deployment of mechanised solutions, both of which under the correct conditions complement and speed up manual clearance. But demining alone was never going to solve the problem in the short term; it is one of a variety of responses required. What is called for is an 'integrated systems' approach, which basically means gathering information on minefields, setting priorities, fencing those you cannot clear immediately, and then systematically clearing the fields on your priority list, as well as keeping up training and mine awareness programmes in the intervening period. Such an approach forms the essence of CMAC's current plans which, if implemented, are expected to reduce casualty rates in Cambodia to almost negligible levels in the next three to five years. In the UK, Explosive Ordnance Disposal (EOD) specialists are still dealing with the unexploded ordnance left over from World War Two. In Poland landmines from the same war were cleared systematically over a 40-year period. Such problems do not go away overnight.

Clearly, though, planning a systematic response to the mine problem in Cambodia and setting up an infrastructure to carry it through will not of itself be enough if international commitment to CMAC's activity is missing. For this reason demining, almost of necessity, becomes a political issue. If international will is weak or faltering, information must be disseminated to strengthen and build it, and CMAC is committed to such objectives. But, these activities do not mean CMAC's hierarchy has been filled with hot-headed radicals, merely with individuals who feel that the international community has a debt to repay. In May 1993 UNTAC Force Engineer Col. Neal Bradley[4] reminded a mixed meeting of UN and NGO workers that none of the millions of mines in Cambodia had been made in the country – all had been imported, willingly supplied by the international sponsors of Cambodia's 'civil war'.

Focusing on the international origins of the Cambodian problem, however, was to some extent inconsistent with the UN's initial stance. In the early days of its mandate much of its response to mines in Cambodia was justified in terms of presenting the problem as something that was Cambodian in its origin, and by definition soluble only by Cambodians. This viewpoint came from the very top: UNTAC Force Commander Lt. General Sanderson, in a television interview,[5] stated categorically, 'This is a *Cambodian* problem.' If the problem was a Cambodian one, then calls for direct foreign assistance would be blunted, and so international attention would be deflected from the fact that some of those members of the Permanent Five in the UN who imposed the peace agreements on Cambodia had in fact also been instrumental in generating and sustaining the civil war during which the 'Cambodian' mines problem had emerged. For those nations who had directly supplied the mines (the USSR, China and others), and for those who had provided direct training in mine-laying techniques to the Cambodian factions (the UK), it was perhaps politically inconvenient to dwell too long on the international complexions of the 'Cambodian' mine problem.

However, for those involved in demining, the need to inform and educate people goes beyond the practicalities of fund raising. It would seem an incomplete activity to devote time and energy to alleviating the damage done to people and communities by landmines in the aftermath of conflict without speaking out about the profoundly unacceptable nature of mines as a class of weapon. The third component of the awareness objective in CMAC's corporate plan,[6] is '… to generate political support within the international community as a whole to minimise [chances of] a recurrence of the problem'. Many senior military figures now agree that urgent action needs to be taken internationally: 'the positive step that the world must wake up to is that we have got to *ban mines now*. Ban the manufacture of them, the use of them, the sale of them. It's the only way I see for the future with regard to the mine problem ….'[7]

What is Mine Clearance? A Day in the Life of a Demining Platoon

On 19 February 1993 the Mines Advisory Group (MAG), one of the demining NGOs operational in Cambodia, was working on a minefield just off Route 10 in Sanang Commune of Banan district, near Rattanak Mondul. MAG teams had been requested to clear the land around several bridges that had been scheduled for repair, so that by-pass roads could be constructed and the work carried out safely. Development work in mine-infested areas cannot be undertaken without such demining capacity. While working on the bridges the MAG team were approached by a local farmer, Tith Maew, whose land about 200 metres north of the road, had been heavily mined in 1989. The land in the area is etched with small paddy dykes, a mere 9 inches tall, the sides of which had been mined to deny cover to any group attempting to attack the nearby police station. Norman Stewart of MAG explained that while such a field was not a high priority, because it was so heavily mined it would constitute some useful field experience for his still relatively 'fresh' Cambodian deminers. He therefore split his platoon, half to conduct breaches into the areas surrounding the bridge in order to estimate the extent of the mine problem and half to work in Maew's field.

We reached the field by a path which ran up the edge of a recently ploughed rice paddy to the left and a thick copse to the right, which masked Maew's field from the road. The copse was known to be mined and laced with trip wires – it too would otherwise have provided excellent cover for an attack on the police station. Under the shade of a tree in a safe 'base area', away from the field being cleared sat Tith Maew and the majority of the demining platoon. When working on a live field most of the team are kept back from the point of actual clearance which takes place in 1 metre wide lanes marked with high-visibility tape, at least 25 metres apart for safety reasons. In this field two lanes were being run.

The process of detection and verification is the job of two-man teams working in the lanes, both of which are supplied with ballistic helmets and flak jackets. One has a highly sensitive metal detector with which he scans the lane as he advances up it. These detectors are so sensitive that they can detect the tiny metal firing pins in even the smallest plastic mines. In areas where combat has taken place one of the main problems faced by deminers is that the 'metal content' of the ground, littered

PMN-2 exposed by the rain, Tith Maew's field, Sanang

with old bullets, pieces of shrapnel etc, is very high. Each piece of metal has to be treated with the caution a potential mine deserves.

Once a piece of metal has been sensed the detector operator indicates the location of the suspect mine to the second man in the team, who advances from a safe position at the end of the lane. This is a question of damage limitation: by keeping only one man in the danger zone during clearance, risks to the team as a whole are minimised. The detector man then retires to a safe position while the 'prodder' man takes over. A sharp pointed metal rod is gently pushed into the ground to probe for the mine. The rod is never be held higher

Starting a new lane

than 30 degrees above the horizontal when prodding: if the rod is held at this angle it is likely to strike the side of the mine, not the top where in most instances the firing mechanism is located. Once contact has been made the ground to the side of the mine is cut away using a large knife and trowel. If the metal fragment is not a mine this becomes clear as the side of the object is exposed. However, if it is a mine the ground around it is gently cleared away. In the west deminers are taught to lie down during this stage, but in Cambodia they tend to squat. Although squatting presents a higher body profile to the potential explosion demining experts agree that if Cambodians are more relaxed in this customary position then they are less likely to make a mistake, and so procedures have been adapted slightly to meet local norms. Once the mine has been exposed it is clearly marked within the lane. Gary Elmer, another of MAG's expatriate EOD specialists and supervisors, noted that many demining accidents happen when people inadvertently tread on mines which have been detected, exposed and marked for demolition.

These two-man teams work for short periods and are rotated with those resting in the safe area. This is to keep the men fresh, and their concentration high. In tropical

The detector man waits his turn

climates such rotation is essential. Thus, much of the deminer's life is spent waiting, watching colleagues at work. However, even when on the 'sharp' end of things the boredom created by the repetition of tasks and procedures is, the deminers say, one of the most common, and deadly, features of the life. This could explain the continual banter and joking in which these expatriate-led teams engage: it boosts morale and builds a team dynamic that is vital in the minefield where reliance on others is literally a matter of life or death. It also helps to alleviate tension when scraping the soil away from the pressure pad of a mine could destroy your hands and face.

MAG policy is that detected mines are destroyed *in situ*. Mines which have lain in the ground for extended periods of time often become unstable. Lifting mines, and storing them in one place for mass destruction, is one more practice that increases risk factors. Arguably, however, it can speed demining, and for these reasons has been taught by some of the UNTAC supervisors.

On the day we visited, the only mines found were lying on the northern edge of the field in a tight corridor next to the paddy dyke. This was the second day the team had been working here: during the previous day 14 mines (PMN-2s) had been discovered in the first 2 metres of the corridor adjacent to the dyke. These had been destroyed at the end of the day's work. That morning the next few metres had revealed another six, which were blown just after we arrived on the site. This was a little after 10 a.m., by which time the team had cleared the first 12 metres of paddy.

Over the next four hours the teams swept a further 10 metres of paddy, covering the ground in the centre of the field with ease, occasionally stopping to prod and verify metal pieces. But the rhythm of the work on this site brought the same results in each lane. As the teams came to the last 2 metres in the area adjacent to the paddy dyke the metal detectors cried out madly, and prodding revealed the sinister green curves of PMN-2s. This type of anti-personnel mines is one of the commonest found in Cambodia. It originates in the former USSR, and will detonate with only 5 kg of pressure applied to the black plastic pressure pad. Here the mines had been laid in a 'professional' triangular pattern which is relatively unusual in Cambodia. Robb Jones, MAG's other expatriate, noted that this field had been laid either by the Vietnamese, renowned for their disciplined but dense defensive mining, or by a CPAF officer who had received very good training from them.

As the afternoon wore on I watched the teams exposing mines. The last 3 metres of paddy revealed a further eight PMN-2s. Almost the last mine uncovered brought home the message about the boredom/complacency factor. All the mines in this field to that point had been discovered within a 2 metre band from the dyke. Suddenly, as the team approached the dyke on their

penultimate lane, a mine was discovered outside this 2 metre corridor, lying in a straight line from the side of the last triangular pattern uncovered. I was nowhere near the lane, but my (bored) assumption that they would find mines only inside the 2 metre band, after nearly two days of just that pattern, had been proven very badly wrong, and I felt quite shaken. There is no place for assumption in a minefield.

With 14 mines exposed, and the day coming to an end, it was time for demolition. The explosives work is gradually being handed over to the Cambodian supervisors of the platoon, in a programme of devolution of management and responsibility that is MAG policy. The demolition process, a method known as 'main lining', involved placing a 400 gram TNT block next to each of the exposed mines. It was explained to me that with this much explosive the mines 'simply vapourise'. The TNT blocks were wrapped around with detonator wire, which carries its charge at 6,000 metres a second. From each block, the pink cord stretched back into the safe area of the field. These individual detonator lines were taped to the main line which ran parallel to the dyke. The main line was then linked to a detonator, itself attached to an electric cable which ran back to the firing box that was carried away from the minefield and set down at a safe distance. We all retired to a paddy dyke and took cover.

A few seconds before the blast Gary shouted 'Stand by', and then 'Firing now'. No matter how prepared you are, the force of the demolitions is always surprising. We looked up (to check for falling debris), and then looked forward. The smoke cleared. In a country where relief and development work can be slow, frustrating and even inappropriate, there is something very tangible about the destruction of landmines and the return to the community of land previously laid barren.

MAG were not the first deminers to work on this site. Tith Maew, the farmer, had tried to reclaim his land in July 1992. At that time he estimated that some 90 per cent of his 1.5 hectares of rice paddy was unusable due to landmines. With his six months' military experience Maew had removed all the mines he could see – about 100 POMZs and 40 PMN-2s. Their burnt remains could still be seen in the corner of the field. He was lucky though: others from his village had died demining their land. Throughout the day children had been herding cows around the area, knowing it to be unsafe. Maew himself had lost six cows to landmines. *They were totally destroyed*, he said; *I could not even sell the meat. I am very happy that MAG have cleared my land, I'd like to say thank you.* A broad smile spread across his face.

Humanitarian mine clearance is a time consuming, costly and dangerous process. It aims to achieve 100 per cent clearance of mines from the areas designated, and

Page 84 Prodding: a deminer uncovers a PMN-2
Page 85 Demolition

this marks it out as a very different activity from that carried out by the military during combat situations. Military operations might best be described as 'minefield breaching', for which a variety of methods are available (manual, mechanical, explosives) all of which aim to create a small safe path through the minefield wide enough for vehicles or personnel. Since the aim is to get through in relative safety rather than to clear an area entirely, mines can be moved to the side of the safe path, and left. One of the main problems with mechanised as opposed to manual approaches to minefield clearance is that the research and development funding allocated to this area has, to date, come only from the military seeking mechanical solutions to breaching problems. The HALO Trust's project on the road to Kuok Chas village in Banteay Meanchay graphically revealed the different ethos between breaching and clearance operations. Peter Newman, Project Manager for HALO's operations in the province, explained:

Demining is a very slow process – it's taken us a month to clear 200 metres of road, in a strip 25 metres wide. Progress is slow, but it's humanitarian – it's 100 per cent clearance, and that's what takes the time. Military breaching – give me one night and I'll get you a footpath through to the village. But that would not be 100 per cent clearance, and you take your chances with casualties.

The road Newman was referring to is a total of 650 metres long, and joins the village of Kuok Chas with a main road. The trench line near the road revealed the position of an old Vietnamese fort, built to protect Kuok Chas from the threat of attack from resistance factions (operating from the north west). Further Vietnamese positions were installed up the road, and the area laced with minefields. The locals, still requiring access to the main road, rerouted a footpath which bent its perilous way around the minefields. Progress on the job had been good, at around 150–500 square metres per day, but it depended on the type of terrain (e.g. the amount of foliage, which had to be gently cut away for fear of booby-traps), the number of mines found, the 'metal content' of the ground etc. When we visited the site the expatriate in charge estimated that there was another three months' work left before the task would be completed.

Demining NGOs

The Mines Advisory Group (MAG) is one of the three specialist demining NGOs actively working in Cambodia at the time of writing. MAG has a very close relationship with Handicap International (HI), primarily a medical agency which has also been directly involved in initiatives to demine Cambodia during the UN time and beyond. Both agencies are committed to advocacy on the landmines issue, and it was on this level that the relationship blossomed in Europe until, in 1992, HI assisted in introducing MAG to UNHCR, which subsequently funded a survey by a team of MAG specialists in Battambang in mid 1992. Following the survey, MAG submitted proposals to the European Community for a demining project to work in partnership with HI's sister agency Action Nord Sud, which specialises in community development work. The funding of such an integrated proposal was, 'the first time ever that demining had been accepted as an integral part of development'.[8] It was a significant breakthrough. The EC has subsequently funded a similar co-action between demining and development in Pursat and Banteay-Meanchay, using the HALO Trust and the Irish development agency, CONCERN.

The first obstacle faced by MAG was the need to retrain its Cambodian deminers, all graduates of the UNTAC courses. The deminers of MAG's first 22-man platoon had completed training in April 1992, and had not been deployed until recruited by MAG the following October.[9] As demining is a practical skill which requires

Mines ready for explosive demolition

The road to Kuok Chas: as a deminer slowly works his way up an overgrown lane, villagers were given permission to use their 'safe path' through the minefield. Although their proximity to the minefield is dangerous, in practice it is impossible to deny them access

the reinforcement of on-the-job experience after training, retraining was essential. Furthermore, MAG wished to include extra-curriculum areas to those taught in the UN courses, such as Explosive Ordnance Disposal (EOD). The teams started work in December 1992 and they have been active in surveying, marking and selective clearance of minefields ever since. Sites cleared have included areas designated to become schools, hospitals, health centres, water sources, community market areas, and bridges. The priorities for clearance are set with reference to the needs of MAG's partner agencies and their development work, as well as participation by the local community, which means local leaders as well as ordinary people. This community-based approach , and the commitment to train Cambodian staff and hence 'Cambodianise' the operation over the coming years emphasises the developmental character of MAG's work. In 1993 MAG complemented its demining work with an ongoing 'mine awareness' programme in the villages of its target areas designed to help people avoid injury when living and working around minefields. This uses several highly visual and graphic mediums. Two further development agencies, World Vision and the Danish Cambodia Consortium, funded expansions of the MAG team in 1993 as the link between demining and development became increasingly obvious.

Perhaps the most important characteristic of NGO demining work, as exhibited by MAG and the HALO Trust, is the insistence that tasks should be chosen and evaluated in terms of the qualitative value of the area cleared, rather than in quantitative terms (numbers of mines lifted, total area cleared, etc.). Quantitative indicators are to some extent meaningless. For example, the two days MAG spent on Tith Maew's field produced over 500 square metres cleared of some 34 anti-personnel mines. Not a bad quantative performance, but the qualititative value for the community was rather low – one prosperous farmer had his field partially restored, and the children who herd cattle were marginally safer as a result. On other occasions I have visited MAG clearance operations where no mines had been found all day, but as this was part of an area clearance operation on a community project its overall value was significant. In fact, even if an entire area is cleared for a community project and no mines are found, this is not a failure: the key point is that land has been returned to the community that had previously been denied them because of the fear of mines perceived to exist there.

The whole concept of a demining NGO is very new. MAG, for example, has been in existence only since 1990. For the NGO community in Cambodia this has been one of the 'learning areas' to which Benoit Denise referred, as mentioned earlier. At the beginning of the UN time in Cambodia, Denise had asked many NGOs whether or not they felt demining was an appropriate area for them to be involved in. The vast majority said that they didn't feel it was because they either perceived mines as a purely military issue, or becasue they saw them as something that was the 'responsibility of the UN' and thus not something they should consider. Events overtook such opinions, but certain prejudices still had to be broken down. 'People working in specialised agencies are still a bit suspect of the demining NGOs not being "proper NGOs", perhaps because their people are former military personnel …'[10]

Such suspicions were not limited to NGOs: funding agencies also had to be won over. However, this is a battle that MAG and its fellow demining NGOs, the HALO Trust and Norwegian People's Aid, seem to be winning. As noted above, MAG has undergone continued expansion since arriving in Battambang, as the value of its work has been realised. Equally, the HALO Trust's successes in demining in Banteay-Meanchay, resulting in the restoration of villages, roads and the facilitation

Mine awareness: learning to live with mines

of specific community development tasks (such as schools) have also resulted in increased funding and the recruitment of additional teams. HALO, the longest serving demining group in Cambodia (which started work in April 1992, using the first team of Cambodian deminers trained by UNAMIC), was set to raise two more teams by June 1993 to complement those already working in Banteay-Meanchay and Pursat, funded by the EC.

The third specialist demining NGO, Norwegian People's Aid (NPA), is very closely associated with the Norwegian government, which has a strong commitment to the mine issue. Throughout 1993 it worked in a co-action with the United Nations Development Programme (UNDP), also in Banteay-Meanchay province. NPA cleared the areas which were considered priorities according to the UNDP work plan and thus made it possible for the UN organisation to carry out its development projects (water, roads, etc). The Norwegian government funded the team's costs (vehicles, salaries, etc) while UNDP covered the in-country running costs. The agency employed two 32-man platoons of Cambodian deminers, and it too was planning an expansion when we visited its office in early May 1993.

The performance of demining NGOs in Cambodia has helped to establish not only the organisations but demining itself as an important developmental and humanitarian issue in the international aid world. All three demining groups are currently investigating further demining projects in other countries (Laos, Mozambique, Angola, etc).

However, the very success of these demining NGOs in scoring international funding, caused some concern among UN staff, for whom a lack of funding remained the most serious threat to the successful long-term outcome of their operations, and that meant the success of the Cambodian Mine Action Centre. The issue turned around considerations of sustainability: the employment of expatriate demining specialists in several foreign NGOs, it was argued, would prove more expensive than establishing an indigenous national demining agency staffed by local people. Lt. Col. Mulliner noted:

> I respect and understand the NGOs and the way they operate. They get international funding and they are quick to respond because they are small (efficient) organisations … a government can happily fund an NGO with a limited amount of money for a year, and see a result at the end of it; they don't have to commit themselves for five to ten years. So it's obvious that the NGOs are going to be a more attractive option at the moment ….[11]

However, to understand fully the relationship between the demining NGOs and the UN it is necessary first to review the work of the latter, both as MCTU (Mine Clearance Training Unit) and CMAC. The apparent dif-

POMZ: one of the most common mines found in Cambodia

ferences in approach represented by the NGOs and the UN (hands-on operations working at grass-roots level, as opposed to a training approach and top-down planning) underpinned the key debate about demining Cambodia.

Have criticisms of the UN's approach – that it was slothful, lacking in foresight, and basically uncommitted to the Cambodian people and 'their' mine problem – been justified? Equally, have the NGOs been a successful but overly expensive short-term and non-sustainable option? Or were such polarised views, as were often found in the press, really of any value in considering the efforts of both UN and NGOs as they attempted to demine Cambodia? Indeed it can be argued that both the NGOs and the UN shared a common vision for the future of demining in Cambodia, since both were committed to Cambodianising their operations after a satisfactory handover period. Perhaps the crucial difference lies in the fact that the NGOs may be more successful in achieving this goal since their field operatives have far greater control over the planning process and are less susceptible to international political agendas. At the time of writing it may be that the UN's ultimate reluctance to continue to staff CMAC after the end of the UNTAC mandate period (15 November 1993) may result in the NGOs being employed to guide CMAC

through the medium-term period (five years) during which time it is hoped, through in-house training, to Cambodianise the agency entirely. If this is the outcome fear about 'competition for scarce demining resources' between the NGOs and the UN's creation, CMAC, will be exposed for what it is – a false debate. However, compared with the costs of war making, talk of shortages of demining resources for a country so devastated by international politics as Cambodia should be considered as nothing short of immoral.

Mandate, Money and a Certain Lack of Will? The UN's Approach to Demining Cambodia

First of all, the United Nations didn't provide mine clearers *per se*, except in the limited sense of having people to clear areas of operation for UNTAC activities. Very early in the peace we acknowledged the fact that the solution to the Cambodian mine problem was to train as many Cambodian mine clearers as we possibly could and create an environment in which they could sustain that activity beyond UNTAC. This is a 30 to 40 year problem.

Lt. General Sanderson,
Force Commander, UNTAC[12]

Why has so little been done for Cambodia? Lack of foresight, lack of understanding of the size and nature of the problem, lack of the right people in the right place at the right time? Lack of, or reluctance to present, a provisional budget showing the true needs of the country? Probably a combination of these reasons, coupled with the disastrous position of some governments not to put their soldiers at risk, has led to such small international activity in the field of demining.

Handicap International Statement[13]

In the Paris Accords[14] UNTAC's demining mandate was left vague and open to wide interpretation. Perhaps the most surprising omission was any detail of how the Cambodian deminers the UN said it was to train were going to be put to work, even in the short term. Worse still, there was no mention of how the UN was going to create an environment in which such demining activity could be sustained after it left Cambodia. Acknowledging this point Lt. Col. Focsaneanu noted, 'What was UNTAC's mandate? It was basically to hold elections and thereby generate a new constitution. That's what it was set up to do. CMAC was General Sanderson's idea … it was an UNTAC initiative. So now a lot of people are criticising CMAC, but there could have been no CMAC.' Thus, even the idea for what was later portrayed as the flagship of the entire UN demining effort in Cambodia, emerged only once the mandate period was underway,[15] a pragmatic response to a *de facto* situation where the UN appeared to be prepared only to engage in training. CMAC should have been the rational outcome of a planning process which had started well before the Paris Peace Agreements in 1991, as had been the case with other components of the UN time in Cambodia (for example, the repatriation plan). Without CMAC it would be have been retroactively impossible for the UN to justify its response to the mine problem in Cambodia. A cynic might suggest that this was one of the primary motivations for its foundation.

Some sense of the overall importance attributed to demining early in the mandate period can be gained by recourse to an overall UNTAC budget prepared in May 1992.[16] This allocated a total of $14,256,000 to mine clearance and training. This budget line should be contrasted with some $88,782,000 allocated for UNTAC vehicles, $10,585,100 for generators, and even $2,496,000 for contractual services (laundry, dry-cleaning, tailoring and hair-cutting services for contingent personnel). Estimates now suggest that the total cost of UNTAC (1991–93) ran to nearly $3 billion. However, a meeting in Phnom Penh[17] in November 1992 revealed that even this relatively paltry demining budget had been cut, allowing MCTU to plan to field only some 40 demining teams, not the 64 originally envisaged. As of March 1993, a year into the UNTAC mandate, and a mere

two months before the elections, only 16 UNTAC-led and financed demining teams were operational in the field.[18] Something had clearly gone wrong, both at field level and higher within the UN where budgetary decisions are made.

The poor performance of the UN did not go without comment. In February 1993 an article appeared in the Thai press[19] which summed up much of what was being said among journalistic, NGO and mine clearance circles. The basic thrust was that the UN's efforts had focused on training and not on demining the country – the task in hand – and that it had been wasteful with the precious resources at its disposal. However, such criticisms did not answer the central question of why it was that the UN was prepared to engage in training alone: even the mandate had suggested more might have been expected when it called on the UN to 'assist in mine clearance'.

There was strong evidence that at the beginning of the UN mandate period none of the member states from which mine specialists had been drawn to staff UNTAC's MCTU were prepared to allow 'their boys' to work in live minefields. The demining of Cambodia was deemed not to be worth the risk of injury even to one expatriate specialist. Levels of commitment to Cambodia were made dramatically clear. For this reason it was left to the HALO Trust to employ the first UN-trained Cambodian demining team in April 1992. Within the UN bureaucracy itself further obstacles existed, which turned around issues of compensation and liability for injuries sustained while working for the UN. Naturally, these restrictions produced considerable frustration on the ground among the UN's deminers, who in many cases were keen to extend their experience, test their training, and contribute towards tackling what was obviously an enormous problem. However, there was little the UN could do – or so it said. Mieke Bos of UNHCR recalls the situation thus, 'The major frustration of that stage was that we were all doing surveys and reconnaissance and training, but not one single mine was being lifted.'

UNHCR's frustrations paralleled those mounting within the NGO community, and eventually led Handicap International to see if a way around the obstacles could not be found. If they could get just one UN-led demining team working, it might set a precedent, and create sufficient 'embarrassment' within the system to ensure that other teams were allowed to start work. Benoit Denise recalls these events very clearly:

> In July 1992 there were 600 Khmer deminers, trained and not working … UNTAC had supervisors, but it didn't want to use them on field activities. There was money available for demining … and there were confident people, both Khmer and expatriate. There were mine injuries every day, but *nothing was happening*. We didn't really want to get involved

HALO Trust, Kuok Chas, Banteay-Meanchay province, 1993

directly in demining, but it was because of our shame with the situation that we decided to take responsibility and sign the first contracts with Cambodian deminers.

We made a deal whereby we would be financially and administratively responsible for demining. UNTAC would provide the supervisory personnel for two teams of 32 deminers. The idea was, of course, to clear land, but also (more importantly) to show that *something could be done*, because UNTAC was really strongly saying 'we will not get involved in actual demining' ... [Then] when we were all ready to sign these contracts at UNTAC HQ, at the last minute, UNTAC said no because it did not want its name to appear on a demining contract. This just illustrates their fear of getting involved. Later there was real shame among the MCTU guys on the ground when they realised their general would not sign this agreement. So we made another draft contract, this time only between UNHCR and HI with just a letter from UNTAC to UNHCR confirming that they would provide technical assistance (supervisors). *But they were really doing everything they could to remain out of demining*. So we signed the contract and the two teams started working. This agreement was made on

20 July 1992; by mid September UNTAC had started to hire its own teams. So it went from two to ten demining teams working, in one and a half months, because UNTAC could not any longer maintain the position of saying, 'we are not allowed to do this'.

It is too much of a coincidence to believe that the UN's new-found ability to overcome its own difficulties, and those of member states, was not achieved as a direct result of the HI/UNHCR initiative. If the UN thought, consciously or unconsciously, that it could get away with the appearance of being committed to deal with Cambodia's mine problem, events had overtaken it. Demining had become too hot an issue to ignore: too many people had seen the need. This sea change was a major accomplishment, but it wasn't until the end of that year that there were substantial numbers of UN supervisory teams on the ground. Even when expatriate supervisors had been located further delays were created by the need to recall the trained Cambodian deminers, and conduct refresher courses. In the meantime the numbers of unemployed deminers grew as the UN continued to train. MCTU's figures[20] confirm that at the end of February 1993 there had been a total of 1,960 deminers trained from the ten UN schools throughout the country: of these only 416 were employed directly by the UN, with a further 190 working for the demining NGOs, and 1,354 were officially described as 'awaiting employment'. The basic problem remained a lack of UN personnel to supervise the Cambodian demining platoons: only the French, Dutch, Bangladeshis, Indians and Pakistanis were prepared to release men for these tasks in live minefields. But an obvious solution appeared to have been overlooked: the training of Cambodian supervisors.

The concept of CMAC, which had originated in April 1992, was for a Cambodian institution that would tackle the 'Cambodian' mine problem in the long term. Cambodian supervisors were intended as an integral part of this structure, yet training courses for these vital Cambodian personnel were not started until January 1993, ten months into the UNTAC mandate period which was set to run for just a year and a half. In the words of the then commander of MCTU's regional cell in Battambang, 'The supervisor's courses are in some senses the crux of the entire MCTU effort. If they fail in their objectives of providing Cambodians fit to lead demining operations in this country after the withdrawal of UNTAC then the future is not good.'[21]

Other specialist functions were also overlooked, and training courses such as MCTU's Explosive Ordnance Disposal (EOD) training, were introduced in a rather haphazard way. Many areas of Cambodia are littered with still live, and thus lethal, explosive ordnance. Every survey done in Cambodia in advance of the UN mission had been at pains to stress this point. The Dutch MCTU supervisory group which had been working for ten weeks, from the end of November 1992 demining a minefield opposite Beng Ampil camp in Rattanak Mondul, was suddenly ordered to stop work, and abandon the half-cleared field, select their best deminers for EOD training, and start teaching the course. Their surprise testified to the sense of panic, and lack of planning, that seemed to be gripping MCTU at that time.

Charges of poor management also surround the issue of the purchase of three UNTAC vehicles, registration plates 7997, 7998, and 7999. These mine-clearance bulldozers, known as D7s, were purchased from the American corporation Caterpiller for $1.5 million, at a time when the machines had not even been field tested. Furthermore, they had been designed for anti-tank minefield breaching operations in a sandy soil environment.[22] In Cambodia the requirement was for anti-personnel minefield clearance in a heavy, often root-infested, clay soil environment. The machines arrived in November 1992 and trials were conducted for the next four months, tying up at least one team of MCTU supervisory personnel for the entire period. At the end of day, the trials revealed what had been obvious from the start, that they were useless to mine clearance operations in Cambodia. The D7s were, in the words of Lt. Col. Focsaneanu, 'a useless piece of kit'. Not sur-

prisingly, the UN sought to conceal the error by cultivating a myth that the machines had been donated by the Japanese government rather than purchased.[23] Mechanised clearance will have a part to play in the resolution of Cambodia's mine problem, but the UN should not in effect have subsidised the research and development costs of such machines, for private-sector companies, by trialing them. Nor should three of these machines have been purchased at a time when resources were so short that the original plans for 64 demining platoons had to be scaled down to 40.[24]

Another prime example of haphazard planning and management was the allocation of priority areas for those UNTAC demining teams that did eventually make it into the field. This point demands detailed attention since it intimately affects Rattanak Mondul, the district at the heart of this book.

The allocation of priority tasks for demining is perhaps the single most important stage in any demining operation. Given the length of time it takes to demine land, the costs of training and running such labour-intensive operations, the risks involved for the deminers, etc, it is vital to ensure that the demining that does occur benefits the maximum number of people for the maximum time period. However, the UN's allocation of priorities revealed the hand of political considerations rather than a rational analysis of the greatest humanitarian and developmental needs. At a meeting in CMAC in November 1992 senior UN personnel admitted that demining teams were 'tripping over one another in the Svey Chek area'. Nevertheless, after the meeting the director of the HALO Trust went to a further meeting with the head of the US Mission to the SNC, to discuss a proposal for a further $1 million for demining in and around the Svey Chek area. What was going on?

Svey Chek, north of Sisophon, the provincial capital of Banteay-Meanchay province, had been one of the most fought over, and thus mined, towns in Cambodia. It was also the 'stand-off point' between areas nominally controlled by the non-communist resistance[25] and the State of Cambodia. Svey Chek was the last State of Cambodia controlled town on the north–south highway of Route 69; the next town reached is Thmar Pouk, at that time the headquarters of the KPNLF. As a result of the ideological 'correctness' of the non-communists as far as the US and other UN member states were concerned, considerable investment was made in both demining activities and the communications infrastructure in and around the 'non-communist zones' during the UNTAC mandate period. At the end of February 1993 nine of the UN's 15 supervisory teams capable of live clearance were operating in these areas, together with five NGO teams: in sum over 63 per cent of Cambodia's available demining resources were concentrated in one sector of one province. As public criticism mounted, the MCTU's weekly situation reports (from March 1993) ceased to contain data on which province the teams were working in, merely giving village names.

This situation contrasted strikingly with that in the largely State of Cambodia controlled Battambang province, where only one UN demining platoon, led by the Dutch in Rattanak Mondul, was allocated throughout 1992 and the first quarter of 1993. Battambang-based NGOs, local government officials and the residents of mine-infested areas like Rattanak Mondul could not understand why the UN 'only came, and looked, and then drove away again'. Furthermore, the area cleared by the Dutch in the ten week window of their operation had been on nobody's priority listings! MCTU in Battambang believed the area was for refugee resettlement (which was news to UNHCR, the agency responsible for the repatriation): the local authorities privately confided that they wanted to put a Thai cotton factory there. In April 1993 Mieke Bos of UNHCR confided, 'Its a little bit mind-boggling … I can't really explain to you why Rattanak Mondul didn't take off earlier than it did, because we in UNHCR have been, like you, banging our heads against the wall.'

Surprised, and somewhat angry that the UN would be so callous as to put political considerations above a rational allocation of such vitally important resources (at a time when casualty rates in Rattanak Mondul reached seven victims in one seven-day period), I went in search of alternative explanations. However, none was on offer that could excuse the disproportionate allocation of demining resource in the Svey Chek area. For example, while Warrant Officer McCracken of CMAC suggested there were sound technical and practical reasons why so many teams had been allocated to Banteay-Meanchay and so few to Battambang, none of the factors he cited as being important in the decision to send teams to the former were absent from the latter, apart, that is, from the high political profile of being able to demine in areas where all four Cambodian factions claimed territory.

On 26 March 1993 Sergio de Mello, the then Interim Director of CMAC and UNHCR Special Envoy to Cambodia, speaking at the second meeting of the Governing Council of CMAC, attempted to erect a smoke screen. He claimed, according to the minutes, that Rattanak Mondul had been 'the scene of constant ceasefire violations'. This tactic, retroactively justifying the UN's allocations, might have been accepted by those without first-hand knowledge of the area; however, the allegation that Rattanak Mondul had been the scene of constant ceasefire violations, rendering demining impossible, while convenient, was patently unsupportable to those who knew the district well. There had been some ceasefire violations, but these had been entirely restricted to the military zone areas, further to

the west. The only violation that had impinged on civilian life in Rattanak Mondul had been a shelling incident and ground assault in the eastern areas of the military zone in mid December 1992. Even then, it had only been the flight of UN civilian police personnel which had led to a mass exodus of civilians. Lt. Col. Mulliner, speaking a month later, eventually agreed that there had been a misallocation of resources, and that as a result he was looking to rationalise matters by moving 11 platoons to the Battambang area, leaving a more appropriate contingent of seven teams in the Svey Chek area. By the middle of 1993 these teams were in place, all operational in Rattanak Mondul. Rattanak Mondul's 'insecure' history appeared to have been forgotten.

Nevertheless, the issue of priority setting for demining during what remained of the UN time was a hit-and-miss affair. Constant requests for NGO and UN field personnel to submit priority listings never seemed to produce a rational plan. As late as April 1993 Lt. Col. Mulliner noted that since MCTU had now expanded capacity, he just needed, '… someone to tell me where the priorities are'. In the meantime, apart from redressing the 'Battambang imbalance', he would continue to expand in the areas where MCTU had historically worked, '… in the absence of anybody telling me to go elsewhere'. Benoit Denise believes that UNTAC's real needs in setting priorities were to work in safe areas (not unreasonable), but more significantly to work in areas where they could be readily observed working, and where access for visiting UN dignitaries and the press was easy. It was left to Lt. Col. Focsaneanu at CMAC to formulate a national plan for priorities in the middle of May – 14 months after the arrival of UNTAC, and a mere six months before the last UN personnel were set to leave Cambodia.

Politics also played a role in the distribution of the ten training schools MCTU had established. Wishing to be seen as impartial in their dealings with all the factions, UNTAC set up schools in the areas controlled by the non-communist resistance (Phum Ku – ANKI, and Banteay Meanrith – KPNLAF) and the Khmer Rouge (Pailin), as well as the obvious and historic regional and population centres, all of which were controlled by the State of Cambodia. Once again, this was hardly a rational use of resources: three separate training establishments were set up in the one province of Banteay-Meanchay. Furthermore, the concept of national reconciliation might have been better promoted if UNTAC had created 'a neutral environment' whereby each faction felt equally at home in the other's territory, as had been the original plan. In fairness, MCTU did rationalise its operation towards the end of its mandate period, closing all the schools apart from the one in Battambang, where members of the non-communist factions trained without problems alongside their former enemies from the CPAF. However, in Pailin where the Khmer Rouge had asked British demining specialists to set up a school,[26] no deminers were trained. In line with its whole policy towards the UN, the Khmer Rouge refused to allow the British specialists to operate: after months in conditions of virtual house arrest the UN representatives were withdrawn.

As 1993 wore on and the UNTAC demining initiative finally expanded as the supervisor's courses produced Cambodian-led teams, security problems in the pre-election build up started to impinge on the work. Although in general the CPAF's co-operation had facilitated the majority of UNTAC's demining successes during the mandate period, in the central province of Kompong Thom, scene of some of the heaviest fighting during the peace process, and in coastal Kampot, MCTU experienced difficulties with the CPAF authorities who, fearing that tactical minefields might be demined, threw up obstacles at the provincial level. More seriously, in Siem Reap the Khmer Rouge mounted a campaign of violence and intimidation against the Dutch-led demining platoons, located in Ampil commune 14 km east of the town. This culminated in an attack by 70 Khmer Rouge on the deminer's camp on the night of Saturday 3 April 1993 during which the camp was burnt down, UNTAC

MCTU Training School, Siem Reap: deminers are shown the correct technique for prodding in a minefield

equipment being stolen, and the Cambodian deminers threatened with their lives. The Dutch commander, Captain Fiers, felt that this attack was not an attack on the demining initiative *per se* but related to the general collapse in the security situation in Siem Reap at the time, in advance of the elections, and to the Khmer Rouge's policy of targeting the UN and its personnel. I asked whether the Bangladeshi contingent could provide protection, to which Fiers replied, 'They can't even protect themselves,[27] let alone the election people who are their primary concern.' On the morning of 6 April 1993 I flew with Fiers on his way to MCTU HQ to update Mulliner on the situation. 'It's all over for demining in Siem Reap now;' clearly very upset; 'you should write a book about demining in another place; this is not a normal country.'

Clearly, Cambodia was not, as the UN wanted to believe, a country in post-conflict mode with a mines problem to resolve. Whether you called it, as did UNHCR's Mieke Bos 'continuing ceasefire violations', or a state of war, no one would dispute that there was a 'non-existence of peace in Cambodia' during the first half of 1993. Lt. Col. Mulliner acknowledged that while MCTU were now making progress with demining, 'new mines were being laid in most areas'. Mieke Bos confirmed that such fresh mine laying had occurred in Kompong Thom, and commented:

> to have successful demining, you need peace, otherwise its pointless. We've had the first examples of *fresh mines being laid in fields that have been cleared by UNTAC*. I mean what the hell are we doing here if people are going to lay new mines in a demined minefield? I find that totally criminal. I don't think there's another word for it because if you take into consideration how long it takes, the risks that these poor deminers have to take, the excruciating, tiring, boring work that they have to do and then finally you can give the green light and say OK this field has been demined, you can start ploughing it, and then the next thing you hear is that people are laying fresh mines. That's when Sergio de Mello would get totally frustrated and come out with statements like 'the laying of fresh mines should be considered as a criminal act, and should be prosecuted accordingly'.

After the May elections UNTAC handed back to the new Cambodian government some of the weapons that had been given up during the mandate period. Among these were significant numbers of anti-personnel mines.

CMAC: a Cambodian Solution, a Cambodian Institution

At the end of July 1993 MCTU was absorbed into CMAC, giving it huge operational capacity as well as concrete grounds to start claiming financial support from international aid donors. While the agency's genesis, among the confusion of the UN's response to demining Cambodia during the mandate period, appeared almost as an afterthought, even those observers who had been critical of the UN approach to the mines problem in Cambodia came to believe that with CMAC a viable long-term solution could emerge. Without doubt, this optimism was directly attributable to the dedication and hard work of Lt. Col. George Focsaneanu and his small core of staff, whose efforts shone out as a bright spot among the myriad of UN activity in Cambodia. Yet at the same time as CMAC was emerging as one of the lasting and beneficial legacies of the UN time, its senior officers were amazed to find themselves, towards the end of 1993, struggling for the very survival of the agency. The crucial question remained the commitment of the UN and its member states to Cambodia, and the resolution of the mine issue. But to some extent, too, it seemed to come down to a complete lack of understanding within the higher echelons of the UN as to what CMAC was, what had been achieved, and what was needed to secure its future.

Sadly, it seemed that it wasn't until CMAC was teetering on the edge of collapse that the international community finally understood the importance of the organisation. To some extent, as a source in UN HQ in New York confided, the UN had been 'blinded by the success of the elections' and were too busy holding up the Cambodia operation as an unmitigated success to look closely at such *minutiae* as the life or death of CMAC. By late October 1993 Lt. Col. Mulliner's comments, made six months earlier, had assumed a prophetic tone. He had said:

> No one seems to have grasped that MCTU and CMAC transcend UNTAC. It will go on before, during, and after the elections. It should be one of the most enduring and important legacies of the UNTAC time here, but it has just one paragraph in the Paris Peace Agreements ... you read Akashi's statement on UNTAC's birthday celebrations [March 1993]: he didn't even mention mine clearance. Not once. Akashi, I'm afraid, has his eyes turned totally towards the elections; his interest and definition of success or failure for the UN will be if we have elections or not. Whatever happens in the election, the mine clearance remains.

The Cambodian Mine Action Centre (CMAC) had come into being officially on 10 June 1992. Although part of UNTAC in terms of personnel and funding, the aim was to create a sustainable Cambodian institution with the overall 'corporate aim' being 'To achieve a state within Cambodia where people can go about their lives free from the threat of mines'. This was to be achieved

CMAC: Cambodian deminers at work in Rattanak Mondul

in the long-term, by implementing the 'integrated systems' approach to the mine problem, a question of a combination of strategies: of information about mines (gathering, recording and disseminating – vital for the priority setting process); mine awareness (both for Cambodians and internationally to increase the general awareness of mines and the problems they create); minefield marking (of fields lower down the priority listings that would have to wait years before being cleared); minefield clearance (using a variety of different techniques – manual, mechanical, dogs and combinations thereof); and lastly training to sustain these activities. CMAC was also envisaged as being the central co-ordinating agency for demining in Cambodia, with the vital functions of ensuring that quality control standards were maintained, national priorities cleared in a rational way, and demining resources maximised in the service of the entire nation.

However, during the UN time CMAC's ambiguous identity had been one of the agency's major obstacles – was it a UN organisation, an NGO, or part of the Cambodian government? As Focsaneanu noted in March 1993:

CMAC … is (currently) a part of UNTAC, but CMAC needs to be a stand-alone organisation to really grow and get going. The problem is that UNTAC will not release its assets to CMAC because it requires those assets to provide operational control for UNTAC requirements. I mean that's the reality of life.

The problem for CMAC during the mandate period was that without the release of those assets, and primarily the human resources MCTU controlled – the deminers themselves – it remained essentially a paper organisation. During the UN time CMAC was restricted to information collection and minefield mapping,[28] as well as generating, but not implementing, a national mine awareness programme, and working on policy issues. The heart of the business was conducted from the headquarters of the MCTU office responsible for operations: minefield clearance, marking, training, support services and administration. As Lt. Col. Mulliner noted, 'if you put those functions together you get one organisation'.

But the merger of MCTU and CMAC could not, and did not, resolve the agency's problems overnight. Throughout 1993 funding remained a crucial concern. In March, when I interviewed him, Focsaneanu wanted to be absolutely sure that I understood its importance:

Funding is the number one CMAC problem. If funding doesn't occur by the time UNTAC leaves, CMAC is going to die and all the work that has gone on is going to be forgotten, which would be a real travesty … [currently] … CMAC does not have a goddamn cent, therefore all of these deminers, the school, all of the data base, will be worth f*** all when UNTAC leaves. That's the point I'm trying to get to you. Focus on the goddamn funding …

Without funding independent of UNTAC it was clear that CMAC would face extinction at the end of the mandate period. But if CMAC was so important, why had funding not been forthcoming? The most obvious, if somewhat surprising, reason was that funding had not been requested. In April 1993 Lt. Col. Mulliner explained, '… it's not the fact that we've been turned down; we haven't asked. We haven't sold ourselves in the way that we should have done, for example we haven't got a promotional video.' However, towards the end of the first half of 1993 such obvious gaps were being addressed. For example, in early May Fox officially put the CMAC promotional video, designed to win funding from international aid agencies and governmental donors, out to tender, with a deadline for completion of 31 July. Although such a measure should have been taken months earlier the unwieldy nature of the UNTAC bureaucracy in Cambodia caused still further delays. Although tenders were received by CMAC in early June it wasn't until the middle of August that an English production

company, Bicycle Trail Films, was informally told they had been awarded the contract. The UN purchase order formally requesting their services took a further six weeks even to make it to a fax machine in UNTAC HQ, Phnom Penh. The film was eventually delivered to CMAC in February 1994, some seven months after Focsaneanu's original deadline.

However, lack of funding meant more for CMAC than just the inability to run its own demining programmes. One of its crucial functions is its co-ordination role, with a view to ensuring national priorities are met and technical quality control standards followed – standards that are a matter of life and death both for the deminers and future users of the land being cleared. As UNHCR's Mieke Bos pointed out, if CMAC did not become the central conduit for demining funds, the ability to exercise this co-ordination and quality control function would be seriously undermined. Without control of the purse strings of Cambodian demining, CMAC would lack the authority to function effectively. The dangers of such a situation had already become obvious to senior UN personnel on the ground. In January 1993 Major Vishw, the commanding officer of MCTU's forward HQ in Battambang, was very concerned about further demining organisations, particularly commercial outfits, arriving in Cambodia and not only by-passing national humanitarian and development demining priorities but ignoring standard operating procedures established during the UN time to ensure safe practices and high-quality clearance. Such a situation had already occurred, and the Major could barely conceal his anger. The United States Agency for International Development had funded a Thai demining contractor to clear Route 69, the highway that runs north–south from Thmar Pouk to Svey Chek in Banteay-Meanchay. The standards of clearance and safety were farcical, the Major said. The deminers were told merely to lift the mines they had located with their prodders, and place them on the side of the road which was to be resurfaced and repaired with US aid money. They were paid a paltry $1 per day.

Even when funding was eventually approved, bureaucratic and political problems prevented CMAC from accessing it. In April 1993, when half a million dollars was made available for the agency from the US government, UNHCR's Mieke Bos revealed that CMAC, the awkward 'hybrid' organisation, was having difficulties receiving the money. In the end funding was held in a 'trust fund' for CMAC at UN HQ in New York. At the time of writing (November 1993) CMAC still has no direct access to these funds. During the first half of 1993 CMAC's ability to secure international funding was also hampered, ironically, by the elections. Focsaneanu quite candidly accepted that for major international donors most funding decisions would turn on the results of the elections. Until a stable context emerged, and assurances of accountability from CMAC were received, donors would prefer to make short-term commitments to fund demining through NGOs and others rather than to invest in a long-term, national solution to the problem. As 1993 drew to a close and the new Cambodian government consolidated its position, donors remained hesitant about funding CMAC: at this stage they had become cautious about the very survival of the agency itself. Yet without such donor confidence in CMAC such fears would become self-justifying. In early November 1993 the Australian Ambassador to Cambodia noted that the $1 million his government had allocated to CMAC was being held back until it was confident the agency had a future.

To some extent this lack of confidence had its origins in the agency's 15-month set-up phase, when it had remained a paper organisation. During 1992 UN personnel pointed out that CMAC had suffered from 'stagnation', which derived from a lack of direction and commitment from the UN, and even Cambodian politicians, to CMAC. For example, no high-flying UN official was recruited to take on the job of CMAC director, which as Benoit Denise noted was essential if the agency was to market itself internationally. CMAC had to make do with sharing an already overstretched man, Sergio Vierra de Mello, the Special Envoy of the United Nations High Commissioner for Refugees, as 'interim director'. The charismatic de Mello left Cambodia in April 1993 for another 'Special Envoy' job, this time in Angola. In the meantime the interim director's job was passed to the UNTAC Force Engineer, Col. Neal Bradley, another man who, in Mulliner's words, had 'many other responsibilities': CMAC was far from being his primary concern, which still lay with the overall success of UNTAC's mission. Following the elections Bradley, against the strong advice of many informed participants, made CMAC a statutory body of the new Cambodian government, storing up problems for the future of the agency. Bradley's hurry to Cambodianise the agency not only left it without the leadership of a skilled international bureaucrat, of the type Denise had seen as necessary to head up the agency in the medium term, it also failed to give CMAC a director who could dedicate his full time and energy to it. The appointee, Ieng Mouly, an able Cambodian politician and member of the Buddhist Liberal Democrat Party elected to the constituent assembly in May, had also been appointed Minister of Information in the new government. Sadly, many of the other Cambodians who had been appointed to CMAC's governing council, all representatives of the various factions that had made up the SNC during the mandate period, had demonstrated a lack of commitment to CMAC. Benoit Denise of HI, the sole representative of the NGO community on the Council, noted that 'very few of them are really interested because they are high political players and are not really involved in, or concerned about, demining …'

During the third quarter of 1993, as CMAC finally achieved full operational strength,[29] fears started to mount among its senior expatriate leadership as the UNTAC specialists who had been seconded to it following the merger with MCTU were gradually withdrawn, apparently not to be replaced. During an international NGO Forum meeting held in Phnom Penh in mid-September concerns were voiced that Cambodian supervisors had been driven into taking over the management of demining platoons before they were ready for these responsibilities. Even within the administrative structure, Cambodians had been left to some extent floundering without sufficient levels of external support. The pace of CMAC's Cambodianisation had been forced to fit in with the politically driven timetable, which focused on the electoral process under which UNTAC had been operating: it did not reflect a task-oriented planning response. In Rattanak Mondul local village leaders had begun to notice the falling standards of CMAC's minefield clearance, which were the regrettable, but inevitable, consequences of this process. In one incident in September 1993 a monk lost a leg walking over land that had recently been 'cleared' by a Cambodian-led team; subsequently, in the following weeks, CMAC personnel were involved in a series of accidents, accidents that expert observers on the ground attributed to an increasingly lax attitude on the part of the Cambodian supervisors towards the safety standards enshrined within CMAC's own operating procedures.

Given the importance of CMAC's role and the very real dangers that such a forcing of the pace of Cambodianisation produced both for its employees, and for future users of the land it was charged to clear, such inappropriate planning can only be described as highly irresponsible. Such a situation could and should have been avoided. Senior UN officers had known at least since November 1992, what CMAC's long-term staffing and funding requirements would be.

However, Bradley now seemed keen to present CMAC to his superiors in the UN as a 'task achieved', and perhaps for this reason had downplayed the agency's ongoing need for external support. The prevailing view at the UN in New York regarded UNTAC as a great success: Cambodians had had a great deal of money spent on them during the peace process, and now, to some extent, it was time for them to stand on their own . Certainly Bradley's decision to make CMAC part of the new Cambodian government must have reinforced impressions within the UN hierarchy that the goal of Cambodianisation had been successfully accomplished. Indeed, July 1993 had been the unrealistic target date established in the CMAC Short Term Operational Plan, issued in November 1992, to turn CMAC over to civilian

Cambodian control. However, the effect of making CMAC an entirely Cambodian institution, ahead of its ability to live up to that noble aspiration, not only deflected attention from its ongoing requirements for external support but also enhanced the reluctance of governments to pledge bi-lateral funding and made it extremely difficult, for several practical reasons, for foreign governments to commit military specialists to assist on a technical front, even if they had understood the continued need for such assistance, and were willing to give it.[30] Some journalists drew the inevitable conclusion: the UN had never been serious about CMAC; there had been 'a washing of hands in Cambodia'.[31]

In October 1993 Bradley informed Focsaneanu and his staff that all expatriate UNTAC staff seconded to CMAC were to leave Cambodia by 15 November. Focsaneanu and his men refused to accept the situation and instigated an international lobby which, primarily through diplomatic and NGO networks, succeeded in a few short weeks in raising the profile of CMAC in several western nations. Despite the fact that a General Assembly meeting was in progress at UN HQ in New York, CMAC became a major issue, the response indicating that what previously had seemed indicative of a lack of commitment essentially boiled down to a lack of accurate information. To give focus to this campaign, on 18 October 1993 Mouly (Director of CMAC and Minister of Information) issued a widely circulated directive which ordered the cessation of CMAC demining activities on 1 November. The reasons cited included the shortages of funding, the lack of 'definition of the UN financial control umbrella to allow transfer of donor funds', and the need for a 'technical advisory group' of expatriate specialists to oversee the work in the medium term. Ieng Mouly continued:

> The decision to stop demining has not been taken lightly as the negative impact on Cambodia and the Cambodian people will be extremely detrimental. After 18 months of effort to set up a Cambodian Mine Action Centre, it makes no sense to me, both as a concerned Cambodian and as its Director, that in the next two weeks an organisation which can save thousands of lives and provide an environment conducive to growth and prosperity will be allowed to wither … The reality is that this vital organisation will cease at a time when its survival is essential to Cambodia's own survival.

At the time of writing the future of CMAC remains uncertain. The outcry generated by the directive of 18 October resulted in an in-country extension, until the beginning of December 1993, of the core of 30 expatriates who made up the 'technical advisory group'. However, the *de facto* shortages of funding meant that demining did in fact cease in November 1993, and a

Demolition

period of 'retraining', on half pay, was carried out. That the UN was forced at least temporarily to give Focsaneanu the extension he demanded was in part a function of the perfect timing of the lobby. Pilger wrote:

> The day after CMAC announced its closure, the UN General Assembly passed a resolution calling for an end to the 'worldwide scourge' of landmines. 'Of all the tasks involved in setting a nation on a new road to peace and prosperity,' declared Secretary General Boutros-Ghali, 'perhaps none has the immediate urgency of mine clearance'. The resolution[32] was based largely on evidence from Cambodia that mines killed more people than any other weapon. It was 'imperative', said Boutros-Ghali 'that mine clearing should continue in Cambodia after the UN left'.[33]

However, unless CMAC was reconstituted as a UN body, as was the case with the co-ordinating agency established in Afghanistan, it would be extremely unlikely that such CMAC controlled mine clearance would be directly overseen by UN personnel seconded from member states, although several such states had expressed a willingness to consider such a role for their nationals.[34]

Furthermore, even if the 'bi-lateral solution' overcame the series of obstacles standing in its way, several observers felt that the levels of staffing under consideration – a presence of 30 expatriates which would be gradually phased out over a two-year period – would still not be sufficient to ensure a responsible Cambodianisation of CMAC. Realistically, this 'bi-lateral' solution may prove politically too difficult, in which case the demining NGOs would be asked to provide the specialist staff necessary to see CMAC through the five years that are seen as being the necessary transition period. While NPA, MAG and the HALO Trust were willing to respond to this need, even an 'NGO solution' to the CMAC crisis posed serious difficulties. Not only might NGOs be left as the reluctant fall guys, responsible for completing the UN's unfinished business in Cambodia, if they were also being asked to assume responsiblity for its operations in the field they too needed to have certain assurances of influence and control within the agency's management hierarchy – assurances which would be hard to gain now CMAC was part of the new Cambodian government. Perhaps more seriously they had to be cautious about taking on such a huge long-term responsibility in an environment where sources of funding sufficient to sustain an appropriate involvement seemed to be as uncertain as ever. As Matthew Middlemiss, HALO's regional director, noted in early November 1993, 'While we are willing to help out, we can't afford to do so unless we have concrete assurances that we won't be left holding the CMAC baby as the spotlight on Cambodia fades over the coming years.'

Conclusions

CMAC can and should work. This is a long-term problem, and an appropriate sustainable solution has been found, given the fact that Cambodia is not Kuwait, i.e. it has no great economic or strategic importance to the member states who control the purse strings in the UN. In comparison with the enormity of Cambodia's mine problem in humanitarian terms, and considering the intimate connectivity of the mine problem to many other developmental issues, the total budget requested in the CMAC corporate plan is minimal in international terms. $12 million per annum for the 1992–97 period. From 1970 until 1975 the United States government alone spent $1 million a day on military and economic aid to prop up the corrupt Cambodian administration of Lon Nol, in addition to $7 billion spent during the 1969–73 period on the illegal bombing of Cambodia by American planes.[35] An avoidable tragedy is in store if these relatively small sums of money, and appropriate numbers of expatriate advisers, are not made available by donors who in a very real sense should be considered responsible for the 'Cambodian' mine problem.

So funding is of vital importance, and we must get the message across to the international community that this country will not be demined without financial assistance from abroad. And if it doesn't get the finances there will continue to be 300 mine casualties every month until all the mines are exploded by casualties. And if the world can sit by, and accept that, then fine. But if the world can't, it will be too late to wait for casualties to start rising again, and some volunteer organisation to come in and say the number of amputees in Cambodia is ridiculous, it's already the highest in the world now, and it's still rising. Why can't the world do something about it? Well the world can do something about it, and now is the time to do it, because we can leave Cambodia with CMAC. But it needs money and commitment.
Lt. Col. N. F. Mulliner, Phnom Penh, April 1993

6
Prosthetics and Society:
A Return to Dignity?

Estimates suggest that at least 25,000 and perhaps as many as 35,000 Cambodians are amputees, the vast majority of them mine victims. Cambodians now have the dubious distinction of being the world's most disabled people.[1] Given current mine casualty rates this is a characteristic the country is unlikely to shed in the near future. In such a situation the provision of prostheses is clearly of vital importance. This chapter reviews the efforts of humanitarian agencies to meet these needs over recent years and considers the problems faced by amputees in Cambodian society. It is clear that the successful reintegration of those whose lives have been shattered by mines, depends on not only in the provision of prostheses but on a host of broader socio-economic and cultural factors. While the provision of prostheses is undoubtedly important other factors maybe more significant determinants of individual mine victims' new social experience. Reintegration is seriously challenged, for example by socio-cultural Cambodian prejudices against the disabled, and on the economic front, the limited education of the majority of mine victims is a barrier to skills training.

Marked differences have been observed between the social position of amputees in rural and urban settings. In part these differences are attributable to economic factors – it is easier for a rural amputee to contribute, albeit at a reduced level, to the family economy in village life than for an amputee to find work in the city. Not only does the ability to contribute economically make a difference to personal confidence and self-image, but the ability not to be a burden to one's family seems to be the key in determining the ease with which the amputee is reintegrated into social life. Given the fact that mines have a special relationship with the poorest, this is hardly surprising when families are living so close to subsistence levels. Furthermore, in mine-affected communities such as Rattanak Mondul the ubiquitous knowledge that mines can strike at any time acts as a great leveller on the able bodied, encouraging perhaps a more tolerant and accepting attitude to the disabled than among city dwellers whose lives are far removed from the daily threat of mines.

Among the NGOs involved in Cambodia it is those specialising in prosthetics – particularly the Vietnam Veterans of America Foundation (VVAF) and Handicap International (HI) – who have realised the integral logic of engaging in advocacy about landmines as an obvious corollary of running prosthetics programmes in the field. In a sector that has been marked by intense rivalry and competition between agencies there is remarkable cohesion on this one point:

> People are not really aware of the problem [of mines] … now we need these prostheses, but of course it would be much better to start at the point of mines, because if you have no mines there will not be as many amputations. It's the same as polio … if you have vaccinations, you don't have to think about orthotics. Better to go to the roots than to tackle the problems they produce.[2]

Meeting the Need: Which Way to a Solution?

The first agency to tackle the problem of the provision of prostheses in Cambodia was the American Friends Service Committee (AFSC), which started operations in Phnom Penh in 1981. It was joined a few months later by Handicap International (HI) who, due to problems with the Phnom Penh authorities concerning its prosthetic programmes in the Thai border camps, was obliged initially to work under AFSC, providing only technical

Begging: Battambang market

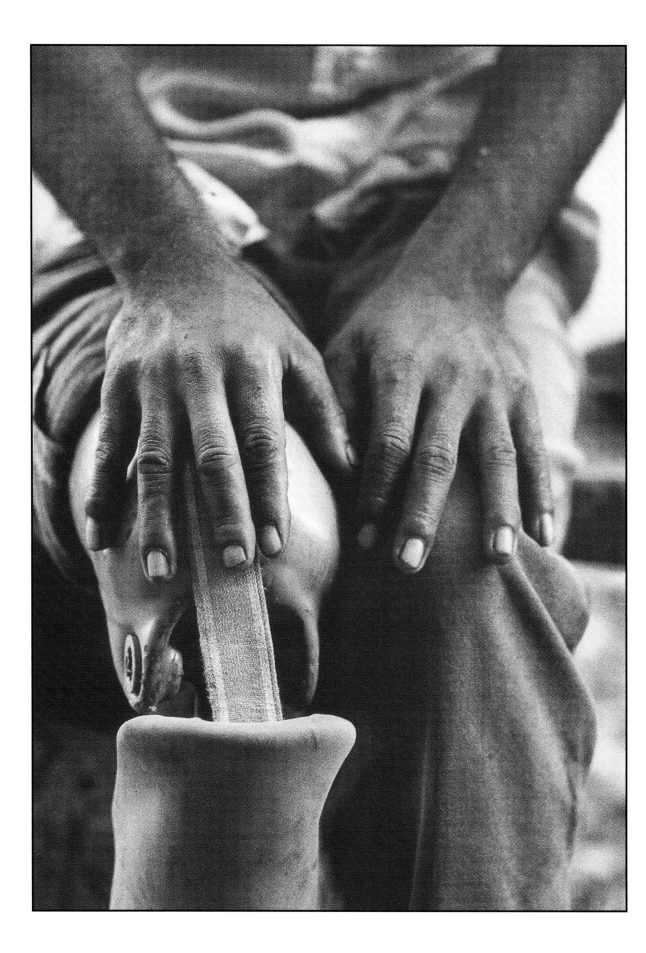

expertise. As well as fitting prostheses, AFSC and HI made an early decision to focus on the training of Cambodian staff so as to make their efforts sustainable in the long-term. In February 1982 there were no Cambodian prosthetists or technicians in the country, and these agencies swiftly realised that the future success of Cambodian prosthetics would depend on the development of indigenous capacity. By the early 1990s the one-year training course they developed had produced a pool of 100 trained 'technicians' skilled in the wood and leather technology that was to become the hallmark of these early initiatives.

Due to the security situation in country it was initially possible for the agencies to provide these services only in Phnom Penh, at the Wat Than 'National Rehabilitation Centre'. However, in 1987 permission was granted to set up workshops in various regional and provincial centres, and HI decided to focus the bulk of its activities in the provinces. However, during the first few years expatriate personnel were not allowed to live outside Phnom Penh, and the workshops were entirely Khmer self-managed by technicians who had already been trained at Wat Than.

Given the conditions in Cambodia in the 1980s, where recovery from the devastation of the Khmer Rouge years was hampered by both the civil war and the western-led international aid embargo, both AFSC and HI agreed that a 'low-tech' approach to prosthetics would be most appropriate. Their response centred on the production of a wood and leather limb – leather sockets, and wooden shaft and foot pieces. Not only were such materials locally available, but the process of manufacture required only a low level of capital input, no electricity, and materials with which Cambodians were familiar. Such an approach was appropriate since most of the trainee prosthetics technicians, all employees of the Ministry of Labour and Social Action (MLSA),[3] had received very little formal education, in many cases due to the disruptions of the Pol Pot years.

This approach, while arguably appropriate for conditions in the 1980s, became far less so for the 1990s, particularly after the signing of the Paris Peace Accords in 1991. Significant changes had started two years before. The withdrawal of Vietnamese troops in September 1989, itself partly a function of the dramatic reduction in eastern bloc largesse in the region, made the State of Cambodia (SOC) realise that it needed to identify additional sources of support if it was to meet the needs of its war-torn country. One of these sources came in the form of the International Committee of the Red Cross (ICRC).

In 1979 ICRC's refusal to give up its relief work on the Thai-Cambodian border led to its being unable to reach an agreement with the Phnom Penh regime about developing programmes in Cambodia itself, although a

presence was maintained in the capital throughout the 1980s. However, in 1989 the Phnom Penh authorities invited ICRC to start medical programmes in some of Cambodia's hospitals. Other activities followed including, in May 1991, prosthetics. Clearly the SOC officials, while happy to have received assistance from AFSC and HI in the 1980s, were starting to realise that their efforts alone were not going to be adequate to meet the needs of Cambodia's amputees. At the close of the decade those needs were growing sharply as mines claimed ever increasing numbers due to the escalation in the war that followed the Vietnamese withdrawal. 'Between 1982 and 1989, these two NGOs had made just over 1,000 artificial limbs – two thirds of them for the same patients.'[4] Furthermore, other technologies were now available that could not only produce limbs faster and cheaper but result in a lighter, more comfortable and cosmetically more appealing limb. ICRC had experience in one such technology, using polypropylene, which had been developed during 1989 in its programmes in Afghanistan and Chad. The SOC was impressed, and requested that ICRC take over the HI-assisted regional workshop in Battambang.

In April 1993 Philippe Steiner, head of the ICRC's orthopaedic programmes in Cambodia, recalled that the

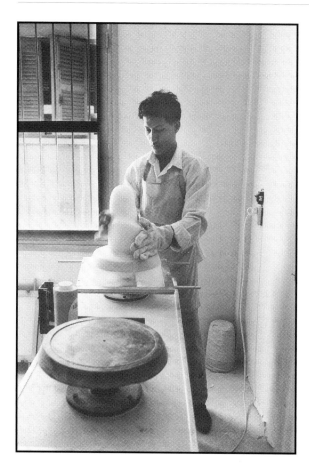

Vacuum forming a polypropylene socket for a new prosthetic limb

agency's concern had been to meet local needs quickly, in what might arguably be termed a 'relief' mode. The initial goal was not the development of indigenous capacity, a focus on the process of prosthetics production, but the output of limbs. On 31 September 1991 ICRC opened its regional workshop in Battambang. The 'hi-tech' solution adopted has resulted in far higher outputs. It involves an electrified workshop with a high level of investment in equipment and imported raw materials (polypropylene sheets), and a production-line approach. In the first 16 months of its operation the Battambang workshop, assisted by a separate components factory in Phnom Penh, produced well over 2,000 prostheses for patients from all four western provinces, 96 per cent of whom were mine victims. In February 1993 the workshop was producing around 130 limbs a month, and aimed to expand production still further.

However, ICRC's high-volume, hi-tech approach did not mean that it had no interest in developing a sustainable long-term solution to the problem, which as HI and AFSC had realised must be seen in terms of developing indigenous capacity. In October 1991 ICRC signed a five-year agreement with the Ministry of Labour and Social

Action which envisaged the Cambodianisation of the entire operation by 1996. After bitter arguments AFSC and HI also came to realise that ICRC's approach offered the most appropriate solution to Cambodia's prosthetics needs in the 1990s. In the same month these three agencies signed an operational agreement which agreed roles and acknowledged that the ICRC polypropylene limb system was to become the standard technology in the development of a national prosthetics infrastructure. Over the ensuing two years HI and AFSC started to move over to the polypropylene system.

The key factors in making a successful prosthesis are the fabrication of a well-fitted and comfortable 'socket' (into which the end of the patient's amputated leg – or 'stump' – fits and good alignment of the artificial limb to ensure a natural gait both of which are more easily achieved with the polypropylene system. ICRC's well-respected Phnom Penh based ortho-prosthetist, Heinz Trebbin, commented, 'Not only is polypropylene cheaper than wood and leather, the technical quality of prosthesis made from the latter is no way as good ... leather is not a good material for a prosthesis because the moment it gets wet, it gets deformed.'[5] If a prosthesis is not comfortable an amputee will not wear it. The weight of the wooden prostheses also goes against them, as does the tendency to rot in damp environments (such as the paddy field).

But perhaps the most important battle that the polypropylene system had to win revolved around the creation of an international dependency based on the system's reliance on imported polypropylene sheets. Polypropylene is made locally in Cambodia but not in the high-specification sheet form required for the prosthetics process. With an assured demand it is hoped that this Cambodian factory (sold in 1992 to Thai business interests along with many other going concerns) will start to produce the sheets required. Also, polypropylene is an efficient material with which to work. For example, waste cuts are capable of recycling by means of shredding into small granules which can then be recast into sheets from which limb components can be made. ICRC's components factory in Phnom Penh is further testimony to its commitment to the creation of local capacity. This factory produces enough limb components to service national demand (it supplies other agencies on a no-charge basis). Perhaps the most surprising factor overcoming this 'dependency' argument was the fact that HI and AFSC had been importing the leather used for their prostheses from Thailand anyway, the quality of Cambodian leather being too poor for prosthesis manufacture!

However, at the close of the 1980s the State of Cambodia government appealed for help to more agencies than just the ICRC. For instance, in January 1990 Dr Peter Carey of the Oxford-based Cambodia Trust, in a meeting with the Cambodian Prime Minister Hun Sen, asked what his government saw as its most pressing humanitarian needs. Carey writes of the meeting:

> He [Hun Sen] had just returned from visiting the battlefront at Mongkol Berei [Banteay-Meanchay] where he had seen grievously wounded children caught in mine blasts. His reply was unequivocal: help with demining and the provision of modern prostheses to cope with the ever swelling numbers of mine casualties, victims of the unrestricted mine warfare then being carried out by the Khmer Rouge against the civilian population of Cambodia's western provinces.[6]

The Cambodia Trust responded by introducing the HALO Trust to Cambodia and by developing its own project to tackle the prosthetics need, the Cambodia Trust Limb Project. In February 1992 it opened a workshop in Calmette Hospital, Phnom Penh, making limbs with polypropylene sockets (like ICRC's) and limb parts recycled from old stock purchased from the British National Health Service (a technology that had only just been phased out in the UK, known as Modular Assembly Prosthesis). In the first year of its operations in Cambodia over 900 limbs were produced, at an average of 75 per month. The backlog in providing prostheses for Cambodia's amputees was starting to be shifted.

At this time other agencies also opened prosthetics projects, including the Indo-China Project, funded by the Vietnam Veterans of America Foundation (VVAF), and the American Red Cross. While the latter adopted the ICRC technology at its workshop in Kompong Speu, VVAF was convinced that the aluminium socket and 'Jaipur (rubber) foot' technology was the most appropriate solution to the Cambodian problem. Developed in India, this uses and recycles readily available materials

A Cambodian technician hammers out an aluminium socket

found in a Third World environment and involves a very simple, low-cost manufacturing process. Attached to a hand-beaten aluminium socket, the foot produces a prosthesis that seems remarkably easy for amputees to come to terms with. However, while progress was being made on the ground in Cambodia, some extremely bitter arguments raged in the UK between proponents of the Jaipur technology and supporters of the Cambodia Trust, an argument which, superficially at least, generated enough momentum to warrant a BBC television documentary broadcast in 1992.

But such vying for the 'perfect solution' is ridiculous. The ICRC system, for example, did not arrive as a complete and fully researched technology 'for Cambodia'. The strength of the current system is that it partly evolved on the ground. The AFSC/ICRC/HI operational agreement divided responsibility among the agencies for development of Cambodia-appropriate components for the national limb. Thus, ICRC were responsible for developing the knee joints, pylons (leg shafts) and ankle pieces, while HI worked on the design and manufacture of the feet. The process is intended to be ongoing, and is increasingly participative with

The first step. Limb fitting in Phnom Penh: 10,000–16,000 Cambodian amputees have still to receive their first prosthesis

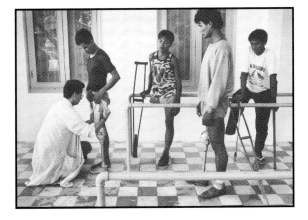

newcomers like the Cambodia Trust providing technical input in what has become a co-operative endeavour. Perhaps most damning to those who proclaimed the 'perfect solution' with regard to the Jaipur foot technology is the fact that the foot's originator was reported as saying that he would have used polypropylene for the limb sockets if he had had access to it, freely admitting that aluminium is less suitable.[7] However, this is not to negate the valuable contribution of the Indo-China Project's work on the ground. Its centre at Kean Khleang in Phnom Penh fitted a further 750 amputees in the year following the project's opening in late 1991, and has carried out other rehabilitative work that has been widely admired in the Phnom Penh prosthetics community and beyond.

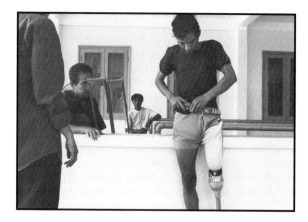

Nevertheless, the duplication of technologies has produced some duplication of effort, and overall a less than efficient allocation of prosthetics resources. While perhaps the majority of Cambodian amputees have no prosthesis, some, especially in Phnom Penh and surrounding areas, have two or three, in different technologies. Benoit Denise, Director of Handicap International, even reported some amputees getting HI limbs for work and the ICRC leg as a 'social choice model'. While no one would deny that amputees should have the right to choose between the available technologies such freedom of choice should be suspended until all have had access to a limb. Furthermore, in 1992 there were a total of 14 prosthetics workshops in Cambodia, many of which were concentrated in Phnom Penh and areas that are easily accessible to the city. This was simply too many, and a complete turnaround from the situation little over ten years ago, especially in light of the fact that no agency had then tackled the massive orthotics needs that exist in Cambodia.[8] Like demining, prosthetics has a surprisingly 'sexy' image among donors and the media.

Thankfully, however, the various agencies are now working closer together, all sharing a commitment to the development of a durable national prosthetics infrastructure. While the Cambodia Trust and VVAF have not become signatories of the operational agreement, they accept most of it in principle, and all agencies are involved in a joint dialogue with the Cambodian Ministry responsible for developing such an infrastructure.[9] For example, a national plan has been developed that sets a framework for the distribution of agencies countrywide with a view to rationalising the current situation and maximising the utilisation of prosthetics resources available to Cambodians.

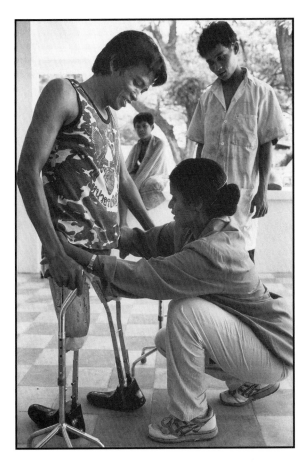

A double amputee is fitted with specially adapted prostheses designed to strengthen his thigh muscles before he is fitted with full-length limbs

But perhaps the most important function of a standardised technology, over and above a duplication of effort by competing technologies sponsored by competing agencies, has to do with the goal of training for the future Cambodianisation of prosthetics. It had long been realised that while the one year training established by

AFSC had been a good start, a three-year course was required to provide training to professional ortho-prosthetist level in Cambodia. The benefits of co-operation among the prosthetics agencies was summarised by Benoit Denise:

> having technicians trained from all over Cambodia in Phnom Penh in one school, in one technology ... to have a central warehouse, a central stock ordering process for materials, improved national distribution of materials to the provinces [is the goal]. If you have three workshops that need aluminium, five that need leather, ten that need plastic, it's very difficult to build one system. I think now the idea to use one technique over and above another is because you want to create one network that you can develop and hand over to Cambodians when the NGOs leave. It's more important to see it from this point of view than to see it in terms of a rivalry between which material is the most appropriate.

However, since agreement on a standardised technology for Cambodia has been accomplished progress is now underway on both the collaborative development of such a training course and the construction of a national school, under the supervision of the Cambodia Trust in the Calmette Hospital in Phnom Penh. In addition to the commitment each agency has to training its own staff and releasing some of its best technicians to attend the ortho-prosthetics training, all will contribute staff time and finances towards the development and operation of the national school when it is established. The aim is to produce a core of some 60 professionally trained ortho-prosthetists who will effectively form the core of the future Cambodian prosthetics and orthotics service by the end of the decade.

Many believe that after the establishment of prosthetics workshops throughout the country, improvements in technology and the establishment of a training school, what is needed now is capacity building within the government, in the Ministry of Veterans' Affairs. Not only is such a goal philosophically important but, as in demining, it is vital since funding for expatriate heavy organisations cannot be expected to be maintained at current levels indefinitely. The historic and current corruption of Cambodian government officials, partly a product of the Pol Pot years, partly a product of the impoverishment of a regime that cannot pay even its senior members, and partly a cultural problem, needs to be addressed by the new Cambodian government. Nevertheless what is needed now from external aid donors is financial support for the new ministry through properly structured salaries and the recruitment of professional advisers to conduct in-house training that will ultimately enable the ministry to assert itself and produce a situation

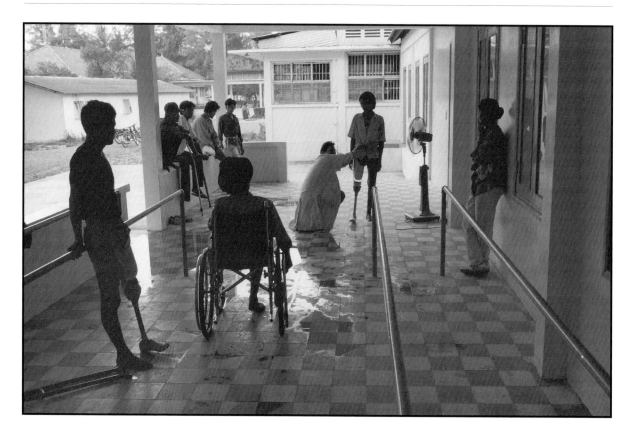

where the Cambodian government calls the shots on the development and efficient co-ordination of a national plan to resolve the Cambodian prosthetics problem. At present it is NGOs that are making the decisions about what is 'best for Cambodia', a problematic situation which has evolved in response to the weakness of the Cambodian structures.

In evaluating the extent to which current needs are being met, one can see that the foundations of a sustainable system have been laid and great progress has been made not only in terms of increasing production but also in terms of developing a technology suitable for Cambodia. In 1993 it was estimated that somewhere in the region of 10,000–16,000[10] people were still awaiting limbs. With total national production of limbs standing at roughly 6,000 per annum (all agencies, 35 per cent wood and leather), it will take several years more before every Cambodian amputee has access to a prosthesis.

The 'Access' Issue

Most of Cambodia's amputees live in remote, mine-affected rural areas, and have no idea of the prosthetic services on offer. Often this is the first time they will have had to deal with the *Barang* (foreigner).[11] The assumed superiority of the *Barang* in the social order means that ordinary Cambodian peasants cannot comprehend the concept of the *Barang's* being in Cambodia to serve them. Nor can they understand the fact that, for once, they will not be charged for a medical service. Benoit Denise [12] cited examples of amputees in Takeo province living a mere 30 km from HI's provincial workshop who had no idea of the existence of the free service. Part of the problem lies with the weaknesses of the MLSA officials in the districts and communes, who are officials in name only. Clearly, the referral system desperately needs to be improved, especially for vulnerable groups such as women and children. UNICEF, whose mandate is partly to target programmes to such vulnerable groups, has been very proactive in responding to the need and has funded a pilot 'search' programme by the Cambodia Trust which as of April 1993 had assisted 46 women and children from particularly poor backgrounds. The programme involves visiting local villages, explaining the services on offer, and transporting the amputees to and from the workshops. In the case of children, whose prostheses need to updated every six months or so, such intensive assistance is necessary if an artificial limb is ever to meet the most basic need, a restoration of mobility.

For women special encouragement to come to the prosthetics workshop is needed. In ICRC's Battambang workshop women and children account for only 4 per cent of the patients seen to date.[13] Partly this is due to the shame and embarrassment often felt by women amputees, some of which may stem from a cultural reluctance to enter the male-dominated world of the prosthetics workshop where the fitting process may require strangers to touch their legs. In addition, agency personnel suggest that the vital role of women as the lynchpin of family life in the villages, and the reluctance of men to take on these responsibilities even for the two to three weeks the woman may have to stay in the prosthetics workshop, can prohibit their access. Such issues, partial solutions to which may include the recruitment of female technicians and prosthetists, are problems which the prosthetics agencies have to address on a daily basis.

In the western provinces ICRC has engaged in similar work to that of the Cambodia Trust: sending vehicles out into the districts, explaining the programmes, referring patients, and employing female staff in the workshops. However, since part of the operational agreement signed between the NGOs specifies that all Cambodians employed are government 'counterparts',[14] any changes in gender balance within the staff employed in the workshops has to be instigated by the Ministry of Veterans' Affairs, which at the time of writing struggles with concepts such as equal opportunities, as witnessed by the extreme reluctance to hire disabled people.

The fear of having to pay for the limb, as with any other medical service, is also so ingrained that time must be spent to convince the amputees that no charge will be made. Peter Carey cited the example of a middle-aged nun who may become the Cambodia Trust's Kompong Som centre's first patient:

> The [blessing] ceremony also brought us our first patient – a nun from the local *wat* [temple], who had stepped on a mine six years ago and had been on crutches ever since. When she discovered that she would be provided with a free artificial limb she could hardly believe her ears since she had expected to have to sell her house to pay for it![15]

Since the fitting process can take anything from two weeks to several months amputees, who are often from the poorest sectors of society anyway, require free accommodation and food allowances in order to be persuaded to stay at the workshops long enough to even receive their free limb. The ICRC workshop in Battambang had had to insist that patients leave their prostheses in the workshop at night, as several were leaving early with half-finished limbs because they felt they couldn't afford to stay any longer. For rural amputees the loss of earnings associated with time away from the village and familial economy has to be carefully balanced against the perceived advantages of receiving a limb. In

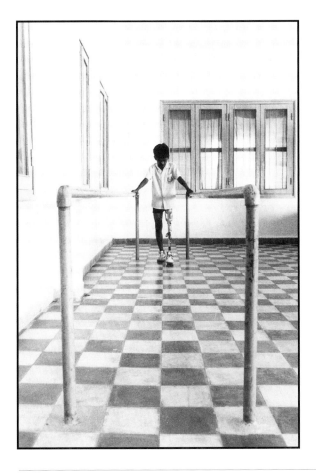

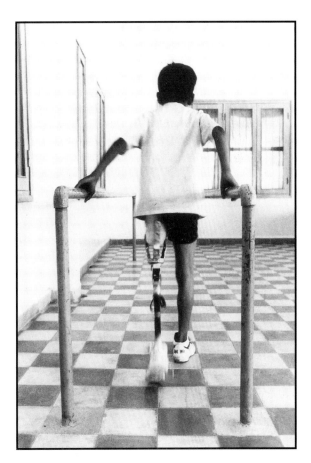

Phnom Penh the Cambodia Trust has a special fund to meet amputees' food and travel costs, and to assist patients who require further operations on difficult or infected stumps. Since these people are often ex-soldiers this activity marks out the Trust as one of the few NGOs prepared to overcome political fears about working in a military hospital and to put humanitarian considerations first. Such background support services have to be costed into the provision of prostheses if an effective service is to be provided.

Restoring What Mines Have Taken

The first stage in the manufacture of the standard ICRC prosthesis is to take a plaster cast of the amputee's stump to which the prosthesis will be fitted. This cast is then filled with plaster which produces a positive image of the stump. Plaster is built up on to the cast in certain areas and taken away from others to ensure that the amputee will be able to put his weight on to the right areas of the polypropylene socket. The positive cast is then taken to the vacuum table. This is the key stage in the process, for it is the technique of 'vacuum forming' that enables the workshops to produce high-quality limbs in such volumes.

The polypropylene sheets, which are ready cut into small sections, are heated in an oven. When they are pliable and soft they are taken from the oven and wrapped around the positive stump model, which is attached to a vacuum pump. When a rough seal has been made around the stump by the technician the vacuum pump is turned on and the hot plastic moulds itself to the stump model, creating a perfect fit. This forms the basis of the socket for the new prosthesis. A softer, thermoplastic (polyethylene) is used to form a 'soft socket' to make a lining for the hard polypropylene socket. Again,

the soft plastic is moulded around the plaster cast to create a comfortable fit.

For a below knee (bk) prosthesis the socket is then attached to a metal pylon by means of a plate system with holes for small screws which can be used to fine-tune the prosthesis in the physical therapy room. The pylon is attached, via an ankle unit, to the rubber foot piece, the pylon length and foot size having been determined by measurements taken at the same time as the plaster cast. With a prosthesis for an above knee (ak) amputation the procedure is exactly the same, except that the socket is attached to a thigh-piece pylon, which attaches to a knee joint, calf pylon, and ankle and foot pieces.

The next stage of the process happens in the physical therapy room where the amputee is introduced to the 'draft' prosthesis for the first time. It's at this stage that checks are made on socket comfort, and limb length and alignment – adjustments to the latter being made with the screw system and also small polypropylene wedges inserted between the plates. The system is far easier to align than the wood and leather or aluminium technologies mentioned above, and this is one of its great advantages. The physical therapy area of the ICRC workshop in Battambang has an elaborate range of walking environments – steps, gravel pits, beams, parallel bars and uneven surfaces to challenge the amputee and test the limb's suitability. For those who have not worn a prosthesis before, especially those with old stumps, it may be necessary to build up muscle tone in the stump before walking can be achieved. Thus there is also a weights section. When the physiotherapists and patients are happy with the limb it is sent back to the workshop for finishing.

The adjusted prosthesis is then taken back to the plaster room and the socket, foot and shaft plastered round, preserving the adjustments made. This forms the basis of yet another 'positive' from which the final limb will be made. First, however, the foot and the top of the

socket section are removed, to be joined later to the finished calf section. The positive is taken to the vacuum table, and heated polypropylene is moulded to form the calf section. The prosthesis is finished by reuniting the foot and socket pieces to the calf. The finished below knee prosthesis is thus hollow, the load being borne by the polypropylene forming the calf. In the case of above knee prosthesis the procedure is similar, resulting in a single thigh and knee section linking up with a calf, ankle and foot section below. This time, however, the load in the calf is borne by a metal pylon inside the calf piece, a thin 'cosmesis' not capable of load bearing.

In the socket the load is borne not on the end but on the muscles half-way up the stump, thus the prosthesis can be worn comfortably by amputees whose stumps are not of 'good quality' (i.e. with a healthy flap of muscle tissue covering the bone end to provide padding). Due to poor standards in most Cambodian hospitals, many stumps are far from ideal, especially where reinfection problems have led to repeated 'salami' amputations. However, the ICRC system ensures that most amputees are able to walk away from the centres – the senior prosthetist in Battambang estimates that only 1 per cent of amputees have to be referred for further surgery before a prosthesis can be fitted.

The process of making the 'draft' prosthesis takes at least a week, and a further week is needed to finish the adjusted limb. The period in between, in the physical therapy area, can take anything from a day to several weeks. The fastest through-time at the ICRC centre in Battambang is little over two weeks. For a first prosthesis on a recent amputee, no matter which technology is being used, the length of use is usually only about a year. This is because the stump is not yet stable and will shrink, leaving the socket too large. When the stump has stabilised the readjusted prosthesis should last for as long as four years. It is hoped that as overall production mounts, the backlog of Cambodian amputees who have never had a prosthesis can rapidly be eroded. At ICRC in Battambang, as at the other limb centres, amputees are told to come back if they have any problems with their limbs. The expatriate physiotherapist recalled: 'Several have had to bring their legs back for repair, having broken them while playing football. They were a little bit sheepish, but we were delighted of course!'

A Return to Dignity?

Twenty-six-year-old Same Ewye was clearly delighted with her new prosthesis as she walked skilfully around the physio area at the ICRC workshop in Battambang. Though she had received the limb only four days before, she was already walking easily without any pain and with only the slightest of limps. These were some of the first steps she had taken since a landmine accident in 1986 while working as a *Gor Bram* (K5) labourer in the northern part of her home province of Siem Reap. Her left leg had been amputated below the knee. But to what extent would the limb change her life, her social position, her expectations and her future?

Ewye is from Phnom Srok, the famous silk-weaving district, where she lives with her mother. In a sense she is very lucky as her ability to earn a living has not been affected in the slightest – she can still feed her silkworms and weave their silk, just as her able-bodied friends do.

For Ewye the most important legacy of her accident has been the fact that she no longer expects to get married. She clearly accepts this as her fate – she told us that she was very happy living with her mother and friends in the village, and that she didn't want to have children anyway. However, even though her accident occurred seven years ago she still feels a strong sense of anger about what has happened to her. She confided that she had a sweetheart before the accident, and they were planning to get married. After the accident he left her. With a demographic balance as distorted as Cambodia's (two women for every one man – a result of the losses of war and the Pol Pot years that claimed more men than women), which results in high rates of desertion and polygamy, the chances of an amputee woman marrying are remote in the extreme. Ewye is lucky as her family has clearly accepted her changed situation and, as will be argued below, familial reactions and support are vital element in the successful reintegration of the amputee, whether male or female. Kevin Malone, who has worked in skills training for the handicapped both in the Thai border camps and in Battambang, recalled several cases, particularly in Site 2, where women and girls who had had accidents and who were no longer considered 'marriageable assets' were reduced to little more than domestic slaves in either their own or host families.

Plong Khemara (my friend and translator) told me of a story that had been doing the rounds in the bars in Battambang about a woman from Omal (the rural commune on the south western edge of town). She had had a below knee amputation and had recently received an ICRC prosthesis. Dressed in her long sarong her disability was not obvious, since she could walk perfectly. One evening she was standing watching the dancing at a wedding party in the village, and met a man. He invited her to join him at his table. They had some drinks together and were getting on well. He thought he would try his luck and touch her leg with his foot, in an attempt to judge just how well they were getting on. He stroked her prosthesis with his foot and as she didn't complain he thought his advances had not been rejected. Later, she invited him to her home and it was only when she sat down and took her prosthesis off that he realised her disability. Realising she was an amputee, the man made his excuses and left. The tale may or may not be true; either way it is a revealing barometer of social attitudes. While the story if told in the west, might leave the listener expecting that the man would overcome his surprise and stay with the woman, in Cambodia no one would be surprised at his hasty desertion. The opposite would almost be unthinkable.

But amputation devastates the matrimonial prospects not only of women. In the Battambang Military Hospital I asked a group of young, single ex-soldiers, all amputees, about their marital expectations. They laughed at the foreigner's stupidity. In Cambodia young men have to give the bride's parents a sum of money – the younger and more beautiful the bride the more is expected. In part this is a marker of the groom's ability to provide for his new wife, and is a very important custom. Twenty-six-year-old Yuern Jong explained that he had been poor before his accident, but for any parents to accept an amputee marrying their daughter, he would have to provide at least twice what an able-bodied man might be expected to pay. He stated quite simply, 'I have no money, and will get no wife.' 'How much would you have to pay to get one?', I asked. 'Even for a wife that is not beautiful, at least 2 dumlong (a measure of gold worth about $1,000 at the time)', he replied. I wrote the

following in my notes after leaving the ward, 'With no land, familial support or cash, the outlook is bleak, and even a return to their home provinces, which all wanted, seems a distant prospect.'

For those already married mine accidents can result in marital rejection. In a society where the overriding majority of families from which mine victims are drawn are already living on the edge of poverty the loss of economic capacity can appear as the final blow. In the border refugee camps sometimes the opposite was true – amputee men did sometimes find themselves marrying able-bodied women. Becky Jordan,[16] who worked in the camps noted that although life could never be described as 'easy' the UN rations and the security that being married provided for women meant that amputees had fewer difficulties finding wives. However, in her current work which involves following up on a case-by-case basis all EVIs (UNHCR jargon – Extremely Vulnerable Individuals) after their repatriation to Cambodia, Becky discovered a rather alarming story of rejection as these families were repatriated. In early March 1993 she came across ten families where amputee partners had been deserted after repatriation. In one incident a male double amputee who had married in the camps was deserted by his wife, leaving him with two very small children to fend for. The family had been repatriated to Battambang

and had made their own way to Sdao in Rattanak Mondul, where the man had an aunt. After a few days the woman fled to Pursat (her old home) and married again. The amputee had an old wheel chair. Wanting to find out what had happened to his wife he put his small children behind him in the chair and wheeled them the 150 km or so, over the pot-holed roads, to Pursat. It took him four days. They slept on the roadside. When he discovered what had become of his wife he turned round and wheeled himself back to Sdao, which took a further six days. Becky had met the man on the road (he refused a lift), and followed him up later in Sdao. The wife had indeed totally rejected her husband, and the children, and he had no way of providing for his family. Becky asked him if he had any other relatives in the Battambang area who might be able to help. It emerged that he had an uncle who owned a workshop in Phnom Sampao, 20 km back up Route 10 towards Battambang. 'Had he contacted him about a job?' was the obvious next question. 'No', came the reply; he had felt too ashamed.

HI's programme in Battambang in 1993 involved both caring for paraplegics in a newly-built centre and visiting communities to seek out individuals such as this double amputee to assist them on a case-by-case basis. Becky confessed that this might not be considered 'developmentally sound' by purists – as the assistance often involved a cash gift for those with a concrete plan for the future ('trickle up', Becky called it). In this case the amputee was persuaded by Becky to visit his uncle, who offered the man an apprenticeship, and HI agreed to provide the tools. Sometimes the fear of rejection, relating to an internalisation of societal prejudices, can be one of the major barriers holding people back. And as Becky noted:

> … giving people prostheses is not enough. A prosthesis does not facilitate reintegration. Most of the double amputees don't have the will to learn to walk with prostheses anyway, like the guy we helped, he had some that he never used. It's the bigger picture that has to change for reintegration of Cambodia's amputees, and that means tackling their poverty and these social attitudes.

Becky had encountered these attitudes herself. Cambodian friends had warned her that she should not work with amputees since 'the stumps give off gasses which affect the brain'. Workers from the Cambodia Trust had also experienced extreme prejudice when trying to get some leatherwork stitched for a particularly difficult prosthesis in the central market in Phnom Penh. When the leatherworkers found out what the leather was for they refused to do the work – eventually, the leather had to be stitched at the trust's workshop. The refusal to do this work had to do with a belief that by touching something destined for an amputee, someone who by definition has obviously experienced bad luck or has poor *karma*, then somehow, by association presumably, this bad luck would 'infect' the leather-worker.

The Cambodian belief system is an extremely complicated amalgam of philosophies and reflects cultural influences from several regions. While the culture would now be described as Buddhist, in fact beliefs are a mixture of Buddhism, Hinduism[17] and local animistic beliefs which predate even the Hindu era in Cambodia. As in other south east Asian cultures, one of the most deep-seated world views is a hierarchical one, whereby those with position and wealth are worthy of respect not only for their current position but also for their intrinsic merit which has led to that position. Thus it is that Sihanouk is still revered as the 'God King'. The position into which one is born in such a socio-cultural system is believed to be determined by merit accumulated in past lives, a concept of 'fate' which has more to do with Brahminism than the law of *Karma*, which the revered Cambodian Buddhist leader Ven. Maha Ghosananda describes as being a law of 'action, here and now, in the present'.[18] Conversely, those with low position and poor fortune must have some intrinsic failing, a lack of merit from former lives. In some senses this concept of merit and fate accounts for some of the apparent lack of compassion with which amputees and other disabled people are treated in Cambodia.

There is a terrible self-fulfilling aspect to such belief systems for amputees in Cambodian society. As in all societies, the burden of conscription in Cambodia falls heaviest on the poorest, the least educated, and those least able to cope with the socio-economic implications of disability. In the *Gor Bram* (K5) days, while every family was supposed to contribute one member for this 'national service', those with even a modicum of wealth paid the poor to take the risks of forced labour in mined areas. As has been shown in Rattanak Mondul, poverty itself leads to people being forced to take known risks with mines. Thus mine injuries, and the amputees they produce, are a function of a cycle of poverty in which mines have become yet one more aspect in a hostile environment for the poor. And once maimed, the amputee can become locked into a cycle of social stereotyping which of itself will determine a marginalised economic position for the amputee and family. Amputees are perceived as useless and unproductive, no longer whole in a physical and religious sense, a thieving, drink-and-drugs-abusing residuum, a marginalised tribe of social waste, to be despised and cursed. Such social prejudices are often internalised (usually because they were the victim's own views of the handicapped before the accident), and the amputee's self-expectation slumps. In this fashion, social attitudes are self-fulfilling and self-justifying.

One of the strongest forces (potentially) for addressing such social prejudices, Cambodian Buddhism, at the moment serves only to reinforce the low status image of the amputee. Current practice in Cambodia is that no man who is an amputee may become a monk. Ven. Maha Ghosananda has admitted that traditionally Cambodian Buddhism has been known as, 'the small vehicle. We admit only those who are able mentally and physically … only the able man can become a monk. If you are not able to support yourself it is very difficult.' But part of this exclusiveness is due to the fact that many of Cambodia's new generation of monks are 'ignorant … newcomers, they know nothing' since most of the old monks were massacred during the Pol Pot years. Ven. Ghosananda agreed that amputees should be allowed to become novice monks in the future, as this would help to break down social stereotypes about amputees.

Buddhist culture sets much store on inner and outer 'wholeness' – an amputee cannot be ordained as a monk

As Becky Jordan has found out, sometimes these societal perceptions of the amputee as economically useless, and hence destined to a low position in life, override even the reality. One woman left her husband on their return to Cambodia, believing he was incapable of supporting her, only to see him do well and open a radio repair business. Benoit Denise[19] concurs that attitudinal problems need to be addressed:

There is big work to be done on people's attitude towards the handicapped, both among the population as a whole and among the amputees themselves. They don't have the *spirit*, they have low expectations, they say 'I am an amputee, I will never succeed in the community'. Sometimes Cambodians are surprised by all the energy we put into helping disabled people. It's not something natural for Cambodians … for example, look at the paraplegic centre in Battambang … there we have people lying on beds, they can only move their hands, they cannot move their legs or arms, and when you explain to Cambodians that these people

can produce, and can have an income-generating activity, its a bit of a shock for them to realise that these people, who can perhaps only move their hands, can do something … it needs an information campaign to break down such social stereotyping.

Positive, productive role models within society might go a long way towards accomplishing such a goal but concrete assistance is also required. Jordan believes that skills training for the poor amputee is probably more important than prosthetics. But even skills training may prove a redundant exercise if evaluated purely in 'output terms' (how many people get jobs after graduating from the courses). Mary Knoll, an American Catholic agency that has been working in skills training in both Kean Khleang and Wat Than in Phnom Penh, has experienced extremely poor levels of success in terms of getting people work. Again, attitudinal prejudices concerning amputees play against them in the job market. To overcome this Kevin Malone,[20] a consultant involved in planning World Vision's skills training project in Battambang, looked to 'clustering' graduates of the newly opened school in workshops in the commercial hearts of each of Battambang's rural districts. Such workshops would be staffed by graduates with a range of skills taught in the school (small engine repair, welding, bicycle repairs, battery charging, etc). In fact, the question of how graduates will employ their skills has become one of the key determinants in student selection – people are chosen in batches from the same area who are interested in studying a range of skills. Those students selected from the town area of Battambang itself will be found apprenticeships in workshops in their trade area in the town. Part of the task of Kevin Malone's 'extension team' will be to encourage workshop owners to take in amputees. Equally, workshop owners need to be sensitive in their dealings with amputee apprentices – Malone knew of several cases where amputees from the Jesuit Refugee Service's skills training programme left apprenticeships because they felt that they were being 'picked on' for their disability, though Malone believes this may have been only the usual rough deal that junior apprentices get from their masters.

For amputees to succeed in their trade they will have to do consistently better than able-bodied competitors in order to break down prejudice, and these are the standards the Battambang school is aiming for. Malone remembers one amputee watchmaker who had graduated from a skills training course in Site 2. He had been given the job of repairing a KPNLAF colonel's watch, which he subsequently broke. The colonel nearly killed the man, and swore he would never trust an amputee again. Jordan agrees with such a comprehensive view of skills training as an integral part of a broad rehabilitative and reintegration programme whose continuum starts with improved medical care, provision of prostheses, and includes a host of other activities including political advocacy for disabled rights,[21] and the formation of self-help associations for the disabled.

Perhaps the biggest single employer of Cambodians during the 1992–93 period was the United Nations. In particular, some 40,000 jobs were available for Cambodians to staff the electoral process which culminated in May 1993. Such jobs involved a high level of social 'visibility' during the elections and were a perfect opportunity for positive discrimination to help counter prevailing prejudices against 'useless' amputees. However, while the UN were keen to entice able-bodied Cambodians away from extremely low paid but vital jobs in the civil services (including education and health care),[22] they showed no eagerness to recruit from the ranks of the disabled, a social class desperately in need of such opportunities. While it may be impossible to prove a policy of discrimination by the UN in Cambodia, a UN Human Rights official,[23] when presented with anecdotal evidence about the way some amputees had been treated when they applied for jobs with the Battambang UN Electoral Component, described the stories as amounting to, 'a discriminatory practice in principle'. Several of the amputees had suitable skills,

yet none even made it to interview. When she pursued the matter with the UN in Phnom Penh, Jordan was treated as a trouble-maker and deflected with buck-passing platitudes.

Without changes in social attitudes the plight of the amputee in Cambodia will remain a poor one, with or without a prosthesis. But the lives of Cambodian amputees, as with any other 'social class' do not reflect a blanket of rejection and desperation. As the case studies in Chapter four revealed, things are generally very different in rural areas: with the exception of Sor Bun Tuern, injury had not led to rejection, familial life had adapted to the injury and the community had accepted it. Benoit Denise explains:

amputees in the countryside have a much easier life than people living and working in urban areas. They do seem to have jobs, growing rice etc … and so they're participating in the activity of their family. And they're an income generating person … they are not a burden. It is very difficult for someone to get a paid job in Phnom Penh, or in a city, so the people living in the urban area are mostly begging … in a rural area there is a bigger solidarity within the family, and people really depend on each member of the family to do something … let's take someone with a below

Skills training: preparing the handicapped for a productive future

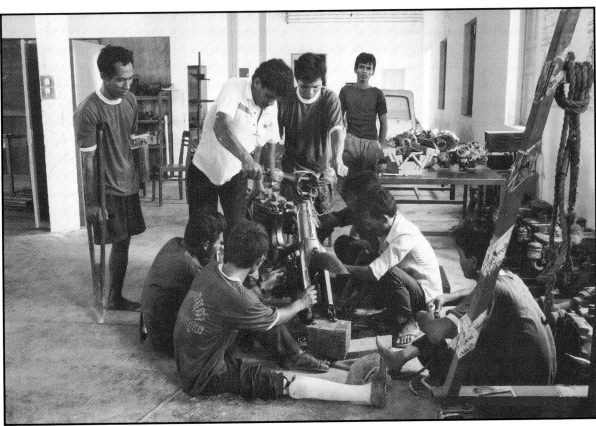

knee amputation (as two-thirds of amputees in Cambodia are), working as a peasant he can work to 80–90 per cent of what he was doing before.

On the journey to work down Route 10 to Rattanak Mondul, World Vision's rural health team recalls regularly seeing a double amputee who lived in Beng Ampil but who owned a rice field in Sanang commune, Banan. They first noticed him one morning wheeling himself in a wooden wheelchair the 5 or 6 km from the camp to his field. Subsequently, they often saw him *en route* or splashing around on his stumps in the paddy, planting rice, his wheelchair parked on the roadside. As in every society reactions to disability vary from person to person, but generally a pattern of acceptance and easier reintegration into familial and community life seems to exist in the Cambodian countryside. Malone concurs: when planning the Battambang skills training centre he surveyed the disabled in every commune of the province. The most startling result of the survey for him was the extent to which the rural handicapped were such an important and active part of the family economy. 'Life in the countryside means that by necessity the disabled have to help out, and there's plenty for them to do,' he said. The occupational part of the survey revealed the disabled, including of course a large percentage of mine-injured amputees, engaged in the full range of rural employments typical in Cambodia. For example, one polio victim with a wasted leg earnt his living by digging wells. This was so much the case that the school faced a problem of finding handicapped students from rural areas able to leave their families for a year's study.[24] When, questioned, amputees said that the commonest response they received from their neighbours in these rural communities was *'ah-neu't'* (pity, compassion) – a marked contrast to the scorn exhibited in the cities. Nevertheless, acceptance may have its limits even in rural areas. Malone recalled one wedding he went to where the bride's father, usually the focal figure, was handicapped. The man never showed his face

at the proceedings and stood in the back, allowing his best friend, an able-bodied man, to take on his duties – not wishing to 'spoil' his daughter's day.

As Malone and others have noted, the very powerful social role of the family as a unit of support in Cambodian society is undoubtedly central to the successful reintegration of the amputee. But what determines familial acceptance? Obviously, individual psychological factors will play their part. However, from our experience it would seem that the crucial determinant of acceptance by the family in the Cambodian case is the location and context within which the injury occurred.

When injuries occur locally in areas where mine accidents are an accepted occupational hazard and a characteristic, or symbol, of a shared problem, as in Rattanak Mondul, families and the broader community are far more likely to be accepting and the sense of shame of the victim is lessened. The accident is an integral part of communal life, not something removed from it, and the 'victim' can almost always return to a productive life. However, the majority of the dispossessed 'urban' amputees, were injured while serving as soldiers in places far removed from their homes – homes left years before when they were little more than boys. They had been cut off from those homes, and even before they were injured their lives as soldiers dispossessed them from traditional roles and locations. When accidents occur in these circumstances it is something very remote from the experience of their families, something very distant from their first communities. Even within Battambang province, one of the nation's worst mine-affected areas, there are communities that are terrified of mines and for whom the risks the people of Rattanak Mondul have to accept are as foreign as they are to the average reader in Australia or Europe.[25]

For those originally from urban areas there never were many employment opportunities anyway (otherwise they wouldn't have ended up in the army). As amputees their horizons shorten still further. Their comrades from rural areas who languish in the cities to some extent cut themselves off from their old communities. Often it is their fear of rejection, rather than the reality of it, which keeps them away. Often the little land the family might have owned will have passed to other brothers, and no one has the space to make provision for a relative who will be seen as a burden, and who may bring bad luck and even bad spirits. With no possibility of finding a niche in the economy he once would have referred to as local, the rewards of begging in the towns, where he is unknown and therefore relatively unashamed, may present itself as the least worst option. But isolated from the family support system, dispossessed from the land – the traditional source of livelihood for the poor Cambodian – the amputee can lose all sense of hope, purpose and position. At this point the stereotypes become self-fulfilling – drinking, drug abuse, gang violence, create still further alienation between the amputee and the urban society at large.

For the former soldiers such a nomadic, almost parasitic, lifestyle is not that different from their years in the army. Wrenched from their homes and the authority the home represents in Cambodian life, given guns but not a living wage, the 'culture of making demands' for the necessities of life may have become almost second nature. And these aggressive predatorial roles are now set to be played out on an increasingly hostile stage. As in all recently urbanised societies, the traditional communal roles, obligations and relationships of agrarian life have become disjointed – the amputees are a dispossessed underclass in a society where all cohesion, beyond the power of the dollar, of which they have none, has gone. In Cambodia the Pol Pot years and the privations of the 1980s have only exacerbated these trends, creating a stifling individualism and cut-throat materialism artificially pumped up with UN dollars. Substitute US for UN and the echoes of the Lon Nol years are all too obvious for those with a memory. In these circumstances the amputee beggars cut a stark image on the Phnom Penh streets, newly clogged with imported Japanese cars.

The View From Below

In the three years I have worked with Cambodians I have never seen a Cambodian openly angry. Towards the end of March 1993, Nic and I were talking with and photographing amputee beggars in Phnom Penh. We were speaking to one, Chea Savourn, a 36-year-old former soldier who had come to the capital only three days before to beg enough money to support his family and, he said, set himself up as a barber eventually. Not only did he lack the money to buy rice seed to plant on his small ricefield in Kompong Thom, but the fighting had come so close to his home he had decided to leave until the rains came, when he would temporarily return to grow a crop. Savourn had lost his right leg above the knee in 1986 – the result of a mine blast – and had an ICRC prosthesis that he had obviously used a great deal. The family was sleeping on the street, opposite the run-down French-built railway station near Achar Mean Boulevard which at night started to look like central Bangkok with its brightly illuminated hotels charging Western rates, its dancing restaurants and nightclubs, its beautiful Vietnamese prostitutes dressed like Paris models, and the new Mercedes cruising the streets. Savourn was shocked by the wealth, angered by it. As we were leaving, a Cambodian video store owner burst out of his shop and started wildly gesticulating with hands made heavy with gold, shouting at Savann, our

A livelihood denied: abandoned by his wife and family, an amputee veteran begs in the market

translator, 'Why were you speaking to them? Don't you know they're disrespectful thieves, they're lower class, rude peasants who are always making problems in this neighbourhood? If the police had come by just now I'd have had you all arrested.' Savann wanted to calm the man, and tried, but he was having none of it.

Such snapshots of amputee life in Cambodia contrast so strongly with the case studies from Rattanak Mondul that some of the notes I made while researching the book are given here. While the Rattanak Mondul victims have suffered a great deal, and are living with great difficulties, theirs are stories of survival and acceptance. They do not paint a completely representative picture of the social experience of Cambodian amputees. This section redresses this imbalance. These are some of the views from below.

The Beggars in the Market, 25 February 1993

Beggars are a common feature of most Third World markets, and those of Cambodia's major towns are no exception. However, the beggars in these markets are often ex-soldiers, reduced to this way of life by landmine accidents which have stolen their limbs, their social standing and their hope of a livelihood.

Battambang market, located in the centre of the town, is a bustling, madly overcrowded labyrinth. The beggars usually congregate in the middle section, which is open and home to the food stalls and the fruit and vegetable vendors. The market is dirty and smells the sweet smell of decaying produce which litters the floor. On either side, in cathedral-like end sections, the narrow alleyways are crowded with stalls selling a whole range of goods. Imitation Rolexes from Thailand, precious gems from Pailin and Vietnam, local cloth, and seamstresses making garments to order, washing powders and 'Darlie' toothpaste.

As the hot season comes on the place is intense and breathless, and the amputees, their caps outstretched at the entrances, or loudly banging their crutches on the floor as they move through the shoppers, add to its intensity, a constant reminder that the prosperity the market represents rests on fragile foundations. They are living reminders of the war that still festers on the outskirts of the province.

We wanted to talk to these men, and invited a couple to join us for a drink at one of the stalls. The owner eyed them suspiciously as they sat down. 'Who will pay?' she asked, 'He will,' says Sophal, our translator, pointing to me. Other amputees eyed us from across the market, calling out for money, not noticing we were sitting with their colleagues. One of these men hobbled up on his crutch and sat down. Sophal was nervous. The amputees laughed and joked with one another as we passed out cigarettes.

They all had similar stories to tell. All had had landmine accidents. 'We were attacking Pailin,' 'I was on patrol,' 'We had moved forward and I was setting up a radio antenna,' 'We had moved camp and I was looking for fish in the paddy field.' 1981, 1986, 1990, 1991, five months ago. None had done any work since their injuries, except for the daily ritual of begging.

Some were in Battambang only to have a limb fitted at the ICRC centre. Others had come in search of

relatives. Some had come from other provincial towns, or even Phnom Penh, because they had heard that it was easier to beg for a living in Battambang. Only one had been born in Battambang.

What they all shared, however, was a lack of family or community support for some reason. In some cases all their relatives were dead, in others they had rejected them. Nearly all had come from poor families and communities: lacking land and resources there was no point in returning, although all wanted to. There were many prostheses in evidence, some only recently received from ICRC, and for the first time since their accidents the amputees were moving without the assistance of a crutch. Although they valued this mobility (one with a below knee amputation said he sometimes plays football in the evenings) and the sense of dignity the legs gave them, they told us that the prostheses don't really help them to get a job.[26] If they had some land then it would be different, but lacking their own land they were dependent on wage labour, and no one was prepared to hire an amputee, even if he had a good degree of mobility thanks to a new prosthesis. They freely admitted that what they needed was a skill as it would be far easier then to get work. 'Begging is a bad way to earn your living,' they said. None of them wanted to carry on begging, despite the fact that the daily income from begging (in the range of 4,000–6,000 riels – $1.6–2.4

– they told us) compares very favourably with workmen's day labour rates.

But with the government allowance for handicapped ex-servicemen typically running at about 30,000 riels a month ($12), intended only as a supplement, those with families needed to get money somehow. 'You know,' said Ieng Sopart, looking at me intensely as he drew deeply on his cigarette, 'they compare my life to a dog.' 'Why do people look down on you?' I asked. 'It's because some beggars are very aggressive, and make fights with the shopkeepers, and use bad language to them,' said Paen Teth. 'They give us all a bad name, and people hate us. They think we cannot get the money for our families and so we are the lowest people.' A few months before I remembered having seen Teth drunkenly lurching his way around one of the Thai-owned restaurants in Battambang, banging his metal crutch on the ground and demanding money from the UN and NGO workers. He was thrown out. I had resented his intrusion at the end of another frustrating day, I just wanted to be left alone, to forget I was in Cambodia. He was one depressing image too many.

The Ministry of Labour and Social Action Hostel, Battambang, 27 February 1993

The hostel for landless war-injured soldiers has 62 families registered, although in reality only 42 stay there. The others have left to live with family in their home districts. Those remaining can truly have no place left to go. Whether the Battambang provincial government is operating a philosophy of 'less eligibility' in providing social assistance, similar to that which guided the English poor law reforms in 1834, or whether it simply does not have the resources, the effect is the same. The hostel is a disgrace. But perhaps the real disgrace lies in the fact that one year after the arrival of numerous western NGOs and the hordes of vastly overpaid UN personnel such conditions have been allowed to persist. From the balconies of the hostel the amputees and their families watch the daily bustle of the white air-conditioned vehicles speeding by, all intent on some important mission. Clearly, not one has bothered to stop. Unlike those riding in the cars, time is the only thing these people have.

The two-storey concrete building lies on the east side of Battambang, on Route 5, which links the town with Phnom Penh. In true Cambodian style its architects valued open plan, and the interior on all three floors consists of a large tiled space, with a stairwell in the rear of the building. The families sleep communally for the most part, claiming a section of these vast floors. A few have hammocks but most relieve the harshness of the tiles with a bamboo sleeping mat only. Some have attempted to gain a degree of privacy by erecting partitions made out of plastic sacks that once contained Vietnamese cement. For the most part no tenderness or intimacy can go unobserved.

On one floor a woman was washing her family's stretch of tiles, but the overall impression was of neglect, worn and dirtied paint that probably dated from the Lon Nol era, and the odours associated with overcrowding and a lack of sanitation. In the stairwell two women had cleared the refuse to make some space to cook lunch. Everywhere children were running, and limbless men in faded uniforms smoked cigarettes. They looked surprised to see a foreigner visit their home.

For Paen Teth, whom I had met a few days before in the market, the hostel is home, although he has sent his four children to live with his brother who has inherited the family's small house in Kompong Chnnang province. 'There's too much noise and ill-discipline among the children here,' he said, 'you can't have children growing up in a place like this.' Nevertheless, the hostel is still a roof over his head. 'I always thought of myself as one of the lowest people in Battambang, but the other day I saw some amputees who had come here from some other provinces. They were camping out under the trees on the riverside. That's a lot worse than staying here.'

Teth fears that this situation might change in the near future. The provincial government has said it is planning to instruct the Moung Russey District people to make some land available for the amputees. The latest rumour is that the centre will be closed by the end of the year and the building sold to 'foreigners' (probably Thai businessmen who bought up many of the Ministry of Health buildings last year). The government stands to make some money on the deal, though it will have to be clinched before the elections. The amputees say that if the building is sold the government may give them a small amount and tell them to go to their home provinces. All of the hostel's inhabitants are landmine victims. Without cash, a home and land, a return to less prosperous provinces holds no appeal. Perhaps they too will end up watching the white cars from the riverbank.[27]

The Beggars on the Riverbank, 1 March 1993

Most cities have their shanty towns and dosshouses where the poor and the marginalised find shelter from the elements and eek out a living in any way they can. In London they live in cardboard boxes under the bridges on the embankment by the side of the Thames. In Battambang they do the same, but what marks out these dispossessed Cambodian families is the fact that they are all former soldiers, all victims of landmines.

Sophal says their huts look like the sort of houses he would keep a dog in as we draw up on the riverbank, a *stone's throw from the UN water collection unit which trucks away the brown waters of the Sang Ke River to the various military encampments the foreign soldiers have set up around the town. Sophal is right. These families are living in tiny shacks, flimsy frames made from broken branches and small pieces of sawn wood covered in bits of plastic sheeting, cardboard and ancient pieces of corrugated iron. In most there can be barely room for two people to lie down. Where do the children, of which there are many at the site, sleep, I wonder?*

Our arrival causes some stir, and the crippled men and their families gather round. I pass out cigarettes which, as Steinbeck rightly observed in a different context in a different age, establishes a relationship quickly. In all there are seven families here. Some have come to get prostheses, others because the begging is easier here, and others because they have nowhere else to turn.

Seng Ran told us his story. He is 31 years old. His left leg amputation is the result of a landmine injury sustained during heavy fighting with the Khmer Rouge at Phnom Ky Pruk in his home province of Pursat. He and his wife have been living on the riverbank here for three months. His home village lies just outside Pursat town, and he lived there with his mother and older sister from the time of his discharge from hospital until his departure for Battambang at the end of 1992. He says he left because he couldn't make any money in Pursat: 'I felt afraid of everything because I used to live there before the accident. Now I am poor and have no way to get money I am ashamed. I decided to come here where it is easy to beg for money, and no one knows me. I don't feel uncomfortable here.' The village leader in Pursat had tried, unsuccessfully, to get him a small plot of land.

Before leaving Pursat Ran had sold the right to collect his monthly pension for the whole of 1993. He had received only 50,000 riels for these rights to a pension that is worth 10,000 riels a month. The amount of the pension paid depends on the rank of the soldier when injured, as well as the size of his family, etc. Ran was just an ordinary soldier although his allowance is a lot less that that paid in Battambang, a difference that reflects the relative differences in wealth in the two provinces.[28]

Ran has no plans to move, in fact he has no plans at all for the future apart from staying here and begging.

Conclusions

The provision of a prosthesis in a society such as this can in no way, of itself, ensure a 'return to dignity'. For those with no option but to return to urban areas where they may be forced to live outside the support structures of family and community, a prosthesis is only of value

for improved personal mobility and a sense of wholeness. No one would deny that these functions are not valuable. Claude Athiet, ICRC's Technical Manager in Battambang, tells the story of the Afghan amputee who made his own leather cosmetic covering for a basic wood and leather limb, to make it look more lifelike. The man used to wear traditional flowing robes that entirely covered his legs – the only people to see them were his immediate family. A good-looking prosthesis is undoubtedly an extremely important asset for an amputee. But without a fuller range of reintegrative programmes the disproportionate attention that prosthetics has been receiving in Cambodia may become rather meaningless, and the images of dispossessed amputees on hi-tech prostheses become the rule rather than the exception. As in demining, the provision of prostheses in Cambodia, and national planning for the rehabilitation of the enormous numbers of amputees, need to be Cambodianised, and this means strengthening Cambodian structures and human resources, both technical and managerial. Beyond Cambodia it means lobbying donors to commit to such long-term goals, and fund them. It is the minimum that is owed Cambodia's handicapped, the victims of an imported problem.

7
Landmines – The Global Problem
Rae McGrath

The worldwide post-combat residue of landmines has been termed a major ecological disaster and few knowledgeable observers would argue with that assessment. It is surprising, therefore, that environmental lobbying groups only very recently have shown interest in the problem. In many of the poorest countries of the developing world mines are not merely instrumental in denying vital land to farmers, pastoralists and returning refugees, but have covered large tracts of the earth's surface with non-biodegradable and toxic garbage. Yet it was only through the joint-NGO campaign, begun by humanitarian and human rights agencies in 1991, that environmental groups became active on the issue – why?

The answer lies at the heart of the issue – landmines are very much a First World weapon despite the claims of the western manufacturers and military that they are primarily the weapon of choice for indisciplined guerrilla armies of the developing world. Mines are certainly used by these armies but they are developed for the mutual benefit of the manufacturers and armies of industrialised nations. However, these nations, prior to the break-up of the USSR and the beginning of the fighting in former Yugoslavia, had never experienced the impact of mines on their own territories – their battles were in the fields of political influence, trade and profit, dirty tricks and proxy wars. The superpowers and would-be superpowers used the land of other nations to fight their battles – Asia, Africa and Central America provided battlefields for the industrial world to play global monopoly. Here lies the reason that even active and radical environmental groups such as Greenpeace took many years to react to the problems caused by mines - they simply were not aware that the problem existed.

This, of course, raises another question: how could millions of mines be scattered over more than 20 countries, killing and maiming tens of thousands of civilians, without anyone in Europe or the United States knowing?

In fact, a small group of people *were* well aware of the impact of mines on the population and environment in countries where they were used. But these same people had good reasons to ensure that the world at large remained unaware that a problem existed – they were manufacturers, salesmen, military officers, intelligence agents and politicians. The reasons for their silence are familiar – 'national security', 'need-to-know', 'global strategies' or, translated into common English, power, corporate interests, profit and the mad, immoral global chess played with human pieces by 'great statesmen' such as Henry Kissinger. And so, despite the fact that Laos had been randomly seeded with mines and submunitions since the early 1960s and that China, the USSR, the USA, the UK and most European countries had been major suppliers of mines and training in their most damaging deployment in Cambodia, the horrific damage wrought on the helpless and largely poor target communities remained an obscene secret.

It is a frightening fact that only another 'great game' of international spies – Afghanistan – made the world aware of mines as a humanitarian and environmental issue. When the Soviet armies crossed the Oxus in 1979 they brought with them the lessons of south east Asia – of Vietnam, Cambodia and Laos – lessons learned from intelligence assessments of US actions. One of those lessons was that anti-personnel mines have a special role for forces fighting popular armies on home ground. The Soviets honed that strategy to extremes which linked high technology with traditional manual mine laying. The impact was devastating although, after a decade of massacre and destruction, the Soviets were no more successful than the USA in their attempts to impose their will over that of popular and committed indigenous forces. There is a story, probably apocryphal, that a senior Soviet officer told a group of victorious Mujahideen as the invading forces withdrew from Afghan soil 'we may be leaving but our mines will kill your grandchildren'. Whether or not the story is true, the statement is undoubtedly fact.

The Soviets protected military garrisons and key infrastructural and administrative facilities with enormous hand-emplaced minefields normally consisting of PMN and PMD-6 buried pressure mines, and POMZ-2 stake mines operated by tripwires. These minefields were mapped and recorded, not, however, out of any spirit of responsibility, merely because the Soviet troops lived within the minefield, they needed to know the location of safelanes and, in case of emergency, the necessary data to make fast breaching as safe and effective as possible. There lay the limit of Soviet mine dissemination which may be termed 'responsible'[1] – the use of anti-personnel mines by the Soviets against the Afghan civilian population and, it could be argued, the future of Afghanistan, must constitute one of the greatest war crimes of this century. Soviet strategy was a classic of global thinking, in other words strategy without the inconvenience of considering what is now known as collateral damage. The process was as cruelly logical as it was inhuman: the Mujahideen enjoyed popular support from the rural community and received their arms from Pakistan; without that support the Afghan resistance would be unlikely to remain a viable fighting force; therefore, (a) make the land incapable of supporting the rural population and the Mujahideen, and (b) make supply routes impassable.

Achievement of those aims required a special type of weapon with sustainable properties; bombing and artillery would not serve these purposes, but anti-personnel mines would. The Soviets had an impressive arsenal of mines with which to wage their war against the Afghan people. One of those devices, the PFM-1 *Butterfly* scatterable anti-personnel mine, was deployed in millions from helicopters and fixed-wing aircraft, not just over areas occupied by resistance forces, but across wide swathes of mountain pasture and fertile valley farmland. In purely technical terms the PFM-1, a development of the US-manufactured *Dragontooth* and *Dragonseed* mines used in south east Asia, was probably the least dangerous mine deployed by the Soviets. It had a designed active life of only six months and a comparatively small explosive capacity capable of causing much less severe injuries than other mines. Employing a binary liquid explosive charge detonated by accumulative pressure, the PFM-1 had been designed to interdict enemy movement using air deployment. After an estimated period of six months the liquid charge deteriorated and the device became inactive. But the impact of the *Butterfly* far outweighed its physical properties as a weapon. First, it did not look like a mine and, normally coloured a strangely bright green, lay on the surface in such densities that one western aid worker commented '...[they looked] more like locusts than butterflies'. This mine initially bred rumour and fear among Afghan communities because of its unusual design. Second, it claimed a disproportionate number of child victims – although there were good technical reasons for its design, the appearance of the PFM-1 made it attractive to children. Finally, the *Butterfly*, despite its limited active lifespan, had a long-term impact – there was no external indication of its state, and farmers were forced to assume that the mines in their fields were live.[2]

But it was the overall scale of mine dissemination of all types which ensured the destruction of rural Afghanistan would continue for decades after the Soviet withdrawal. In the same way as the US action against Laos was the first use of widescale air-delivered and untargeted mines, so the USSR strategy in Afghanistan was the first mass deployment of ground emplaced mines aimed specifically at a civilian population. A deadly mix of high-technology devices (including sonar-activated initiators capable of triggering bounding and directional fragmentation mines to create a killing zone[3]) and simple pressure and trip wire mines created an obstacle to even the simplest life-supporting activities, such as water and fuel collection. The cost in rural communities was appalling – a 1990–91 survey[4] of mined areas included the following area situation analysis:

> Surveyed areas of Reg district (Helmand Province) have experienced a particularly high incidence of mines casualties in the past two years, a total of 162 people, of which 112 were fatalities. 21% of fatalities in the area were among boys under ten years.

> Mortality and injury data presents a frightening scenario – more especially because Kandahar [Province] is seen by some agencies as an early target for repatriation. Taking the figures for Spin Bolak [District] at their face value and using the 1988 household size estimate for Kandahar of 10.9 it can be calculated that the surveyed community has suffered a percentage loss of 1.95% in two years as a result of mines. An additional 3.6% have suffered injuries due to mine explosions.

> It would appear from the data that the most common mines, said to be laid in all areas [Ningrehar Province] are anti-personnel pressure devices ... With the exception of Shinwar and Rodat, all areas report a high incidence of tripwire initiated mines, probably POMZ-2 ... The overall scenario indicated by the survey conforms to what could be expected of a rural area affected by large concentrations of hand laid anti-personnel devices over an extended timeframe. Hillsides in all the surveyed locations are said to be heavily mined, and travel by foot is overwhelmingly cited as the most dangerous occupation... Reported casualties are extremely high, 80% of surveyed areas claimed up to two fatalities during the two months prior to survey ... the fatality rate over the surveyed areas in two years is over 0.4% of population, the overall casualty percentage for the same period is 0.56% ... casualties range over the whole spectrum of gender and age.

> ... the report from this facility [Shadheed Maulawi Haqani Surgical Hospital Miram Shah] notes that 'statistics and diagnosis for the shaheed (trans. "martyrs") are not available ... the most serious injuries would be found among them.

> The long-term affects on the Kuchi [Afghan tribal nomadic herders] as a people and the possible residual impact on livestock movement and trade in

Afghanistan as a whole requires further study. The potential scale of those problems are indicated by the large number of nomadic groups who have abandoned their traditional way of life completely and either live as refugees or rely on scarce labouring jobs for their survival.

The introduction to that survey report posed the question:

Are the international community willing to watch as five million refugees return to an inhuman lottery where as little as 0.23 kg of foot pressure on the wrong patch of ground indicates a loser? Not just on their first day home, or their first week, but for the rest of their lives – and their children's lives?

The unspoken answer appears to have been in the affirmative because, despite funding from international donors which eventually led to the deployment of approximately 2,000 Afghan deminers of varying quality and with differing levels of control, the commitment to paying for the eradication of mines has never come remotely near the financial input given to the provision of arms over more than a decade of war by governments who claimed to have the interests of the Afghan people at heart. The United States, for example, invested more than $2.5 billion in covert aid to the Afghan resistance, aid that was justified on the grounds that USA supported the right of the Afghan people to self-determination, and yet, following the Soviet withdrawal and the subsequent fall of the communist government, since which mines have been a major obstacle to repatriation and the reha- bilitation of rural Afghanistan, the *total international* support for mine-related projects is less than $20 million per year including support for prostheses programmes.

Afghanistan still faces a landmine problem on a massive scale. Even the best estimates indicate that it will take a minimum of six years at a funding level in the region of $17 million per annum to clear priority community areas. This estimate does not include the clearance or marking of pasture land and 'low priority' areas, nor does it include the cost of village-based community awareness programmes or victim support.

During the early 1990s international attention focused on Afghanistan and Cambodia, but these were only two of many countries where mines would dictate a future in which civilians would face death with every step.

In Mozambique the success or failure of the interna- tional community in developing a credible remedial strategy to deal with landmines may still prove to be a decisive factor in determining whether or not the peace process succeeds. Rural rehabilitation, the repatriation of refugees and resettlement of *deslocados*, depends in many areas on an effective programme to clear mines and limit casualties. However, planning has centred on clearance of mines from roads and infrastructural facilities and no priority has been given to rural programmes which would act, in addition to the practical value, as important confidence-building inputs for the Mozam- biquan people. Much of the delay in establishing, or even effectively planning, an integrated programme of mine eradication has been blamed on the participants in the ceasefire commission and their failure to reach agreement on implementation of steps to ensure the future of the peace process. There is a factual element in this criticism but it is also true that senior United Nations officials with a responsibility for mine-related activities have failed to take advantage of rural-based mine clearance projects proposed (and assured of funding) by humanitarian agencies. Involved non-governmental organisations, the Halo Trust and the Mines Advisory Group, have submitted proposals strongly supported by operational aid agencies which have faced long and unresolved delay in obtaining approval from the United Nations (a prerequisite of donations to the projects). Apart from the direct advantage of such programmes to the rural community and aid agencies there would be a consid- erable secondary benefit for United Nations strategists in terms of practical lessons and advice from such field- experienced NGOs.

By late 1993 there was a clear indication that the United Nations was preparing to set a disturbing precedent by awarding a major contract for the clearance of mines from thousands of kilometres of roads to a UK mines manufacturer. In addition to the obvious moral question marks over such a policy[5] it is common knowledge that the company concerned plans to sub- contract all or part of the work to other commercial operations, effectively ensuring that each company will take its profit from the funds before a single mine is cleared. This is not an argument against the United Nations funding commercial mine clearance agencies in situations where the required operations can be subjected to adequate contractual control; the key issue is that the contract should be made directly with the implement- ing company.

Taking an overall view of the situation in Mozambique it is clear that a failure to adopt a sufficiently urgent response to the mines situation by the Mozambiquan authorities, the ceasefire commission and the involved United Nations offices may eventually place at risk the lives and futures of many thousands of Mozambiquan refugees, *deslocados* and rural farming families. Neither is it beyond possibility that a failure to implement wide- ranging programmes of mine eradication and community education could be a contributory factor in a breakdown of the whole peace process, especially since such programmes present the best opportunity of paid employment for demobilised soldiers and have important confidence-building potential in a post-war environment. There is little excuse for the failure to respond adequately in Mozambique if one considers the events in Angola which should have influenced the decision-makers in Maputo.

Angola is a classic example of how landmines can have an influence far beyond their mere utility as weapons. In 1960 Agostinho Neto, the father of independent Angola wrote 'To our homes, to our camps, to the beaches, to our fields, we shall return.' He would not have known that his prophecy was unlikely to be fully realised during the twentieth century. It is a fact, however, that even if unlimited funds were to be made immediately available to a country-wide programme of mine eradication, the process of clearance is not likely to be complete within a decade. Angola's first mines were laid by the Portuguese army in 1961, the process has been refined (as have the mines themselves) and the minefields have multiplied in the 33 years that have passed since that first deployment. Mine laying has been carried out by the Angolan army, FNLA/UNITA, the Cubans and the South Africans, and its effectiveness is well illustrated by the casualties – one study of deaths from war actions between 1975 and 1991 found that mine explosions claimed a total of 6,728 lives, 1046 in 1985 alone, more than any other single war-related cause of death.[6] It is probable that one of the original causes for the pre-eminence of mines as weapons in Angola is simply their availability in huge quantities to all combatant parties (this may well be true in other countries as well) rather than any recognised combat strategy. Cuban troops, fighting alongside the MPLA, made random use of mines supplied by the Soviet Union from their earliest combat involvement. But there have certainly been no shortage of western countries willing to ship mines to Angola since 1975 when the United States, under the guise of an emergency aid programme to Zaire, allocated nearly £80 million, most of which was to supply arms to the FNLA, France, Britain, Belgium and West Germany also armed the FNLA and UNITA. The interests behind the USA/European stance were, of course, not the future of the Angolan people but the 'global strategy' which determined that any state aligned with the Soviet Bloc must be destabilised. The MPLA, the government-to-be, was supported and armed by the USSR and its allies. In the case of Angola there were several additional considerations – oil, minerals and the threat that the Soviets might establish military bases on the West African coast. Later, in 1980, the South Africans invaded southern Angola, although they had been conducting military actions on Angolan territory since the May 1978 raid on Kassinga[7]. Their continuing operations in the south made heavy use of mines.

In April and May of 1992 a joint mission to Angola by Human Rights Watch and the Mines Advisory Group reported a desperate situation and called for urgent action[8] by all involved parties, the United Nations and donors. The report gave a clear indication of the scale of the problem:

There is a very serious landmine problem throughout Angola, with certain parts of the country, such as Huambo, Bie, Moxico and Cuando Cubango being particularly severely affected …. Most of the mines have been laid without markings or warning to the civilian population, and a large proportion have been laid in such a way that their victims are almost guaranteed to be civilians. As a result, a very minimum of 15000, and probably more than 20000, Angolans are currently amputees as a result of landmine accidents, and many thousands more have been killed. Even if a lasting peace is established, the human impact of land mines is likely to increase in the short term, with the return home of refugees and displaced people and attempts by civilians to reclaim their villages, fields and pastures, and to travel along roads and paths … Facilities for the evacuation, emergency treatment, hospital treatment and physical and social rehabilitation of land mine victims are inadequate and not improving. Hospital facilities are poor. More than 5000 prostheses are required each year; current production is well under one third of that number. The social needs of land mines are not attended to adequately.[9]

The registration of voters for the September 1992 elections was made extremely difficult in some provinces because of mined roads; it is probable that only the determination of the Angolan people to vote assured the success of the elections, and it could be argued that were it not for the mines the elections would have been more transparently fair, making Savimbi's subsequent claims of vote rigging impossible to believe, even by the most ardent UNITA supporters.[10]

The renewed fighting was not influenced by the experience of the preceding 30 years of war and it soon became clear that, despite the known impact on civilians, both the Angolan army and UNITA forces were deploying mines on a scale that exceeded even the excesses of the past. There was no shortage of stocks, and new arms shipments, including mines, were being supplied to both sides. In November 1993 a Mines Advisory Group mission examined the situation in both government-and UNITA-held areas of Angola. The findings of that assessment presented a situation which formed the basis of an emergency appeal to mount remedial humanitarian action. Seven major towns and cities were found to be totally surrounded by *barriers* of mines: Kuito, Huambo, Luena, Saurimo, Malanje, Menongue and Cuito Canavale.

Malanje, in north-central Angola, is a frightening example of this *encirclement* phenomenon. The city, with more than 12,000 under-ten-year-olds alone, was besieged by UNITA and was almost totally dependent on food aid which, due to mined roads, destroyed bridges and general security, could only be delivered by air. The estimated daily food required was approximately 110 tonnes but World Food Programme were only able to fly in 30–40 tonnes, which was distributed immediately. The effect on the population was an ever-increasing section of the community who were desperate enough to risk traversing the minefield barrier in order to search for food. The cost in human terms in Malanje was easily measured at the single, ill-staffed and poorly equipped hospital where civilian mine casualties number between three and five victims each day and, on occasions, rose to 25 admittances in a single day. There were 112 mine-related amputees between May and November 1993. These were the survivors – the numbers of fatalities can only be estimated, although the following cases indicate the severity of the problem throughout Angola.

Empenara Raphael, aged 12, female, civilian. On 8 November 1993 she was travelling on a crowded cart pulled by a tractor about 30 kilometres from Malanje. The people were taking home their rice to Cametede when the tractor hit a mine on an earth road. Empenara does not know how many people were killed or injured but remembers that almost everyone seemed to be either dead or to have lost limbs. She suffered an above- knee amputation of the left leg.

Franciscos Domingos Resiado, aged 33, male, civilian. On 7 November 1993 he was loading casava in a field near Kesswa, Malanje Province. He had just packed his casava and was bending to lift the load on to his head when he noticed a wire running through the grass. He somehow became entangled in the wire and there was an explosion.[11] Two men were killed instantly and two others were badly injured in addition to Franciscos. The two injured men died later because they were unable to cross the river to get to the hospital. Franciscos suffered an amputation of the right arm to the elbow.

Maria Josephina Gomez, aged 45, female, civilian. Maria was collecting firewood with three other women about three kilometres from the centre of Luena, Moxico Province on 10 November 1993. One of her companions activated a mine. Maria was the only survivor; she suffered amputation of the left foot, and her right leg was fractured and badly injured by fragmentation.

Jose Mario Neto, aged 46, male, civilian. Jose was walking through a casava/banana plantation to begin work farming at Canacassala, Bengo Province when he stood on a mine. He suffered a below-knee amputation of the right leg and severe fragmentation injuries to the left leg.

There have been seven deaths and three other injuries close to that location since January 1993.

Jamie Lulonga, aged three, male, civilian. On 11 June 1993 Jaime was playing with his sister next to his house in Chicala, Moxico Province. His father was with the two children when one of the three stepped on a buried mine. Jaime's father and sister were killed. Nine other people were killed in separate incidents in the vicinity of the village on the same day. Jaime had his left foot amputated.

The mines scattered across the fields and tracks of Angola tell a story of greed and power games which few of the innocent victims would even begin to understand. They come from a wide range of countries, many of which argue that they impose strict control on the export of arms.

Anti-personnel Mines[12]

MI AP DV 59	France
VS Mk2	Italy
M35	Belgium
M409	Belgium
Type-72A	China
M16A1/A2	USA
M14	USA
M18A1	USA
M7A2	USA
PMN/PMN2	Former USSR
PMD-6	Former USSR
POMZ-2	Former USSR
MON50/MON00	Former USSR
PP Mi SR	Czechoslovakia
DM-11	Germany
DM-31	Germany

Large numbers of South African mines have been deployed in Angola, and many unsourced copies of mines such as the M18A1 are also common.

Despite the wide knowledge of the problems caused by mines and the UN moratorium on exports there is no shortage of suppliers still willing to deliver mines to Angola's ports. On 29 December 1993 the *Nora Heeren*, a German-owned ship, left the Russian port of Vysotsk loaded with arms for Angola. On 9 January 1994 she docked at Plymouth in south west England to shelter from storms and to pick up oil. A customs official on routine patrol at the port noticed T62 tanks and artillery loaded as deck cargo and the ship was subsequently impounded awaiting investigation of the cargo. The case came to the notice of the UK media after an anonymous call from an official who believed that the ship's cargo contained anti-personnel mines in wooden cases recorded on the ship's manifest as 'spare parts'. A Greenpeace report noted that the single-page cargo manifest submitted to the UK Customs and Department of Trade and Industry showed nearly 8,000 cases of unspecified 'spare parts' as well as tanks, artillery and 7.62 mm rifle ammunition. Despite widespread protests and questions raised in Parliament the British authorities issued a licence without searching the cargo, and the ship sailed for Angola on 21 January. The *Nora Heeren* is known to have made several voyages to Angola in the previous two years, probably with similar cargoes. This is just one example of a constant criss-crossing of the world's oceans by ships plying a cynical trade with the open or tacit co-operation and support of some countries and a hands-off approach by others. International bans, moratoriums and controls on landmines mean nothing while ships like the *Nora Heeren* can embark from ports in signatory nations without proper searches being conducted to verify cargo manifests. The impact of the trade on countries like Angola is beyond estimation in humanitarian and economic terms.

There is an increasing popular argument in some, primarily western military, circles that it is not the mine but its *indisciplined* use by guerrilla forces which is the root cause of the humanitarian emergency existing today. This is an attractive argument for those countries who see themselves as occupying the global moral high ground; unfortunately it is not supported by recent fact.

The Iran–Iraq War was fought between two uniformed armies commanded by officers who had been trained, in many cases, in the elite military colleges of the world – many had attended the Royal Military College at Sandhurst in the UK, for instance. An examination of the hundreds of minefields which straddle the border between the two countries gives little indication, however, that the protagonists confined their employment of mines to tactically disciplined minelaying. Although some patterns can be discerned in many of the minefields, and perimeters were occasionally marked, the overall strategy of both armies was to deploy mines in massive numbers over wide areas of ground with no concern for the civilian population. Anti-personnel mines were intermixed with drums of napalm and, in some areas, the sheer density of mines far exceeds any possible or imaginable military utility. In northern Iraq/Kurdistan mines are so common that children use mine cases for cartwheels and young women grind salt in the bases of Italian anti-tank mines. It has been estimated that civilian mine injuries tie up 50 per cent of the region's heath-care resources. It is certain that no guerrilla organisation could have assured so effectively the long-term destruc-tion of civilian life and rural infrastructure as did these two well-trained *disciplined* armies. It is also worth noting that military advisors and observers from Europe and the United States were involved in battle-zones for most of the duration of the conflict.

Was the first Gulf War an exception to the rule?

If the Iran-Iraq War was an aberration one would imagine that a war fought between the UK and Argentina would be a model of military correctness, especially as, in the Falklands/Malvinas War, both armies were fighting over land they wished to occupy. And yet, with all the resources and experience available to the British army, they were able to clear only a small percentage of their own and Argentinian-laid minefields.

Despite the arguments of the military (and the man-ufacturers), mines have consistently been designed for unrecorded and random dissemination and, regardless of the stated tactics, have been used in this manner by soldiers of all kinds, The resulting carnage and damage to rural communities is beyond the capacity of those same soldiers to remedy and requires political will, commitment and a high level of funding to ensure an eventual solution. The global scale of the problem can be judged from the following list of affected countries.

1. *Humanitarian emergency exists due to landmines*: Afghanistan, Angola, Cambodia, Iraq, Laos

2. *Major humanitarian problem exists due to landmines*: Bosnia, Croatia, Georgia, Mozambique, Myanmar (Burma), Nicaragua, Somalia, Sri Lanka, Sudan

3. *Humanitarian problem exists due to landmines – of a lesser nature or as yet unassessed*: Armenia, Azerbaijan, Chad, Columbia, Cuba, El Salvador, Ethiopia, Eritrea, Falkland/Malvinas, Guatemala, Honduras, Iran, Kuwait, Libya, Russia, Rwanda, Tajikistan, Uzbekistan, Vietnam

A failure by the international community to fund humanitarian-based mine eradication and to ensure a parallel cessation of the manufacture of, and trade in, landmines will ensure that simply being a civilian in rural areas of any of the above countries will continue to be a high-risk occupation. It is an unpalatable and fright-ening fact that the district of Ratanak Mondul has parallels of human suffering in more than 30 counties around the world.

8
Landmines and International Humanitarian Law[1]

Silent enim leges inter arma
In war, the law is silent
Cicero, *Pro Milone*, IV. xi

Mines may be described as fighters that never miss, strike blindly, do not carry weapons openly, and go on killing long after the hostilities are ended. In short, mines are the greatest violators of international humanitarian law, practising blind terrorism.

Opinion of former ICRC delegate, cited in *Mines: A Perverse Use of Technology* (ICRC publication)

Introduction: a Significant Structural Problem with International Law?

Too often, it would seem, the pessimism of Cicero's remark above, seems to be borne out by the daily reality of war in the modern age. Nowhere is this more obvious than in the 20 or so nations, Cambodia included, that are badly affected by the enduring indiscriminate effects of landmine warfare. In these circumstances the laws would appear to be silent, not only in the midst of the chaos of conflict but after the wars have 'ended' as well, making talk of peace a hollow concept.

For Ches Sary, Sdeng Phal, Tith Poue and countless others the laws were indeed silent, drowned out by the force of the explosions that mutilated their bodies and shattered their lives. However, as the following survey of international humanitarian law reveals, even the existing – and, many would argue, inadequate – provisions of the law do proscribe, in general terms, such circumstances from arising.[2] In practice, what seems to be entirely missing in relation to landmine warfare is any mechanism for compliance with or enforcement of the existing rules, even if in the first place the international will to ensure such compliance and enforcement was present. Furthermore, and perhaps even more disturbing, where such rules do exist there arises in expert legal circles sincere doubt as to their applicability to the vast majority of contemporary armed conflicts.

Part of the reason why pessimistic appraisals of the value of international law have to be taken seriously relates to the fact that, 'the era in which the modern laws of war have largely developed, namely the last 100 years, has also seen extreme developments both in the conduct of war and in the types of weaponry'.[3] These interrelated factors seem to have created what can only be termed a structural inadequacy in the international system of humanitarian law, a legitimate and, some would argue, primary[4] purpose of which must be the protection of the rights not only of peoples (as opposed to the interests of sovereign states), but of individuals, and especially non-combatants.

First, the modern laws of war were developed on the assumption that the regulation of warfare was an activity whose focus involved laying down rules to govern international conflicts – wars between sovereign states. Though the vast majority of wars in the first 40 years of the century were of an international nature, Kende's study[5] reveals that of the 97 wars fought between 1945 and 1969 only 15 were 'interstate conflicts', while 67 were 'internal, anti-regime' and 15 were 'tribal'. Clearly, there has been a trend for wars, or armed conflicts as they are now more typically termed, [6] to become 'non-international' or 'civil affairs'. However, this is something of a misnomer as these recent conflicts have often reflected high levels of international participation. To some extent this has been a product of the banning of the use of force *per se* (unless in self-defence) in the UN Charter (Article 2 (4)) – war being denied the legitimacy it enjoyed in the nineteenth century as merely another tool of state policy.

Thus, especially in the cold war era, there was a tendency to resolve or influence global power balances through 'proxy wars', such as in Cambodia. In the light of these developments in the international community, '… the majority of conflicts occurring in the world today are to a large extent unregulated by the international law of armed conflict. The consequences for civilians are devastating.'[7] Indeed, in 1988 there were an estimated 3 million casualties from 25 wars taking place globally, of whom some 80 per cent were estimated to be civilians.[8] The very nature of such internal wars, often involving guerrilla struggles where opposing parties view the enemy as 'hidden' among the mass of the people, has led to the situation in which civilians are increasingly bearing the burden of armed conflicts.

However, civilians have also suffered as a result of a second trend, a technological revolution that has produced enormous 'advances' in weapon development. Anti-personnel landmines may be just one small corner of the 'market', but they amply illustrate the way technologies have outstripped the protections of the law. In fact, as Rae McGrath suggests in his paper 'The Reality of the Present Use of Mines by Military Forces' (reproduced here as Appendix III), there is strong evidence to suggest that 'the military have less to do with the development of mines than the manufacturers – in other words that mine-laying strategy has become manufacturer/designer led'. If this is not the case then only two other possible conclusions emerge: that 'either the military *aim* to deny land to civilians in the post-combat period and have a *policy* of killing and maiming civilians long after the cessation of hostilities, or international military strategic thinking is so inhuman and short-sighted that they are unaware or uncaring of such considerations'.

Whatever the reasons for the current strategies of mine laying worldwide the results as documented here with regard to Cambodia, and elsewhere, reveal that modern mine warfare has shown a total disregard for international humanitarian law, the customary and ancient principles upon which it is based, and what Rae McGrath calls 'simple human decency'. This last, while seemingly an intangible and emotional extra-legal entity, must be acknowledged as the root motive behind such ancient,[9] and much debated, customary legal principles which have evolved to form and inspire the rules governing armed conflicts 'in almost all societies, without geographical limitation'.[10] The desire to see effective regulation of contemporary armed conflicts, and anti-personnel landmines within them, does not then represent the hazy aspirations of a utopian and marginal 'peace movement',[11] rather it springs from an ancient, customary tradition of soldiers and statesmen to regulate armed conflict. International humanitarian law and the laws of war are not '… an abstract and external imposition on the international system, but rather a direct outgrowth of it'.[12]

Weapon technologies (landmines present a prime example of this trend) and those who develop, control and sell them are fast leading the means and methods of warfare into areas from which the desire for regulation cannot, without immense efforts, claw them back within *traditional fields of restraint*. This requires a struggle of renewal, a struggle for a return to the norms of civilisation. Nothing short of a return will do since, due to the structural changes in the way wars are currently fought globally (the shift from international to internal conflicts), the *de facto* realisation of this loss of control and civilisation have already made their appearances.

However, these ghastly effects have been 'hidden' among the poorest communities and countries of the South, countries like Cambodia, among victims and victimised communities too poor and intimidated to speak out for themselves, or too marginalised to know who to speak to, who to blame. What they do know only too well is that when a young mother two-months' pregnant, like Ches Sary, has her leg ripped from her body while collecting bamboo shoots, something hideous has gone wrong with the norms of social decency – a contract has been brutally broken. This book has sought to bear witness to these hidden obscenities, and to expose them to the light of the 'civilised' societies, from which the mines themselves have issued to wreak havoc in more 'primitive' countries such as Cambodia. In this final chapter the case evidence presented in the book so far will be reviewed against both the treaty law, and the customary principles of international humanitarian law which seek at present to govern armed conflicts.

Classification of the Cambodian Conflict 1979–91

While the years following World War Two witnessed a shift in the pattern of global war making from international to internal conflicts, in many of these 'civil wars' the influence of foreign powers can be clearly discerned. Only rarely is such intervention openly acknowledged, and condemned, as in the *Nicaragua Case*, which came before the International Court of Justice (ICJ) in 1986. However, such interventions complicate the classification of conflicts such as the one under consideration in Cambodia; and such classification is important in terms of seeing which treaty law rules apply and which customary principles are applicable. Professor Roberts has written:

> For different purposes, one could *plausibly* classify the Cambodian conflict 1979–89 as (a) an international conflict between Cambodia and Vietnam; (b) an internal conflict within Cambodia; and (c) a Vietnamese occupation ... There is no absolute answer

... It all depends on what particular activity, by whom, and against whom, is under consideration. There is nothing unique to Cambodia about this: similar multiple classifications are common.[13]

Side-stepping the issue somewhat, the International Committee of the Red Cross (ICRC) refers to the conflict as an 'internationalised internal conflict'.[14]

However, it will be argued here that while a multiple (as with Roberts) or ambiguous (as with the ICRC) classification of the Cambodian conflict may reflect the complexity of this recent history, in essence the conflict is most properly understood as an international conflict, and the customary principles, together with some of the rules, of international law apply as a result. This argument is in essence based on one of the key factors in determining what is or is not a customary rule of international law: state practice. State practice does not merely lie in what acts are done and what acts are abstained from, but in 'what states say in international fora'[15] Clearly, the international actions and reactions as a result of the Vietnamese invasion of 1979 and the subsequent occupation of that country during the following ten years are not being claimed here to amount to the formation of any new customary rule, rather it is argued that since state practice is the basis upon which norms of international law are formed and maintained, it must equally be revealing as a yardstick of the real essence of the Cambodian conflict. These international reactions to the Vietnamese invasion and the subsequent years of conflict must lead one to consider the essential nature of the conflict as being international.

First, the DK regime, and after 1982, the DK-led coalition (CGDK), retained its seat in the UN General Assembly until 1991, a clear acknowledgement of international recognition of Cambodian sovereignty residing in the resistance forces operating out of Thailand. Until the UN peace plan came into operation in 1991 these forces could not be regarded merely as 'factions' in, or parties to, an internal dispute, but as the only legitimate representatives of Cambodia, since this was the way they themselves portrayed the war. The public statements of these sovereign representatives left no doubt as to the nature of the conflict, as they saw it: an international war of liberation against historic Vietnamese expansionism and imperialism. Witness, for example, the public notices saying, in effect, 'Help us rid our homeland of the Vietnamese Aggressor' which were prominently displayed in the UN-financed Site 2 camp in Prachinburi, Thailand, during the late 1980s. By implication, the public statements *and* actions of many other sovereign states, both multilaterally through the UN and bilaterally, indicate an acceptance of this position.[16] In fact, in the light of ICJ's ruling in the *Nicaragua Case* (1986), the only way such extended humanitarian and military inter-

ventionism by third parties to the dispute could be publicly justified at all is in terms of the right of collective self-defence as per Article 51 of the UN Charter, indicating the essentially international character of this conflict had been accepted in practice. Conversely, on the Vietnamese–Soviet bloc side the invasion and ensuing war in Cambodia where represented internationally in these same terms – first as a legitimate exercise in the right of self-defence in response to repeated Khmer Rouge incursions during the 1975–78 period, and later, when the extent of the horrors of the genocidal rule of the Khmer Rouge came to light, under the right of humanitarian intervention.

After the final withdrawal from Cambodia of Vietnamese forces in 1989 the public statements of the CGDK (all factions) still referred to the struggle in essentially international terms as being between Cambodians and Vietnamese.[17] Continued overt multilateral aid and covert bilateral assistance of various forms by other sovereign states for the former CGDK allies and their domestic constituencies similarly implied some form of continued acceptance of this internationalised view of the conflict by other sovereign states. Even if this is not accepted, during the 1989–91 period it could be argued that the ongoing conflict had historically acquired the essential characteristics of an international struggle, characteristics which did not disappear with the retiring Vietnamese mainforce units.

Even if one denies that the international face of the Cambodia conflict is its predominant one, and that it is in essence an internal struggle, as will be mentioned later, many leading commentators have argued that the most important customary rules of international humanitarian law, which have inspired and formulated the most important codifications of international treaty law, are applicable to purely internal conflicts of the level of intensity seen in Cambodia in recent years.[18] To take a yet still further defensive position (one unwarranted, in the author's view by the fact of the case in the recent Cambodian conflict) even if this applicability of inter-

national customary rules is denied, the rights of civilians to some protection in armed conflicts is regarded by many commentators as a fundamental human right: 'In fact, human rights law fills the gaps left by the laws of armed conflict in situations of internal disturbances and tensions not covered by any of the conventional rules of armed conflict.'[19]

The Protection of the Law?

It will be argued here that while the codified international law which relates to landmines is clearly not directly applicable to Cambodia as treaty law,[20] it is applicable in as much as its provisions reflect customary rules. This treaty law is contained in the second protocol (Protocol on Prohibitions or Restrictions on the Use of Mines, Booby-Traps and Other Devices), otherwise known as the 'Landmines Protocol' (LMP), annexed to the 1981 United Nations Convention on Prohibitions or Restrictions on the Use of Certain Conventional Weapons Which May be Deemed to be Excessively Injurious or to Have Indiscriminate Effects (also known in short as the 1981 UN Weapons Convention).

The Landmines Protocol itself makes sense only in the light of the failure of the 1974–77 Diplomatic Conference on the Reaffirmation and Development of International Humanitarian Law Applicable in Armed Conflicts (known hereafter as the 1974–77 Diplomatic Conference) to address the use of specific conventional weapons and incorporate these provisions in the two protocols which emerged from the conference – the famous 1977 Geneva Protocols I and II Additional to the Geneva Conventions of 1949 (referred to hereafter as Protocols I and II). Protocol I, which deals with international conflicts, is extremely significant in that it codified for the first time several important customary norms of international humanitarian laws, arguably the most significant of which for the purposes of this chapter is non-combatant immunity in armed conflicts.

The detailed rules of Protocol I are equally not applicable as treaty law to the situation in Cambodia (only Vietnam, and not Cambodia, ratified it), but they are useful as far as they reflect, and have refined, customary principles. Furthermore, in places, Protocol I also reveals the influence of human rights law, reflecting the blurring of these two streams in contemporary international law. Certain provisions, such as Article 75 of Protocol I are directly derived from the 1966 International Covenant on Civil and Political Rights, and are legally binding 'as a minimum' in all circumstances.[21]

Other sources of customary law that might be seen to have direct relevance to the Cambodian mine problem can be found in the 1907 Hague Convention VIII Relative to the Laying of Automatic Submarine Contact Mines.

Roberts believes that this convention reflects some traditional principles of the laws of war, and that although there is a huge technological and historical gulf between the sea mines being regulated in the 1907 convention, and modern anti-personnel landmines, the principles are especially revealing since the issues are essentially the same.[22]

Lastly, since both Cambodia and Vietnam are bound by the Geneva conventions of 1949, further provisions apply. First, if the Cambodian conflict is viewed primarily in terms of a Vietnamese occupation of Cambodia, which again throws the conflict into the gambit of international relations, then the 1949 Geneva Convention IV Relative to the Protection of Civilian Persons in Time of War comes into play. The fourth convention deals with, and seeks to protect, civilians 'in the hands of the enemy' which is what the effect of the Vietnamese occupation amounts to. Although its central focus is to provide protection from the 'arbitrary power' acquired by one of the belligerents as a result of the conflict, rather than to protect them from the violence of war *per se*, it does so in terms of a reiteration of fundamental human rights which must be respected in all circumstances, and thus to some extent be deemed applicable to the conditions that were resultant upon the occupation by Vietnam. However, even if the Cambodian conflict is seen as a purely internal affair, the 'mini-convention' of Common Article 3 applies, again bringing with it certain minimum provisions.

From this initial survey it should be clear that even as the existing law stands, civilians of countries like Cambodia are not unprotected. In theory, some of the most ancient principles of international law apply. In practice, the disrespect to which these customary principles and rules have been exposed does not diminish their validity as law (the fact that a rule is broken does not signify that it is no longer a rule, merely that it has been broken).[23] The challenge remains to see that the existing law is enforced, and that all too necessary improvements are then made.

Basic Principles

International law consists both of treaty law and customary rules, the latter being automatically binding on states regardless of the extent of their obligations under the former. This was recognised during the latter half of nineteenth century when customary rules were first systematically codified into treaty law, since as Adam Roberts puts it, 'much of the law continued to exist in the form of unwritten customary principles'.[24] This was expressly recognised in what has become known as the Martens Clause which appeared in the Preamble to the 1899 Hague Convention II. Since the treaty law codified

by the 1899 Peace Conference could not possibly hope to cover all the exigencies of war, the Martens Clause represented a safety valve, stating that in unforeseen cases, both civilians and combatants would 'remain under the protection and rule of the principles of the laws of nations, as they result from the usages established among civilised peoples, from the laws of humanity, and the dictates of the public conscience'. Versions of the Martens Clause have reappeared in the 1949 Geneva Conventions, the two 1977 Protocols Additional to the Geneva Convention and the 1981 Weapons Convention.

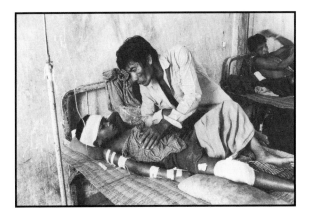

The fundamental principle underlying the laws of war is that *the right of belligerents to adopt means of injuring the enemy is not unlimited*. This involves concepts of limitation and balance: that military necessity must be balanced against, and limited by, the requirements of humanity. This principle was laid down as Article 22 of the Hague Regulations on Land Warfare annexed to Hague Convention IV of 1907, and has been reflected in subsequent treaty law and UN resolutions. The Hague Regulations in their entirety were recognised as representing customary law in the Nuremberg Trials after World War Two, but the concept of the right of limitation in the name of humanity to override military necessity had underlain earlier treaty law, and had been a long-accepted custom of the international system.

From this general principle a number of more specific principles have been deduced which form the keystones of the customary law regime. These are the principle of distinction, the principle of proportionality, and the prohibition of unnecessary suffering and superfluous injury. Often these principles overlap and work together in a collective effort to limit the activities of belligerents. In a recent paper Francoise Hampson[25] expands on these principles as follows:

1. *The principle of distinction*: the law requires that belligerents distinguish between civilians and civilian objects on the one hand and military

objectives on the other. It is only permitted to attack the latter. While this principle protects civilians from intentional attack, it does not prevent their being the unintentional, indirect victim of attacks against military targets. Some protection is given them in that regard by the second principle.

2. *Principle of proportionality*: The principle of proportionality has evolved ... [and now] imposes a positive obligation to consider the possible impact on civilians of an attack against a military objective and to minimise such effects. If the impact would be disproportionate in relation to the concrete and direct military advantage anticipated, the attack must be called off. This formulation [of the traditional principle] would seem to have acquired the status of customary international law.

3. *Prohibition of unnecessary suffering and superfluous injury*: this principle applies to both combatants and civilians. In the case of the latter, there is an overlap with the second principle. Where an attack would cause disproportionate casualties among civilians, it could be said that their suffering is unnecessary and their injury superfluous. The third principle may be of some importance where the injuries are caused a long time after the attack, where it might be difficult to argue that the attack itself was disproportionate. The argument would rather focus on the effects of the weapon used.

It is against these fundamental customary principles that anti-personnel landmines strike.

Distinction: Protecting Civilians and Civilian Objects

The principle of distinction is a fundamental rule and found early codification in the St Petersburg Declaration of 1868 where it was expressly stated that, 'the only legitimate object which states should endeavour to accomplish is to weaken the military forces of the enemy'. Implicit in this is the norm that non-combatants should have immunity from attack, a general principle that also found expression in the Hague Regulations, Articles 25 and 26. The protections of the principle were to be afforded through proper, discriminate targeting of attacks on military objects. This principle found further clear expression in Resolution 2444 (XXIII) 'Respect for Human Rights in Armed Conflicts', of the United Nations General Assembly, which was adopted unanimously on 18 December 1968. The resolution reaffirms some 'principles for observance by all governmental and other authorities responsible for action in armed conflicts', of which the following two, at paragraph 2.3, are of importance here:

(b) That it is prohibited to launch attacks against the civilian population as such;

(c) That distinction must be made at all times between persons taking part in the hostilities and members of the civilian population to the effect that the latter be spared as much as possible.

The principle finds its clearest expression: in Article 48 of Protocol I

the Parties to the conflict shall at all times distinguish between the civilian population and combatants and between civilian objects and military objectives and accordingly shall direct their operations only against military objectives.

Significantly, given the realities of landmine warfare, in the following article attacks are defined as 'acts of violence against the adversary, whether in offence or in defence' (Article 49 (1)), and it is made clear that the respect and protection afforded by the article applies not only to the enemy civilian population but also to those civilians of the attacking or defending power who are endangered by that power's actions. Given the fact that most of the minefields in areas such as Rattanak Mondul were laid as defensive fields by the Vietnamese/CPAF forces, and that the individuals being injured are the very same people these forces were nominally trying to 'protect', these are significant customary provisions. Indeed, they are equally, if not more significant when applied to the actions of the 'Cambodian' state – the resistance coalition for the purposes of this argument throughout the 1980s – whose offensive activities to 'liberate' the country from Vietnamese occupation resulted in both the direct targeting of civilians and their indirect exposure to danger as a result of the indiscriminate usages that occurred, discussed further below.

As Christopher Greenwood notes:[26]

the customary law status of the principle of distinction was never seriously questioned but its reaffirmation in the Protocol was timely in view of the extent to which it had been violated during World War II and subsequent conflicts. Those violations have not ceased since 1977 but no State has denied the binding character of the basic prohibition.

Furthermore, the protocol makes it clear, 'that the principle of distinction applies to all types of conflict, including guerrilla warfare'.[27]

This principle also inspired the 1981 UN Weapons Convention as a whole, and the Land Mines Protocol (LMP) additional to it. Indeed, the desire to afford protection to civilians marks the Weapons Convention out from previous agreements on specific conventional weapons. Thus in Article 3 (2) of the LMP it is stated:

It is prohibited *in all circumstances* to direct weapons to which this Article applies, either in offence, defence or by way of reprisal, against the civilian population as such or against individual civilians [emphasis added]

And later, in Article 3 (4), it is stated that:

All feasible precautions shall be taken to protect civilians from the effects of the weapons to which this Article applies.

In as much as these provisions of the LMP reflect customary principles they may be seen as binding to the parties in the Cambodia conflict.

Walking through the surgical ward at Siem Reap hospital on 5 April 1993, I encountered nine mine victims, all young males, all civilians. Of the nine, seven said they had been injured on paths or in fields, close to their villages, which had been known to be safe since they had never been fought over, and which had been used without incident every day until the victim's accident. One man had been injured returning on the same main path leading out of his village to the nearby forests that he had taken safely only two hours before. Among demining specialists in Siem Reap there was little doubt that such continued mine laying was the result of action

by the Khmer Rouge, action that not only constituted ceasefire violations but conspicuously broke international law by targeting civilians. From their secure home bases in the province there was hardly anywhere Khmer Rouge guerrilla units could not reach in early 1993. Invariably the calling cards that announced their visits were anti-personnel mines.

In other provinces such as Kompong Thom, Banteay-Meanchay, Battambang, and Kompong Speu, both UN and NGO demining experts on the ground believed that targeting civilians for 'anti-morale purposes' was policy and that it has been expressly practised in the Cambodian conflict, amounting to 'terrorism by landmine'. In Kompong Som, Kep Yuthikar, one of the surgeons in the provincial hospital told me how, in 1987, a Khmer Rouge guerrilla unit had mounted a landmine terrorism campaign in the town itself. This had involved placing small mines inside cigarette packets or under money to attract the attention of the unfortunate victims. Several people were killed and injured as a result of this small campaign alone.

That such strategies should have been employed in the Cambodian conflict should not be seen as exceptional rather as McGrath suggests in Appendix III, the deployment of mines against civilians has become accepted by military strategists and field commanders

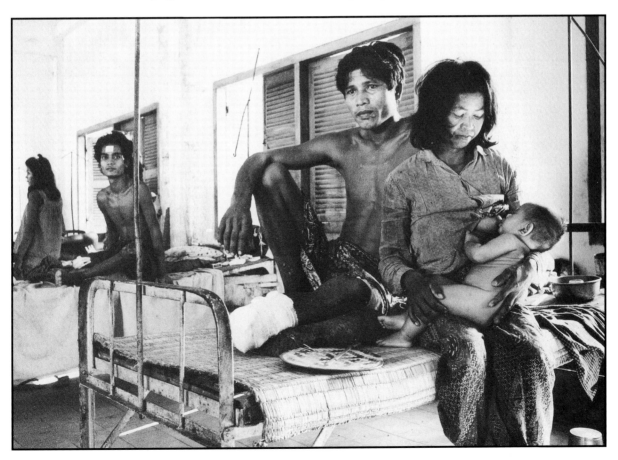

as a standard military tactic in armed conflicts of a *counter-insurgency/insurgency* nature. Furthermore, Cambodian fighters have been expressly trained by Chinese and British forces in the use of mines as an anti-morale weapon specifically targeted against the civilian infrastructure.[28] As will be argued below, given the obligation of states such as the UK and China as 'High Contracting Parties' to the 1949 Geneva Conventions, such activities not only break customary international law, but under Common Article 1,[29] treaty law as well. Such activities are clearly proscribed in Article 51 (2) of Protocol I:

> The civilian population as such, as well as individual civilians, shall not be the object of attack. *Acts or threats of violence the primary purpose of which is to spread terror among the civilian population are prohibited.*

In countless Cambodian villages, the all-pervading fear of mines is one of the bitterest legacies of landmine warfare, victimising not just those who directly suffer accidents but the whole community.

The customary principle of distinction has thus been put under direct threat by anti-personnel landmines and such usage strategies. However, the generalised and non-directed usage, both in defence and offence, in Cambodia, and especially in districts like Rattanak Mondul, results in an *enduring threat* to both civilians and combatants and also represents an indirect threat to the principle because of its indiscriminate characteristics, the effects of which have already been detailed in Chapters 2 and 3. In Article 3 (3), in words drawing direct inspiration from Article 51 (4) of Protocol I, the LMP defines as *indiscriminate*, and therefore prohibited, any usage:

(a) which is not on, or directed against, a military objective.
(b) which employs a method or means of delivery which cannot be directed at a specific military objective.

Previously, in a definition this time directly taken from Article 52 (2) of Protocol I (which is regarded as being declaratory of custom), the LMP described military objectives, in Article 2 (4), as being:

> any object which by its nature, location, purpose or use makes an effective contribution to military action and whose total or partial destruction, capture or neutralisation, in the circumstances ruling at the time, offers a definite military advantage.

Such a prohibition of indiscriminate usage reflects customary positions, in as much as they reflect 'general and well recognised principles', expressed, for example,

with regard to the use of *naval* mines.[30] Judgments in the ICJ in both the *Corfu Channel* (1949) and *Nicaragua* (1986) cases involved rulings which condemned the indiscriminate use of naval mines that might endanger neutral shipping. Just like their counterparts designed for land warfare, these naval mines had no means of self-deactivation. The problem first came to notice during the Russo-Japanese War of 1904–5 when unanchored contact-detonated submarine mines were extensively laid near Port Arthur. These weapons, *by their enduring and deadly nature*, caused extensive damage to neutral, and therefore by implication to non-targeted, shipping both during and *even after the war*. The Hague Convention VIII Relative to the Laying of Automatic Submarine Contact Mines attempted to respond to this threat by regulating the usage of such mines through: the introduction of concepts of self-neutralisation of unanchored mines (Article 1); a reiteration of the definition of a legitimate target (Article 2 – not commercial, non-military shipping); and through insistence that warnings of where dangers zones should be given (Article 3 – a precursor of the modern 'recording and marking requirements' of the LMP, see below).

Clearly, both the convention and the decisions of the ICJ leave little doubt that indiscriminate usage of anti-personnel landmines is prohibited in custom. Furthermore, in as much as the generalised and repetitive indiscriminate usage of landmines over sustained periods of years for *general* area denial in an area such as Rattanak Mondul has the equivalent effect of sustained and random area bombardment, this too has its prohibitive precedents in customary law: for example, in Article 25 of the Hague Regulations, prohibiting the bombardment of undefended towns. This found further detailed and refined codification in Article 51 (5) (a) of Protocol I:

> an attack by bombardment by any methods or means which treats as a single military objective a number of clearly separated and distinct military objectives located in a city, town, village or *other area containing a similar concentration of civilians or civilian objects.*

Communes such as Treng and Ploumeas, notable areas of Andao Hep (Thmar Prous and the north bank of the Sangke River in Andao Hep) and even Sdao, now uninhabitable due to the presence of broad swathes of mines, should be considered as 'other areas' in terms of the definition of Article 51 (5) (a). Furthermore, as Greenwood notes, in the Gulf War:

> the proclaimed policy of the allies with regard to targeting and aerial bombardment (and) ... Statements by allied commanders and heads of government have already made clear that the principles of distinction and proportionality set out in Protocol I are regarded by the allied States as declaratory of custom'.[31]

It would seem clear that one simply cannot mine vast tracts of land, with such mines having no self-neutralisation or self-destruction capacity, and expect these actions and the clearly indiscriminate effects that follow to be considered lawful acts of war. As Rae McGrath concludes:

> in the modern conflict mines cannot be said to be targeted at military formations in any reasonable definition of the word, since the very design of a great proportion of the mines in use and their method of dissemination is such that civilian casualties and long-term infestation are inevitable rather than coincidental.[32]

This principle found further refinement in Article 4 (2) of the LMP, which virtually repeated word for word Article 5 (5) (a) of Protocol I, except it has been accommodated slightly to take account of the particular nature of mine warfare, as discussed further below. The article section reads:

> It is prohibited to use the weapons to which this Article applied in any city, town, village or other area containing a similar concentration of civilians in which combat between ground forces *is not taking place or does not appear to be imminent*, unless either:
> (a) they are placed on or in the close vicinity of a military objective belonging to or under the control of an adverse party; or
> (b) measures are taken to protect civilians from their effects ... &c.

As expert commentators like Greenwood acknowledge, while Article 51 (5) (a) of the Protocol upon which this part of the LMP is based is a desirable refinement of the customary law position, it did go beyond the existing customary position. But in the case of landmines, for those customary provisions and protections to have any continued relevance in fulfilling the role for which they have evolved over time, such refinements must now be considered customary and binding on parties to armed conflicts as such. Increasingly, in expert circles the prohibitions of indiscriminate warfare are now regarded as customary. If they were not, then law has become redundant. Thus, it is undoubtedly the treaty law position to prohibit the indiscriminate mining of vast swathes of territory in districts like Rattanak Mondul on the vague assumption that at some stage in the distant future the enemy may attempt to move through the area. To employ mines as eternal sentinels, standing guard forever along the edges of zones of factional influence, often for the simple reason that mines are available and the resources to pay for the platoons necessary to patrol such vast boundaries are not, is a fundamentally inappropriate and unsatisfactory usage. Such actions are

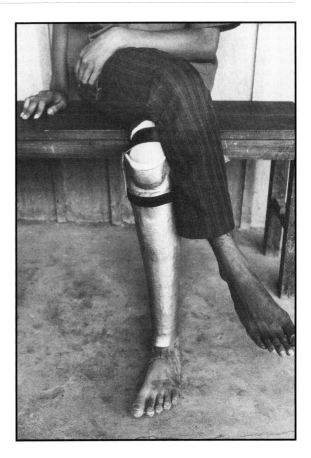

bound to produce long-term civilian casualties and widespread infestation.

Finally, for the concept of distinction to be even theoretically meaningful in landmine warfare, further refinements of the customary principle can be seen as essential, and this was to some extent acknowledged in practice by the authors of the LMP. This is due to the extraordinary nature of mines as a weapon. While other weapons 'approach' their targets, by whatever means, mines 'await' theirs, their 'official' purpose being to impede and deny access to land[33] – a task they will continue to perform with a lethal capacity in the medium to long-term unless fitted with a self-neutralisation or self-destruction device,[34] and few, if any, modern mines have this capacity. Landmines are incapable, once laid, in the words of Article 3 (3) (b) of the LMP,[35] of being 'directed at a specific military objective' in any meaningful sense.

As traditionally formulated, the principle of distinction requires that the military target a discriminate and legitimate objective. However, due to the unique nature and purpose of landmines it could be argued that the principle itself needs to be reformulated to require that the weapons, rather than their objectives, be distinguished as they are deployed, whether in attack or defence. This should be achieved by means of fencing, marking and recording of minefields. Unless these standards are adhered to in the laying of mines it will be acknowledged that a fundamental customary rule has been wilfully broken, since in the absence of almost immediate demining or self-destruction the effects will be the creation of an enduring and indiscriminate hazard. The LMP addresses this in Article 4 where it calls for 'all feasible precautions to be taken to protect civilians', and more specifically in Article 4 (2) (b) where it details these feasible precautions as:

> the posting of warning signs, the posting of sentries, the issue of warnings or the provision of fences.

Also in Article 7, the LMP lays down a recording requirement.

If the principle of distinction is allowed to be reformulated in the way suggested above, then mine-laying actions which break these simple measures would be clearly prohibited under international custom. In fact, mine laying which does not follow these simple guidelines would be hard for a military strategist to justify publicly, since such precautionary measures would not detract from the publicly acknowledged role of the mine in combat.[36]

Arguably, following these guidelines would actually enhance the military efficacy of mines as a weapon, since if the rules were followed mines would only have to be used rarely in areas designated publicly as minefields. Merely marking an area as a minefield would require the enemy force to treat it with the respect that a genuine minefield would deserve. The military effect would be the same, and the use of dummy minefields is a well-recognised and well-regarded practice among conventional armies. Opinion from within the British and Canadian military encountered in Cambodia would indeed not only support the notion of these rules of marking and recording as being the effective meaning of the principle of distinction with regard to landmines, but also as being good military practice.[37] It is only when less publicly justifiable military strategies of mine laying are held to be militarily necessary and/or desirable that the imposition of such rules becomes unworkable, in both conventional and counter-insurgency style conflicts. Even without reformulation of customary principles such indiscriminate practices are already outside the bounds of the law. As McGrath suggests in Appendix 3, it is perhaps the designers and manufacturers who may be to 'blame' for these developments in military strategic thinking and deployments, e.g. with regard to the development of virtually non-detectable mines, a development unwarranted by the publicly 'justifiable and legitimate' usage of mines.

As noted in Chapter 2, in Cambodia hardly any minefields have been recorded and mapped, and where this has occurred the information has often been lost. According to Mike Croll, the Field Director of the British demining NGO the HALO Trust from 1991–3, the only marked and fenced minefield he encountered was around the strategic town of Phum Svey Don Koy, situated on Route 5 at the border of Pursat and Battambang provinces. The marked fields clearly denied access as one approached the concrete and stone pill-box towers that guarded the four corners of the village, channelling the movements of those entering the zone into clearly defined areas. However, around the village itself extensive unmarked fields existed, recorded only in the mental maps of local officials. Once again remarkable negligence seems to have been the product of not only local Cambodian apathy and ill-discipline, but of encouragement by foreign instructors. *The Cowards' War* tells of a Cambodian who had claimed to have attended a British-taught course where, 'a British instructor taught their class how to draw a map of a minefield, but explained that "such maps are rarely drawn and it's hardly practical to bother with them".'[38]

Lastly, it is worth noting that even when mines are laid 'according to the rules', and are recorded, mapped, marked and fenced, the reality in a post-conflict situation sometimes produces insurmountable obstacles to effective demining. The result is that such affected land is effectively lost, for ever:

> After the war in the Falklands-Malvinas, mine-clearing operations were begun at once. But they were found to be so difficult that they were abandoned. Yet the war had only lasted two months and had been waged between two conventional armies. If mine clearance was abandoned in areas that had been clearly identified, what must the situation be in countries where fighting has continued for years and mines have been used indiscriminately and on a massive scale ... Mine clearance is costly and slow ... In Afghanistan ... at a rate of 30 sq km per year, it would take 4,300 years to clear mines from only 20 per cent of Afghan territory manually.[39]

If mines are considered capable of becoming a destructive, long-term pollutant of the environment, even when used according to the rules, then it might be possible to claim that mines by their fundamental nature are prohibited under what Greenwood describes as an 'emerging norm of international law'.[40] Article 35 (3) of Protocol I states that:

> It is prohibited to employ methods or means of warfare which are intended, *or may be expected to cause* widespread, long-term and severe damage to the natural environment.

While Roberts notes [41] that this article is (generally) distinct from the 1977 Environment Convention which is concerned with 'the manipulation of the forces of the environment as weapons', and concerns damage done to the environment by various weapons used, the reality of modern mine warfare might throw some doubt on the extent of the distinction in this case. For in practice mines do modify the environment and take it over, becoming its dominant characteristic. They make the land lethal; they have turned Cambodian farming fields, literally, into killing fields, and sadly they more than meet the criteria for applicability to the Environment Convention – that their effects are 'widespread, long-lasting or severe'. If this is considered applicable to modern-day mine warfare, then it presents the possibility of landmines being illegal *as an entire class of weapon*. While both Article 35 (3) of Protocol I, and the 1977 Environment Convention might be considered as being in advance of custom, as Roberts concludes:

> Although this Convention is the only international agreement which exclusively addresses environmental modification techniques, existing customary and conventional law relating to armed conflicts and occupations could be regarded as applicable, including Articles 22, 23 (a) and (e) and 55 of the Regulations annexed to 1899 Hague Convention II and Hague Convention IV; the 1925 Geneva Protocol; and Article 53 of 1949 Geneva Convention IV.[42]

With perhaps as many as 100 million anti-personnel mines at large, predominantly in some of the poorest nations of the South, it would seem timely to start viewing mines in environmental modification and/or environmentally damaging terms, and as an unacceptable methodology of warfare.

Proportionality: The Prohibition of Disproportionate Attacks

The legitimacy of any military target does not accord combatants an unlimited licence to attack . Again the principle of proportionality stems from the most basic principle that the rights of belligerents to adopt means of injuring the enemy are not unlimited. In this application, the principle demands that the military advantage of an attack on a legitimate target should be weighed against the costs to humanity, and especially any costs occurring to civilians (non-combatants) and civilian objects.

The principle finds clarity and codification in Article 51 of Protocol I, entitled simply 'Protection of the Civilian Population':

> The civilian population and individual civilians shall enjoy general protection against the dangers arising from military operations.

However, it is in Paragraph 5 (b) that the principle of proportionality is stated, prohibiting even an attack upon a military objective:

> *which may be expected to cause incidental loss of civilian life*, injury to civilians, damage to civilian objects or a combination thereof, which would be *excessive in relation* to the *concrete and direct military advantage anticipated.*

This article is incorporated word for word in Article 3 (3) (c) of the LMP, and appears there as a further definition of what is considered an 'indiscriminate use of the weapons' (mines etc.). Christopher Greenwood comments:

> 'The principle of proportionality was also part of the pre-1977 law, although it is expressed in the Protocol in more precise language than that used hitherto .... Nevertheless, the representative of the United Kingdom (*at the 1974–1977 Diplomatic Conference*) seems to have reflected the general view when he described what became Article 51 (5, b) as: 'a useful codification of a concept that was rapidly becoming accepted by all States as an important principle of international law relating to armed conflict .... It is suggested, therefore, that Article 51 (5,b) should be treated as an authoritative statement of the modern customary rule.[43]

By direct extension, therefore, Article 3 (3) (c) of the LMP should be accorded the same status.

These provisions come under the heading not so much of refraining from attacks on civilians but of imposing an obligation that while engaged in attacks on legitimate military targets the civilian population is to be spared as much as possible.[44] This obligation is further stated in Article 57, 'Precaution in Attack', paragraphs 2 (a) (ii) and 2 (b), where commanders are obliged to ensure that civilian casualties are minimised and that if the attack becomes disproportionate it should be 'cancelled or suspended'. Greenwood confirms that these sections of Article 57 should be viewed as custom, and binding on the parties to the Cambodian conflict.[45]

Thus, even if some of the minefields laid in Rattanak Mondul could be considered as attacking or more usually defending a legitimate military objective (as defined above), their military utility should be 'concrete and direct'. Even legitimately laid minefields in Rattanak Mondul almost by definition become prohibited under the principle of proportionality if they are a continued threat to civilians and civilian objects months, let alone years, after they were laid. Commanders should have deployed minefields for discrete periods only, for a particular military purpose (defence against a particular expected attack), and thereafter the mines should have

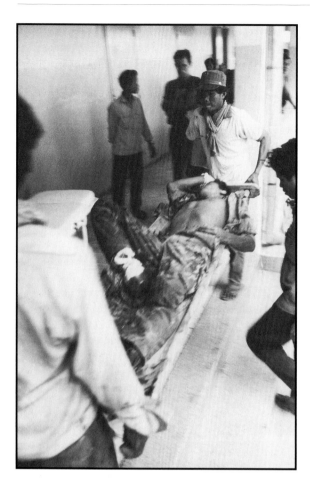

some villages in Rattanak Mondul as many as one-quarter of the animals have perished in the last two years as a result of landmine injuries – an excessive degree of loss from the position of a peasant farmer whose livelihood is marginal even in the best of circumstances. It is crucial in this light to remember the landmine 'multiplier effect' mentioned in Chapter 2. The direct losses caused by mines are only the tip of the iceberg of 'civilian losses' in areas like Rattanak Mondul. A true picture of civilian losses would have to 'cost in' the increased death rate resultant on the poverty induced by loss of access to land, loss of value of land, the real costs of the risk of demining such land, the psychological and cultural trauma of communities due to the climate of fear, and on and on. These are the typical, *not the exceptional*, results of mine warfare, and it is these facts about the weapon which lead responsible figures in the western military to condemn modern anti-personnel landmines as weapons that are almost impossible to deploy in practice in a proportionate manner.

Prohibition of Unnecessary Suffering and Superfluous Injury

There is considerable overlap with the principle of proportionality in the application of this third basic principle. In the case of an attack being acknowledged as causing disproportionate casualties it can also be argued that the suffering produced is unnecessary and the injuries superfluous (in terms of the achievement of the military goal). By focusing on the effects, often long-term, produced by a method of warfare, this principle is particularly valuable when considering the effects of landmine warfare in a context like contemporary Cambodia. Non-targeted, indiscriminate attacks might be considered also to cause unnecessary suffering and superfluous injury, bringing in the principle of distinction once more. Significantly, the third principle is also directly cited in the preamble of the 1981 Weapons Convention, an acknowledgement that in practice mines are of a class of weapons that are deemed to pose a threat to this customary norm of the laws of armed conflict.

But to what extent do mines as a *class of weapon* break the norm of prohibitions of causing unnecessary suffering and superfluous injury? First, the arguments suggested above – that modern mines, due to their design, manufacture, methods and modes of deployment are in practice incapable of being used either discriminately or proportionately – should be reconsidered. It could be argued that as a class of weapon, in generalised terms, they are developed, sold and deployed with the desired intent of causing 'unnecessary suffering and superfluous injury'. Given the standards required for 'legitimate' and defensible usage (that they should be clearly marked ,

been removed. Once civilian injuries started to grow in the district, local commanders (under the customary provisions of Article 57) had an obligation to 'cancel or suspend' the attack, i.e. to demine.

It is for this reason that Lt. Col. Mulliner felt so strongly that anti-personnel mines should be banned (see Chapter 5) unless they have some self-neutralisation device fitted to ensure a short-term life, which would ensure that the mine could only be deployed in a legitimate military attacking or defensive action. Without such a device such weapons are almost certain to wreak disproportionate effects on civilians.

It is clear that civilian injuries surged as people returned to Rattanak Mondul from the Battambang town area when hostilities died down in the last half of 1991 and in early 1992. 1991 and 1992 were the two worst years on record, and injury rates in the first half of 1993 suggested that the figures for those years might reasonably be considered typical, rather than exceptional, for the foreseeable future. By 1993 these injuries were usually occurring from mines laid at least two years before, and in many cases from far earlier in the war. The destruction of livestock (civilian objects) should also be considered as prohibited under the customary provisions of these articles of Protocol I. In fenced and recorded, that they should be used in the short term in defence or as part of an attack against a legitimate military target, etc.), it becomes apparent that there is no 'legitimate reason' for mines' manufacturers to have struggled so hard to make the weapons as light and hard to detect (with 'illegal' plastic casings, for example) as is the case. An easily locatable mine is capable of effective deployment as part of a large marked field and will satisfactorily perform its short-term area denial functions. It could be argued that modern design standards, almost by definition, have led to a weapon class whose inevitable outcome will be unnecessary suffering and superfluous injury.

Currently it is (erroneously) accepted by law makers that such modern-day mines are capable of discriminate and proportionate usage, and this is reflected in the fact that the LMP sets out to restrict the usage of mines rather than to ban them as a class of weapon. For the protection of the laws based on the most fundamental customary principles to have any continued significance in relation to these weapons only a complete prohibition will do, and this must involve a sea change of opinion among decision-makers. *The principles of custom are already on the side of prohibition.*

The first codification of the principle of prohibition of unnecessary suffering and superfluous injury was in the 1868 St Petersburg Declaration, which condemned the usage of explosive projectiles of less than 400 grammes (i.e. lighter than an artillery shell, but heavier than a bullet) because the legitimate military object of weakening the military forces of the enemy 'would be exceeded by the employment of arms which uselessly aggravate the sufferings of disabled men, or render their death inevitable'. Such weapons 'would therefore be contrary to the laws of humanity', since they create an effect more severe than that produced by a normal bullet, which themselves are capable of rendering an adversary *hors de combat*. Similarly, during the First Hague Peace Conference in 1899 dum-dum bullets, which caused similar injuries to those produced by small explosive projectiles, were banned. In doing this, the conference reaffirmed the principle, expressed at St Petersburg, that new weapons need to be evaluated, 'in order to maintain the principles which have been established, and to conciliate the necessities of war with the laws of humanity'.

Article 23 (e) of the Hague Regulations provided for the general prohibition of the employment of 'arms, projectiles, or material calculated to cause unnecessary suffering'. Kalshoven noted:

In this formula, 'unnecessary' signifies that the suffering caused by a particular means of warfare is not justified by its military utility, either because such

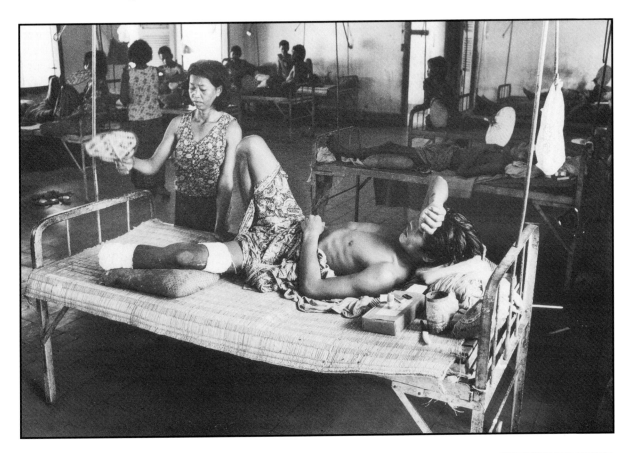

utility is entirely lacking or at best negligible, or because in weighing utility against suffering the scale dips to the latter side and, in so doing, to prohibition.[46]

Clearly, in the calculation of this balance the principle of proportionality comes into play. The principle, now acknowledged as custom, was also codified in Protocol I in Article 35 (Paragraph 2), which comes under the heading of providing the 'Basic Rules' for the section dealing on the 'Means and Methods of Warfare' (Part III, Section I).

Given that only a very small percentage of the overall landmine usage in Cambodia can be considered 'legitimate' anyway under the two other customary principles of international law of armed conflict considered here, it is hard to single out the extent to which mines as a class of weapon have caused unnecessary suffering *per se* in the sense of the principle's historical application to weapon types. Nevertheless, factors such as the disproportionate pull on the enemy's military and hospital resources do start to question the weapon's validity in these terms. This is true when one considers the nature of the injuries produced, the way, for example, in which fragments of soil and other debris are routinely blasted into the flesh, often resulting in secondary complications, including reinfection and osteomyelitis, which may lead to repeated operations and amputations, and extended suffering for the victim. This is especially so when the weapons, which have often been designed to maim rather than to kill, are deployed in poor countries such as Cambodia with already weak medical infrastructures, and when part of their 'military utility' is coldly calculated in terms of their long-term power of impoverishment. Claims made in earlier chapters concerning a proper understanding of mines as weapons of attrition in strategies of total war, and sometimes, as McGrath suggests in Appendix 3, of genocide, would seem to lend weight to a prohibition of these weapons as causing unnecessary suffering.

The Asia Watch report *The Cowards' War* claimed that in Cambodia's recent conflict mines may have claimed more victims than any other weapon deployed, giving the country the world's highest proportion of amputees per head of population of any country in the world. The fact that over 80 per cent of the handicapped in Battambang have been maimed by mines can be seen as further proof that the 'unnecessary suffering' and the social and economic injuries produced by mines are in no way confined to the initial effects on the victim, and the health infrastructure, during the immediate recovery period. These are only the starting point of the 'mines multiplier' effect, an effect in which suffering and injury is spread upwards throughout the entire socio-economic hierarchies of affected nations; through families, communities and finally to the society as a whole. Given that

these long-term effects are calculated as part of the mines' design and can in no sense be described as accidental, can it really be suggested that such effects can be justified as representing a healthy balance between 'the necessities of war' and the 'laws of humanity'?

In areas such as Rattanak Mondul, where communal life is still being undermined and impoverished by mine warfare 'attacks' (whether in offence or defence) which occurred several years before, the concept of 'unnecessary suffering' is especially useful. With injuries to both livestock and humans growing daily, and an overall estimate of around 65 per cent of the district as unusable due to landmines, it becomes clear that whatever military utility mines may have had when laid, this has been clearly overrun by the extent of the long-term suffering and injury produced. This is true to the extent that if one conceives of the end of all military activity as the achievement of a 'victory', then mines as a class of weapon cease to have any long-term military utility. By their nature they render success a failure. As one visitor new to Rattanak Mondul noted in early 1993, 'No one will ever be able to claim a meaningful victory in Rattanak Mondul: they have poisoned the land.'[47]

Prohibition Against Starvation of the Civilian Population

The prohibition of starvation as a method of warfare codified in Article 54 of Protocol I represents a repudiation of a long-established practice (i.e. in siege warfare) which 'was something of an anomaly in view of the principle that civilians are not legitimate targets of attack in their own right'.[48] Greenwood notes that Article 54 represents 'a blend of customary law and innovative provisions which are not easy to disentangle but most of it is likely to become part of customary law with little difficulty if it does not already have that status'. Certainly, Article 54 paragraph 2, is likely to be have that status, and is of particular relevance here. It states:

> It is prohibited to attack, destroy, remove and *render useless objects indispensable to the survival of the civilian population, such as foodstuffs, agricultural areas for the production of foodstuffs, crops, livestock, drinking water installations and supplies and irrigation works*, for the specific purpose of denying them their sustenance value to the civilian population or to the adverse Party, whatever the motive, whether in order to starve out civilians, *to cause them to move away*, or for any other motive.

However, as one authority notes, 'this ... does not prohibit incidental distress of civilians resulting from otherwise lawful military operations'.[49] Nevertheless, under international law, fields may not be mined if such mining results in civilians in the area being left with so little food that they starve or are forced to move away.

As noted in Chapter 3, it is exactly this effect that had occurred in Rattanak Mondul and Banan districts during the 1989–91 offensive in Battambang province. While the populations of these areas were displaced during the fighting, a return to communes such as Ploumeas and Treng in Rattanak Mondul became almost entirely impossible due to the legacy of mines in these areas. Similarly, in Chay Meanchay commune in Banan, only four of the original seven villages were inhabitable at least two years after the episode of fighting that generated the current mines burden in that area. In fact, if it were not for the substantial relief efforts launched by the World Food Programme in such areas, it is likely that increases in death rates attributable to malnutrition would amount to starvation of the civilian population.

Perhaps the most graphic example in Battambang province of mine warfare having broken this customary provision can be found in Sanang commune of Banan district. The 1989–91 Khmer Rouge offensive through the area left the irrigation system sabotaged; the mining of the water gates and canal banks of the Boung Krossar system meant that it became too dangerous to repair, and the productivity of the entire commune was seriously debilitated. An agricultural expert working closely with local officials in the district estimated that roughly half the cultivatable hectarage of the commune was lost. Since these mines were laid only when the Khmer Rouge were retreating through the area in the wake of the CPAF counter-attack in the first quarter of 1991, the only conclusion to be drawn was that their intent was to sabotage the agricultural productivity of the commune and render it incapable of sustaining its civilian population. In other areas in Battambang mines have been randomly sown in agricultural areas with similar intent.

The Internal Face of the Conflict: Does the Law Still Offer Protection?

The Cambodian conflict cannot be considered as a purely 'international conflict', especially in the post-1989 period. While it has been argued here that its predominant face has been that of an international conflict, it would be unrealistic not to accept that the conflict has characteristics of an internal struggle as well. In so far as the conflict is classified as an internal conflict, to what extent are civilians protected from the effects of indiscriminate mine warfare, and to what extent does this warfare 'break the rules' if the internal face of the conflict is considered?

Since the Geneva Conventions of 1949 are now regarded as custom, and given the fact that Cambodia

is bound by the conventions, Common article 3 applies. The Article seeks to ensure basic standards of humane treatment, without distinction, for non-combatants in 'armed conflicts not of an international character'. Paragraph (1) (a) prohibits:

> violence to life and person, in particular murder of all kinds, mutilation, cruel treatment and torture.

Similar provisions are also reflected Article 75 (2) (a) of Protocol I, under the heading 'Fundamental Guarantees'. In the light of the evidence presented in this book the author will leave it up to the individual reader to determine to what extent mines have destroyed these fundamental humanitarian guarantees in Cambodia, guarantees which are designed to apply 'as a minimum'.

Since Common Article 3 is closely associated with human rights law and the traditions of protective law concerned with the victims of armed conflict, known collectively as the 'Geneva Stream', its acceptance into custom has been relatively easy.[50] However, herein also lies its major weakness since it fails to place restrictions on the 'means and methods' of warfare, an area that has traditionally been the focus of the 'Hague Stream'. Whereas the Geneva law seeks to protect the fundamental 'principles of humanity', the restrictions on 'means and methods' of combat in the Hague stream have meant that states are far less willing to accept its restrictions into binding custom. Understandably (from their point of view) states have been far more sensitive in this regard in relation to internal rather than international armed conflicts, since to accept regulation of the former poses challenges to the concept of state sovereignty. For this reason perhaps, Protocol II of 1977 which sought to expand the protections of Common Article 3 in relation to internal conflicts is widely viewed as disappointing, its provisions for the protection of the civilian population (such as Article 13) representing far less comprehensive treaty law than those of Protocol I.

Nevertheless, Gardam points out that a wide range of leading commentators have argued for the application of certain customary norms of international armed conflicts to internal conflicts.[51] For example, Article 13 of Protocol II, reflecting the principle of distinction and non-combatant immunity, is widely regarded as customary, and arguably applies to the conflicts covered by Common Article 3 of the Geneva Conventions. Gardam concludes her discussion of 'non-combatant immunity as a customary norm in internal conflict' by arguing that for conflicts which satisfy 'the high level of application of Protocol II' (i.e. a level of violence and intensity such as the conflict in Cambodia has clearly attained), Articles 48 and 'certain rules in Articles 51 and 57 of Protocol I, designed to give concrete substance to the somewhat abstract rules in Article 48, are also applicable' (to internal conflicts).[52] Such rules include the prohibition of indiscriminate warfare. Kalshoven has argued that the general rule of distinction applies even to 'low level internal conflicts', but that, 'the more effective protection against indiscriminate attacks is restricted to high level internal conflicts', which he designates as 'civil wars proper, in which the armed forces opposing the authorities in power are organised and occupy a part of the territory, and the hostilities are of considerable intensity and sufficient duration'.[53]

As such, most of the arguments made above, from the application of the customary norms of the international law of armed conflict with regard to landmine warfare in Cambodia, in as much as it is an international conflict, would equally apply in as much as it is an internal one. As Gardam concludes, given the trend in practice towards non-internal armed conflicts as the predominant form of global conflict, for the traditional customary protections of the law – the principles of civilisation – to continue to have any relevance it must be accepted that , 'The time is past for States to maintain that the distinction between domestic and international concerns is immutable.'[54]

Lastly, even if the Cambodian conflict is viewed as being predominantly an internal conflict, international actions by third parties to the conflict, in relation to that conflict, are not above the sanctions of international law. In the *Nicaragua Case* (1986), the ICJ found that the United States was in breach of its obligations under Common Article I of the Geneva Conventions for disseminating a CIA manual entitled, *Psychological Operations in Guerrilla Warfare* to the 'Contras'. The ruling of the court was of the opinion that these actions encouraged this group to violate the provisions of Common Article 3, provisions the United States government was obliged 'to respect and to ensure respect for' under Common Article 1. Similarly, it might be argued that the actions of the British and Chinese governments, in as much as their training programmes mentioned above encouraged Cambodian armed factions to violate Common Article 3, were also in breach of their obligations to ensure respect for these rules, described by the court as 'a minimum yardstick'.

Conclusions and Recommendations

The existing customary provisions of the law would seem to proscribe indiscriminate mine-laying practices as documented here, primarily with reference to the *de facto* situation in Cambodia, and arguably even to the concept of modern anti-personnel mines *as a class of weapon*. However, it seems clear that such proscriptions count for very little in practice. Changes in international treaty law are needed that will give teeth to these customary norms in both international and non-international conflicts. If change does not occur then such norms will cease to have any relevance,which would constitute a great loss to the international system and the UN in particular, pledged as it is to defend and promote human rights worldwide.

While there are many measures that can be taken to 'deal' with the problems landmines produce, it is the root evil and that is anti-personnel mines themselves – that must be addressed. Many of those involved in the 'mines world' – deminers, prosthetists and, increasingly, relief and development workers with experience of landmine-affected communities – are increasingly coming to realise that the most effective way of tackling the landmine problem is to improve and/or amend existing international treaty law, and its terms of applicability and enforcement. As has recently been suggested by a leading expert in the field, [55] such changes fall into three categories of option: first, changes that are needed for compliance with the existing law, second, changes that might be desirable to the law itself (in particular the 1980 Land Mines Protocol), and lastly, alternative solutions that might go radically further than current provisions allow for. It is suggested here that while for treaty law to 'catch up' with custom only the third option will do, progress within either of the two other options is long overdue, and may be all that is possible in the short-term.

In a statement issued in October 1992, [56] the ICRC, after reviewing the Land Mines Protocol, noted that malpractice involving mines is far from restricted to the Cambodian case alone:

Unfortunately, as we know only too well, the actual use of mines tends to reflect anything but conformity with these rules. We have seen such a massive indiscriminate use of mines that there are now millions of mines strewn in countries that have been involved in armed conflict. These mines, and those who have been responsible for their use, have blindly killed or injured countless innocent victims and they continue to do so after the conflicts are over. Huge expanses of land are now uncultivatable, preventing people from returning to their homes. The full extent of this scourge has become apparent in countries where mine clearance teams are presently facing an unbelievably slow and dangerous task.

The statement then proceeds to make several recommendations for strengthening the Land Mines Protocol, and increasing compliance with it. First, with only 32 signatories to the 1980 Convention, what the statement calls 'a very disappointing rate of participation', there is a clear need for more states to show their concern for this issue, to ratify the treaty and to encourage others to do so. In particular those nations who have been responsible for the design, manufacture and export of these devices as a commercial or politically driven activity, and those who have purchased licences to produce mines, should feel obliged to sign the protocol and initiate activities to ensure that (even) the current law is complied with, and that the training of armed forces of states or armed parties to internal conflicts reflects that law.

However, there are several areas in which it is desirable to strengthen the existing provisions of the treaty law. For example, a formal application of the law to non-international armed conflicts, which accounts for the combat scenarios within which the majority of contemporary mine-laying takes place, is vital. Measures should also be considered for the inclusion of implementation provisions, as has been suggested by France in its recent request for a review conference for the 1981 Convention. Such measures should also provide for means of verification of compliance with the law. Also in several important areas the Land Mines Protocol is very weak and desperately needs to be strengthened. As a recent paper noted:

> much of this [the LMP] appears to provide civilians with protection, but suffers from 'get out' clauses which prioritise military need over civilian protection; for example, to protect civilians from the effects of mines military authorities must take all 'feasible', 'practicable or practically possible' precautions, and warnings should be given 'unless circumstances do not permit'; thus military necessity is prioritised over civilian protection.[57]

McGrath has written:

> *unless circumstances do not permit* ... what does that mean in practice? What circumstances? That a Serbian corporal doesn't like Muslims – is that an acceptable circumstance? That the Ba'athist regime in Iraq wants to drive the Marsh Arabs out of their homes – surely one of Saddam's commanders could justify those circumstances as not permitting a warning? Effectively the decision depends on the morality of the local military commander, and if that was sufficient to ensure the sanctity of civilians in wartime there would be no need for international laws anyway. In short – the Protocol has value only as a record of the low regard in which the international community holds the lives of poor, unrepresented civilian communities.[58]

McGrath, with Eric Stover, further addressed the issue of the quality of existing international regulations in the Asia Watch report, *The Cowards' War*. With regard to the use of plastic mines,[59] they write:

> Protocol I also fails to address reality. It bans the use of plastic shrapnel, but today many mines are being manufactured with hard plastic casings. Even though manufacturers can argue that the plastic casing is there to make the mine lighter and more durable, it can also turn into shrapnel after the explosion and become embedded in wounds.

Stricter rules should address this situation, including more careful regulation of the duty to register and remove minefields.

Nevertheless, even with such changes the fundamental problems associated with mine warfare would remain. These revolve around the technical difficulties, and dangers, of removing minefields (assuming finance is available and, even if duly registered and marked, which most are not), and the increasing difficulties experienced in detecting modern mine technology (as noted above). To what extent is it practical to expect 'lawless factions', such as the Khmer Rouge to self-impose even stricter controls than those nominally in place at present? Their utter refusal to abide by the Paris Peace Accords suggests an attitude concerning respect for multilateral treaties and international law, shared no doubt by many other armed parties to internal conflicts, which is utterly at variance with any realistic possibilities of imposing effective controls to ensure mine usage 'according to the rules'. In the hands of such people mines will always be a weapon whose criminal potential in practice, will always outweigh 'the laws of humanity'. Such difficult realities require a more radical approach than mere strengthening or revision of existing provisions.

For these reasons a growing body of opinion feels that a radical new approach is urgently required, and that these measures should not stop short of a complete ban. As the authors of *The Cowards' War* acknowledge, 'While such a law might not entirely eliminate the use of mines, it would stigmatise them, in much the same way that chemical weapons are now vilified'. Interestingly,[60] some of the most forthright exponents of a ban on landmines as a class of weapon which cannot be used discriminately have come from within the military. In the words of Sgt. Mjr. Ho Kianga of the New Zealand detachment of the UN's MCTU in Battambang, anti-personnel landmines are 'not a needed item, either militarily or in civilian life'. For the military, other (better) methods are available for area denial purposes.

For Cambodia and many other countries such changes in international law would be too late. The only positive thing that can be said of this disaster is that if the Cambodian experience can serve to show the inhumanity of these weapons and the need for changes to the law, and those changes subsequently occur, then the immense 'unnecessary suffering' wrought on the Cambodian nation will not have been entirely in vain. Without such changes still more nations will inevitably fall foul of landmines. The danger is that these sufferings will pass unnoticed, and that nothing will change.

Appendix 1
Rattanak Mondul: Survivors of Landmine Accidents Residing in the District

Statistics received from the district authorities, February 1993

NB These statistics are based on the records kept by commune and village leaders. As with most Cambodian statistics they are not 100 per cent reliable. Verification of these records showed that while all those shown here do live in the district, many others have also been injured by landmines but their names do not appear in these records. All villages shown as part of Treng and Ploumeas communes are now residents of Beng Ampil Camp, apart from Kilo 38 village.

Name	Age	Sex	Injury	Activity at time	Date	Village	Commune
Chim San	35	Male	Right Leg Amputation	In Combat	12/2/88	Kilo 38	Treng
Chhon Savoeun	32	Female	Right Leg Amputation	Harvesting	2/1/89	Kilo 38	Treng
Phan Phon	42	Male	Left Leg Amputation	Collecting Wood	5/4/86	Kilo 38	Treng
Moun Nouth	16	Female	Left Leg Amputation	Harvesting Rice	8/1/89	Kilo 38	Treng
Chhob Thy	32	Male	Right Leg Amputation	Cutting Bamboo	3/8/92	Kilo 38	Treng
Tot Em	32	Male	Left Hand Amputation	Cutting Bamboo	17/1/92	Kilo 38	Treng
Chhoub Chieng	30	Male	Left Leg Amputation	Fighting	4/6/90	Kilo 38	Treng
Neang Chom	32	Male	Leg Amputation	Collecting Wood	28/10/91	Kilo 38	Treng
Yoeung Chhung	32	Male	Leg Amputation	Collecting Wood	4/9/91	Kilo 38	Treng
Meth Noeun	25	Male	Leg Amputation	Cutting Wood	17/4/89	Kilo 38	Treng
Maew Mom	17	Male	Leg Amputation	Cutting Thatch	23/7/92	Kilo 38	Treng
Bou Thou	30	Male	Leg Amputation	Cutting Bamboo	28/3/92	Kilo 38	Treng
Lon Salin	32	Female	Leg Amputation	Cutting Thatch	17/12/92	Kilo 38	Treng
Kim Khom	22	Male	Left Leg Amputation	Collecting Wood	16/7/91	Pchaeu	Treng
Om Keang	40	Male	Blind Left Eye	Cutting Trees	22/3/81	Pchaeu	Treng
Nouen Muerm	61	Male	Right Leg Amputation	'Guarding' a Trip Wire	11/10/90	Pchaeu	Treng
Ti Toie	25	Male	Left Leg Amputation	Collecting Wood	3/2/88	Pchaeu	Treng
Soc Chea	33	Male	Left Leg Amputation	Collecting Wood	18/2/89	Pchaeu	Treng
Oun Sa Em	28	Female	Left Leg Amputation	Collecting Wood	12/5/91	Pchaeu	Treng
Karoeung Bou	20	Male	Leg Amputation	Collecting Wood	7/9/91	Pchaeu	Treng
Tuern Sarim	25	Male	Right Leg Amputation	Harvesting	2/1/89	Pchaeu	Treng
Chan Sokorn	23	Male	Left Leg Amputation	Cutting Wood	19/4/88	Pchaeu	Treng
Hai Jon	24	Male	Left Leg Amputation	Cutting Wood	26/2/93	Pchaeu	Treng
Lem Nouern	35	Male	Leg Amputation	Fishing	3/2/75	Pchaeu	Treng
Kong Kann	45	Male	Blind in Both Eyes,	Cutting Wood	18/9/91	Pchaeu	Treng
Sang Pia	28	Male	Right Leg Amputation	Soldier	28/11/91	Pchaeu	Treng
Ong Luot	41	Male	Double Leg Amputation	Cutting Wood	31/10/82	Pchaeu	Treng
Prouen Cham	44	Male	Left Leg Amputation	Cutting Wood	14/5/82	Pchaeu	Treng
Deat Sary	27	Female	Left Leg Amputation (bk)	Cutting Cane	28/7/92	Pchaeu	Treng
Nic Khom	29	Male	Left Leg Amputation (bk)	Soldier	27/12/82	Pchaeu	Treng
Eem Lot	58	Male	Right Leg Amputation	Soldier	25/10/82	Pchaeu	Treng
Gneth Gneam	26	Male	Right Leg Amputation (bk)	Soldier	14/2/91	Chea-Montray	Treng
Chan Hang	26	Male	Right Leg Amputation (bk)	Soldier	17/12/88	Chea-Montray	Treng
Cang Lin	29	Male	Right Leg Amputation (bk)	Soldier	4/2/90	Chea-Montray	Treng
Pong Chuern	43	Male	Right Leg Amputation (bk)	Demining	3/11/92	Chea-Montray	Treng
Tith Poue	20	Male	Right Leg Amputation (bk)	Cutting Wood	3/5/92	Chea-Montray	Treng
Siem Tuern	32	Male	Left Leg Amputation (bk)	Demining	26/3/84	Chea-Montray	Treng
Khee Phe	20	Male	Left Leg Amputation	Cutting Wood	12/12/91	Chea-Montray	Treng
Khatt So Piem	29	Male	Left Leg Amputation (bk)	Gardening	27/2/90	Chea-Montray	Treng
Nem Si Peang	32	Male	Left Hand Amputation	Cutting Bamboo	7/4/82	Chea-Montray	Treng
Teang Chieang	26	Male	Leg Amputation	Cutting Wood	21/7/92	Chea-Montray	Treng
Ouk Bou	38	Male	Left Leg Amputation	Cutting Wood	4/5/88	Chea-Montray	Treng
Ping Lath	24	Male	Leg Amputation	Cutting Wood	19/11/92	Chea-Montray	Treng

Name	Age	Sex	Injury	Activity at time	Date	Village	Commune
Ram Ronn	28	Male	Leg Amputation	Cutting Thatch	8/9/92	Chea-Montray	Treng
Som Chuern	33	Male	Left Leg Amputation	Soldier	17/9/82	Chea-Montray	Treng
Hann Neak	52	Male	Leg Amputation (ak)	Cutting Wood	19/5/87	Chisang	Treng
Leap Kik	30	Male	Leg Amputation (ak)	Cutting Wood	5/6/85	Chisang	Treng
Koeut Brem	50	Male	Right Leg Amputation	Building Ditches (K5 – Samlaut)	8/1/85	Chisang	Treng
Dith Loue	48	Male	Left Leg Amputation (bk)	Building Ditches (K5 – Pailin)	10/2/85	Chisang	Treng
Do Ong Rem	30	Female	Right Leg Amputation (bk)	Taking Water	18/4/88	Chisang	Treng
Diem Koll	27	Male	Right Leg Amputation (ak)	Cutting Wood	1/2/90	Chisang	Treng
Sang Sam	45	Male	Right Leg Amputation (bk)	Cutting Wood	13/3/86	Chisang	Treng
Ma Hom Ngel	50	Male	Left Leg Amputation	Cutting Wood	20/12/88	Chisang	Treng
Prak Nuer	60	Male	Left Leg Amputation (bk)	Cutting Rattan	5/8/92	Chisang	Treng
Nang Ni	29	Male	Right Leg Amputation (bk)	Cutting Wood	4/3/90	Kilo	Treng
Mork Pheap	34	Male	Right Hand Amputation	Demining	17/12/90	Kilo	Treng
Sou Sann	28	Male	Right Leg Amputation (ak)	Cutting Wood	13/4/82	Kilo	Treng
You Thon	39	Male	Left Leg Amputation (bk)	Collecting Food	20/6/82	Kilo	Treng
Sea Noum	24	Male	Right Leg Amputation (bk)	Cutting Wood	1/11/90	Kilo	Treng
Hav Leach	64	Male	Right Leg Amputation (bk)	Clearing Trees	7/2/88	Kilo	Treng
Chak Varna	26	Male	Right Hand Amputation	Demining	19/1/88	Kilo	Treng
Sang Em	36	Male	Left Leg Amputation	Cutting Wood	26/3/91	Kilo	Treng
Chom Ran Thong	17	Male	Right Leg Amputation	Cutting Wood	29/9/89	Kilo	Treng
Chhuth Sakonn	26	Male	Left Leg Amputation	Cutting Wood	4/7/88	Kilo	Treng
Thai Lak	55	Male	Left Hand Amputation	Gardening	3/5/88	Kilo	Treng
Tabb Yan	34	Male	Right Leg Amputation	Cutting Wood	21/5/90	Kilo	Treng
Eng Souern	22	Male	Right Leg	Cutting Wood	7/8/90	Kilo	Treng
Watt My	28	Male	Left Leg Amputation	Cutting Wood	1/10/88	Kilo	Treng
Pen Konn	25	Male	Leg Amputation (ak)	Cutting Wood	15/12/88	Kilo	Treng
Dim Joie	29	Male	Leg Amputation	Cutting Thatch	17/3/92	Kilo	Treng
Kim Thouern	34	Male	Left Leg Amputation (bk)	Cutting Wood	19/2/90	Kilo	Treng
Chhin Sokornn	27	Male	Left Leg Amputation	Cutting Wood	4/3/88	Kilo	Treng
Neang Bem	23	Male	Stomach Injury	Cutting Wood	26/6/90	Kilo	Treng
Chuk Chea	49	Female	Left Leg Amputation	Cutting Thatch	3/9/90	Kilo	Treng
Nem Neang	24	Male	Left Leg Amputation	Cutting Wood	14/10/90	Kilo	Treng
Neng Khim	21	Male	Leg Amputation	Cutting Wood	11/12/90	Kilo	Treng
Ta Tuern	34	Male	Left Leg Amputation	Cutting Thatch	4/8/90	Kilo	Treng
Sou Souern	29	Male	Left Hand Amputation	Demining	16/3/91	Kilo	Treng
Roung Pou	38	Male	Left Hand Amputation	Demining	18/7/90	Kilo	Treng
Nout Bun Sen	35	Male	Right Leg Amputation	Soldier	10/5/90	Kilo	Treng
Klay Poue	22	Male	Left Leg Amputation	Wood Collecting	17/2/91	Kilo	Treng
Lin Pou	23	Male	Left Hand Amputation	Demining	23/8/92	Kilo	Treng
Chour Seap	49	Male	Right Leg Amputation	Cutting Wood	1/9/91	Tropangleang	Ploumeas
Sy Yang	51	Male	Blind Both Eyes	Cutting Wood	5/6/80	Tropangleang	Ploumeas
Vann Pong	26	Male	Body Injuries (Kidney)	Cutting Wood	4/9/84	Tropangleang	Ploumeas
Charl Sourn	35	Female	Blind Left Eye	Cutting Wood	15/10/89	Tropangleang	Ploumeas
Chay Moung	61	Male	Right Leg Amputation (bk)	Cutting Wood	1/4/84	Tropangleang	Ploumeas
Chinn Chourn	39	Male	Right Leg Amputation (bk)	Cutting Wood	5/4/92	Tropangleang	Ploumeas
Chea Chan	33	Male	Left Leg Amputation (bk)	Building Wood	1/2/90	Tropangleang	Ploumeas
Perk Poung	26	Male	Left Leg Amputation (bk)	Cutting Wood	1/1/91	Tropangleang	Ploumeas
Tourn Kann	14	Male	Left Leg Amputation	Cutting Bamboo	1/1/91	Tropangleang	Ploumeas
Yim Khun	36	Male	Right Hand Amputation	Cutting Bamboo	5/10/92	Tropangleang	Ploumeas
Poul Ky	44	Male	Right Leg Amputation (bk)	Cutting Wood	5/11/87	Tropangleang	Ploumeas
Tourn Em	55	Male	Right Hand Amputation	Cutting Wood	1/9/84	Tropangleang	Ploumeas
Chim Charm	44	Male	Right Leg Amputation	Cutting Wood	2/1/92	Tropangleang	Ploumeas
Gnau Gneang	32	Male	Right Leg Amputation (bk)	Cutting Wood	7/1/89	Tropangleang	Ploumeas
Som Heang	31	Male	Left Leg Amputation (bk)	Collecting Wood	8/9/89	Tropangleang	Ploumeas
Neam Herm	36	Male	Left Leg Amputation	Collecting Wood	2/7/80	Tropangleang	Ploumeas
Cheurn Chan	34	Male	Double Leg Amputation	Cutting Wood	5/6/86	Tropangleang	Ploumeas
Kim Som Butt	38	Male	Right Leg Amputation (bk)	Cutting Wood	10/5/91	Tropangleang	Ploumeas
Sing Hem	39	Male	Left Leg Amputation (bk)	Cutting Bamboo	3/10/91	Tropangleang	Ploumeas
Herm Sokha	25	Male	Right Leg Amputation (bk)	Cutting Wood	11/7/87	Boueng Ktom	Ploumeas
Young Dol	46	Male	Right Leg Amputation	Cutting Wood	5/4/92	Boueng Ktom	Ploumeas
Maew Mon	20	Male	Left Leg Amputation	Cutting Wood	1/9/87	Boueng Ktom	Ploumeas

Name	Age	Sex	Injury	Activity at time	Date	Village	Commune
Gnou Gnong	20	Male	Right Leg Amputation (ak)	Cutting Rattan	1/12/85	Boueng Ktom	Ploumeas
Vern Chrec	20	Male	Double Leg Amputation(bk)	Digging	12/4/91	Boueng Ktom	Ploumea
Heang Hun	18	Male	Right Leg Amputation (bk)	Cutting Wood	23/10/92	Boueng Ktom	Ploumeas
Neal Hay	36	Male	Blind Both Eyes	Demining	16/4/86	Watt	Ploumeas
Pin Chatt	24	Male	All Body ?	Clearing Ground	11/10/89	Watt	Ploumeas
Poung Ack	52	Male	Right Hand Amputation	Cutting Wood	3/6/85	Watt	Ploumeas
Soc Vann	26	Female	Blind Both Eyes	Cutting Wood	1/3/92	Chipang	Ploumeas
Chann Den Neang	26	Male	Left Leg Amputation (bk)	Cutting Wood	13/7/87	Chipang	Ploumeas
Put Chuuern	37	Male	Left Leg Amputation (bk)	Cutting Wood	1/12/87	Chipang	Ploumeas
Put Pouern	26	Male	Left Leg Amputation (ak)	Cutting Wood	26/1/88	Chipang	Ploumeas
Put Thorn	26	Male	Left Leg Amputation (ak)	Cutting Wood	26/1/88	Chipang	Ploumeas
Hut Preang	53	Male	Left Leg Amputation (bk)	Working in Paddy	4/10/73	Chipang	Ploumeas
Pan Saroun	29	Male	Right Leg Amputation (bk)	Cutting Wood	10/2/87	Chipang	Ploumeas
Sor Bun Tuern	39	Male	Blind Both Eyes, Right Hand Amputation	Cutting Wood	29/5/92	Chipang	Ploumeas
Hut Rokang	41	Male	Right Leg Amputation	Cutting Wood	17/4/87	Chipang	Ploumeas
Meurn Toy	33	Male	Right Hand Amputation	Cutting Wood	4/3/87	Chipang	Ploumeas
Dong Uern	51	Female	Right Leg Amputation (bk)	Cutting Thatch	6/2/87	Chipang	Ploumeas
Cham Sok	37	Male	Left Hand Amputation	Cutting Wood	24/8/85	Chipang	Ploumeas
Chourn Cheoung	33	Male	Right Hand Amputation	Cutting Bamboo	13/4/85	Chipang	Ploumeas
Pek Peng	29	Male	Left Leg Amputation	Cutting Rattan	2/6/92	Chipang	Ploumeas
Lok Ti	27	Male	Right Leg Amputation (bk)	Cutting Wood	16/11/90	Ploumeas	Ploumeas
Lok Rit	22	Male	Right Leg Amputation (bk)	Cutting Wood	8/9/89	Ploumeas	Ploumeas
Loeb Vuthi	32	Male	Right Leg Amputation (bk)	Clearing Farmland	8/1/86	Ploumeas	Ploumeas
Chuerm Poue	20	Male	Right Leg Amputation (bk)	Cutting Wood	7/6/89	Ploumeas	Ploumeas
Ngar Chann	29	Male	Right Leg Amputation (bk)	Cutting Wood	7/2/91	Ploumeas	Ploumeas
Lout Rom	39	Male	Left Leg Amputation (bk)	Cutting Wood	6/9/92	Ploumeas	Ploumea
Lout Heng	29	Male	Right Leg Amputation(bk)	Cutting Wood	8/2/92	Ploumeas	Ploumeas
Dop Diem	33	Male	Right Leg Amputation(bk)	Cutting Wood	8/2/92	Ploumeas	Ploumea
Khieu Loy	35	Female	Right Leg Amputation (ak)	Cutting Wood	2/2/92	Ploumeas	Ploumeas
Long Sokorn	22	Female	Right Leg Amputation (bk)	Cutting Thatch	14/5/92	Ploumeas	Ploumeas
Krev Choum	65	Male	Right Leg Amputation (bk)	Gardening	17/10/91	Ploumeas	Ploumeas
Pim Bar	65	Female	All Body ?	Gardening	12/2/92	Ploumeas	Ploumeas
Pim Reav	43	Female	All Body ?	Gardening	12/2/92	Ploumeas	Ploumeas
Puk Nang	18	Male	Left Leg Amputation (bk)	Clearing Farmland	16/7/92	Ploumeas	Ploumeas
Rouen Chuern	46	Male	All Body ?	Gardening	4/11/89	Ploumeas	Ploumeas
Yok Seang	30	Male	Both Hand Amp & Both Eyes	Gardening	5/12/86	Ploumeas	Ploumea
Chay Lon	49	Male	Right Leg Amputation (bk)	Cutting Wood	23/10/92	Ploumeas	Ploumeas
Et Sophal	32	Male	Left Leg Amputation	Cutting Wood	4/12/91	Beng Ampil	Sdao
Sdeng Phal	12	Male	Right Leg Amputation (ak)	Herding Cows	25/7/92	Beng Ampil	Sdao
Kus Sovann	26	Male	Left Leg Amputation	Demining	27/8/89	Beng Ampil	Sdao
Ang Voeun	21	Male	Stomach Injuries	Gardening	21/10/91	Beng Ampil	Sdao
Ram Rar	8	Male	Injured Chest	Picked up Mine	19/4/92	Beng Ampil	Sdao
Ram Rat	7	Male	Back ?	Picked up Mine	19/4/92	Beng Ampil	Sdao
Ram Ret	5	Male	All Body ?	Picked up Mine	19/4/92	Beng Ampil	Sdao
Chourn Heam	28	Male	All Body ?	Cutting Wood	23/1/84	Beng Ampil	Sdao
Phal Lar	42	Female	Leg Amputation	Cutting Thatch	27/12/91	Beng Ampil	Sdao
Long Khim	28	Male	Leg Amputation	Cutting Wood	27/10/88	Sdao	Sdao
Ny Moa	68	Male	Leg Amputation	Gardening	25/12/91	Sdao	Sdao
Yung Hae	37	Male	Leg Amputation	Cutting Wood	7/10/91	Sdao	Sdao
Kheang Yam	25	Male	Amputation of Part of Foot	Cutting Wood	9/11/91	Sdao	Sdao
Mom Sophea`	17	Female	Right Leg Amputation	Cutting Bamboo	9/9/92	Sdao	Sdao
Kov Saret	32	Male	Amputation of Leg	Cutting Wood	20/8/90	Sdao	Sdao
Som Sen	43	Male	Left Leg Amputation	Soldier	10/10/87	Sreangdong	Sdao
Ney Phoeut	37	Male	Left Leg Amputation	Cutting Wood	16/7/86	Sreangdong	Sdao
Ney Khun	35	Male	Left Hand Amputation	Demining	26/9/88	Sreangdong	Sdao
Noy Kong	63	Male	Left Leg Amputation	Gardening	25/8/88	Sreangdong	Sdao
Mes Samos	27	Male	Injury to Abdomen	Cutting Wood	17/3/89	Sreangdong	Sdao
Chrang Srac	17	Male	Blinded Left Eye	Demining	23/5/90	Sreangdong	Sdao
Prav Tom	26	Male	Left Leg Amputation	Cutting Wood	27/6/89	Sreangdong	Sdao
Yot Sourm	27	Female	Left Leg Amputation	Cutting Thatch	15/6/87	Sreangdong	Sdao
Rath Sokhom	29	Male	Right Leg Amputation, Blind	Border Guard	7/1/85	Samlot	Sdao
Chhoeun Chhom	29	Male	Right Leg Amputation	Guard in Village	8/11/85	Samlot	Sdao

Name	Age	Sex	Injury	Activity at time	Date	Village	Commune
Chhinh Cha	29	Male	Right Leg Amputation	Collecting Wood	23/5/87	Samlot	Sdao
Houen Sarouen	29	Male	Right Leg Amputation	Collecting Wood	14/10/87	Samlot	Sdao
Lim Sen	39	Male	Left Leg Amputation	Collecting Wood	15/3/86	Samlot	Sdao
Khem Sokhom	27	Male	Left Leg Amputation	Cutting Thatch	22/10/92	Samlot	Sdao
Douk Vai	64	Male	All Body ?	Fishing	12/1/84	Samlot	Sdao
Khrong Chhoeun	33	Male	Leg Amputation	Cutting Wood	18/4/84	Samlot	Sdao
Sin Sokon	25	Male	Leg Amputation	Cutting Wood	28/11/85	Samlot	Sdao
Yang Sa Vouern	30	Female	Leg Amputation	Collecting Thatch	3/4/92	Samlot	Sdao
Ches Sary	25	Female	Left Leg Amputation (bk)	Cutting Bamboo	5/7/92	Anlong Pouk	Andao Hep
Chan Din	36	Male	Left Leg Amputation	Cutting Wood	15/8/90	Anlong Pouk	Andao Hep
Souer Sa Muth	34	Male	Left Leg Amputation	Cutting Wood	29/3/84	Anlong Pouk	Andao Hep
Pheach Sa Oeun	26	Male	Broken Leg	Cutting Wood	10/5/90	Anlong Pouk	Andao Hep
Sonn Thi	39	Female	Right Leg Amputation (bk)	Cutting Cane	19/5/92	Anlong Pouk	Andao Hep
Sao San	29	Male	Right Leg Amputation	Fishing	30/3/86	Anlong Pouk	Andao Hep
Na Ny	35	Male	Left Hand Amputation	Demining	8/8/86	Anlong Pouk	Andao Hep
Hou Rath	24	Male	Left Leg Amputation	Cutting Wood	24/8/86	Anlong Pouk	Andao Hep
Vuth Yuong	29	Male	Right Leg Amputation	Cutting Thatch	3/1/89	Anlong Pouk	Andao Hep
Dem Ang	22	Male	Left Leg Amputation	Cutting Wood	6/7/92	Anlong Pouk	Andao Hep
Yem Yan	30	Male	Left Leg Amputation	Cutting Wood	28/5/90	Anlong Pouk	Andao Hep
Lach Dan	25	Male	Left Leg Amputation	Soldier	20/5/80	Anlong Pouk	Andao Hep
Tha Thou	53	Male	Right Leg Amputation	Unknown – Returnee	3/4/85	Anlong Pouk	Andao Hep
Kom Chhan	51	Male	Right Leg Amputation	Cutting Thatch	5/10/87	Orangkhan	Andao Hep
Tith Tinn	32	Male	Right Leg Amputation	Cutting Wood	28/1/89	Orangkhan	Andao Hep
Sen Soeurth	37	Male	Left Leg Amputation	Building Ditch (K5)	5/8/85	Orangkhan	Andao Hep
Huoth Thuern	28	Male	Right Leg Amputation	Herding Cattle	7/1/81	Orangkhan	Andao Hep
Kell Kim	32	Male	Left Leg Amputation	Soldier	10/9/91	Orangkhan	Andao Hep
Bun Ses	58	Male	Right Leg Amputation	Soldier	5/9/79	Orangkhan	Andao Hep
Yin Ry	20	Male	Left Leg Amputation	Cutting Wood	10/4/91	Orangkhan	Andao Hep
Porn Ren	39	Male	Left Arm Amputation	Demining	10/3/90	Orangkhan	Andao Hep
Kuon Chayly	23	Male	Left Leg Amputation	Cutting Thatch	18/11/92	Orangkhan	Andao Hep
Soth Souern	27	Female	Left Leg Amputation	Cutting Bamboo	1/12/90	Orangkhan	Andao Hep
Som Yean	47	Male	Left Leg Amputation	Cutting Wood	5/10/84	Orangkhan	Andao Hep
Prom Bun Khoeurn	41	Male	Left Leg Amputation	Cutting Thatch	7/7/89	Orangkhan	Andao Hep
Som Roth	20	Male	Left Leg Amputation	Cutting Thatch	15/10/89	Orangkhan	Andao Hep
Chim Chor	24	Male	Left Leg Amputation	Digging Ditches (K5)	29/3/84	Tasanh	Andao Hep
San Reth	34	Male	Left Leg Amputation	Cutting Wood	13/3/90	Tasanh	Andao Hep
Noer Nath	19	Male	Right Leg Amputation	Demining	10/3/89	Tasanh	Andao Hep
Poch Sam	28	Male	Left Leg Amputation	Cutting Wood	3/4/91	Tasanh	Andao Hep
Ton Khan	37	Male	Blinded	Demining	3/1/89	Tasanh	Andao Hep
Lan Rey	21	Male	Blinded	Demining	10/2/91	Tasanh	Andao Hep
Leam Bach	24	Male	Blinded	Demining	24/6/91	Tasanh	Andao Hep
Sam Ren	29	Male	Left Leg Amputation	Returnee – Unknown		Tasanh	Andao Hep
Tem Penn	38	Male	Left Leg Amputation	Returnee – Unknown		Tasanh	Andao Hep
San Vean	33	Male	Left Leg Amputation	Returnee – Unknown		Tasanh	Andao Hep
Hun Nen	32	Male	Right Leg Amputation	Returnee – Unknown		Tasanh	Andao Hep
Bun Van	33	Male	Left Leg Amputation	Returnee – Unknown		Tasanh	Andao Hep
Bov Rom	39	Male	Right Leg Amputation	Returnee – Unknown		Tasanh	Andao Hep
Sok Pov	25	Male	Left Leg Amputation	Returnee – Unknown		Tasanh	Andao Hep
Som Bou	26	Male	Right Leg Amputation	Cutting Wood	20/11/91	Thmar Prous	Andao Hep
Leuth Loum	23	Male	Left Hand Amputation	Demining	10/5/91	Thmar Prous	Andao Hep
Prom Pheth	31	Male	Left Leg Amputation	Cutting Wood	29/11/87	Thmar Prous	Andao Hep
Souer Nouth	31	Male	Left Hand Amputation	Demining	20/3/87	Thmar Prous	Andao Hep
Thy Nath	23	Male	Left Leg Amputation	Cutting Wood	10/3/91	Thmar Prous	Andao Hep
Chhim Samouen	25	Male	Left Leg Amputation	Cutting Thatch	19/3/91	Thmar Prous	Andao Hep
Chath Vouem	39	Male	Right Leg Amputation	Collecting Wood	30/9/91	Thmar Prous	Andao Hep
Ya Chhouen	40	Male	Left Hand Amputation	Demining	10/9/87	Thmar Prous	Andao Hep
Dim Nuy	34	Male	Left Leg Amputation	Cutting Wood	5/6/92	Thmar Prous	Andao Hep
Hory Vith	15	Male	Right Leg Amputation	Herding Cattle	2/4/92	Thmar Prous	Andao Hep
San Team	29	Male	Blinded in One Eye	Demining	15/6/88	Thmar Prous	Andao Hep

Appendix 2
Rattanak Mondul: Deaths by Landmines 1979–93

Statistics received from the district authorities, March 1993

NB While it is likely that the large number of young men in the 18–25 age group were mostly young conscript soldiers from the district who died from landmine injuries – probably on active service in the Pailin area (until 1989) and thereafter in the military zone – attention should also be drawn to the large numbers of older men, as well as women and children appearing in these statistics.

However, as the figures for survivors of landmine accidents reveal, the commonest age group for civilians to have landmine accidents while cutting wood etc is in the 20–30 age group. Thus not all of those dying in that age group will have been soldiers. It should also be remembered that these figures are *conservative* – many more people will have perished than are recorded here. This is due to weaknesses of Cambodian record-keeping.

Number	Name	Age	Sex	Date of Death	Village	Commune
1	Chen Kun	25	Female	20/11/91	Beng Ampil	Sdao
2	Kem Ong	49	Male	6/5/91	Beng Ampil	Sdao
3	Mom Vun	19	Male	17/2/93	Beng Ampil	Sdao
4	Horm Sambath	19	Male	15/2/91	Beng Ampil	Sdao
5	Huy Horn	24	Male	20/11/91	Beng Ampil	Sdao
6	Prom Samouen	34	Male	15/2/91	Beng Ampil	Sdao
7	Yeng Vong	28	Male	14/6/92	Beng Ampil	Sdao
8	Yos Mos	12	Male	17/2/93	Sdao	Sdao
9	Moa Phnum	39	Male	7/5/86	Sdao	Sdao
10	Van Rouang	27	Male	18/7/92	Sdao	Sdao
11	Lon Chandy	20	Male	19/3/85	Sdao	Sdao
12	Bung Ha	41	Male	16/4/83	Sdao	Sdao
13	Toy Vany	21	Male	22/2/84	Sdao	Sdao
14	Noun Nouern	38	Male	6/1/87	Sdao	Sdao
15	Ven Jamran	20	Female	12/3/91	Sdao	Sdao
16	Choa Seang	43	Male	1/7/85	Sdao	Sdao
17	Chim Vibol	26	Male	3/2/88	Sdao	Sdao
18	Chif Sung	32	Male	4/4/87	Sdao	Sdao
19	Sor Sung	41	Male	17/8/91	Sdao	Sdao
20	Long Ley	48	Male	15/7/85	Sdao	Sdao
21	Chung Bos	22	Male	12/3/83	Sdao	Sdao
22	Chek Vasna	16	Male	14/2/93	Sdao	Sdao
23	Chin Cheang	39	Male	19/11/87	Sdao	Sdao
24	Sin Thea	60	Male	11/12/88	Sdao	Sdao
25	Vuern Vang	28	Male	16/1/88	Samlot	Sdao
26	Ong Tang	39	Male	4/7/85	Samlot	Sdao
27	Sang Amara	20	Male	20/3/83	Samlot	Sdao
28	Tun Sophal	20	Male	10/12/90	Samlot	Sdao
29	Pung Pean	35	Male	4/10/83	Samlot	Sdao
30	Seng Reng	27	Male	3/11/88	Samlot	Sdao
31	Let Sambat	29	Male	15/11/86	Samlot	Sdao
32	Yuerm Ren	25	Male	15/1/80	Samlot	Sdao
33	Chor Puk	20	Male	1/5/89	Samlot	Sdao
34	Hong Genorlass	29	Male	12/7/90	Samlot	Sdao
35	Rem Leng	20	Male	11/12/80	Samlot	Sdao
36	Rom Saran	20	Male	11/11/89	Samlot	Sdao

Number	*Name*	*Age*	*Sex*	*Date of Death*	*Village*	*Commune*
37	Key Prill	37	Male	23/3/87	Samlot	Sdao
38	Long Sary	29	Male	7/5/84	Samlot	Sdao
39	Toy Chay	27	Male	8/6/87	Samlot	Sdao
40	Duern Treu	21	Male	11/12/90	Samlot	Sdao
41	Leng Sleck	35	Male	19/9/91	Sreangdong	Sdao
42	Doll Kuy	37	Male	2/6/90	Sreangdong	Sdao
43	Kuu Tann	47	Male	4/4/82	Sreangdong	Sdao
44	Him Virac	18	Male	1/8/83	Sreangdong	Sdao
45	Pin Ra	21	Male	11/9/89	Sreangdong	Sdao
46	Noue Vab	27	Male	13/5/81	Sreangdong	Sdao
47	Thim Eang	26	Male	1/9/84	Sreangdong	Sdao
48	Bun Leng	52	Male	1/2/86	Tasanh	Andao Hep
49	Bea Moi	43	Male	24/8/86	Tasanh	Andao Hep
50	Moa Meam	30	Male	30/11/90	Tasanh	Andao Hep
51	Pic Beng	23	Male	16/5/85	Tasanh	Andao Hep
52	Teng Mon	21	Male	21/5/92	Tasanh	Andao Hep
53	Teng Teang	31	Male	1/4/88	Tasanh	Andao Hep
54	Tom Roy	27	Male	14/3/91	Tasanh	Andao Hep
55	Som Venn	28	Male	18/6/88	Tasanh	Andao Hep
56	Bell Cheall	19	Male	18/1/92	Tasanh	Andao Hep
57	Toy Tourm	21	Male	23/3/91	Tasanh	Andao Hep
58	Kan Nouen	59	Male	19/7/92	Tasanh	Andao Hep
59	Thuch Nuen	30	Male	29/5/90	Tasanh	Andao Hep
60	Seng Pet	18	Male	7/3/91	Tasanh	Andao Hep
61	Un Orm	18	Male	12/7/89	Tasanh	Andao Hep
62	Heng Chim	58	Male	9/6/88	Tasanh	Andao Hep
63	Chibb Ouck	18	Male	17/3/91	Tasanh	Andao Hep
64	Chum Ouern	57	Male	24/4/88	Tasanh	Andao Hep
65	Bong Bouern	39	Male	6/4/91	Tasanh	Andao Hep
66	Teth Heath	25	Male	8/2/90	Tasanh	Andao Hep
67	Teng Toy	26	Male	24/4/88	Tasanh	Andao Hep
68	Seang Sean	25	Male	17/1/86	Tasanh	Andao Hep
69	Sonn Suea	22	Male	8/8/83	Tasanh	Andao Hep
70	Dam Cheang	53	Male	9/4/91	Anlong Pouk	Andao Hep
71	De Duern	38	Male	18/8/90	Anlong Pouk	Andao Hep
72	Duern Seb	11	Male	18/8/90	Anlong Pouk	Andao Hep
73	Nor Mabb	12	Male	23/7/91	Anlong Pouk	Andao Hep
74	Pong Pan	11	Male	19/7/91	Anlong Pouk	Andao Hep
75	Morm Suep	10	Male	10/10/91	Anlong Pouk	Andao Hep
76	Chew Savouern	12	Male	13/12/91	Anlong Pouk	Andao Hep
77	Tann Marb	20	Male	15/9/91	Anlong Pouk	Andao Hep
78	Lak Dute	51	Male	11/4/88	Anlong Pouk	Andao Hep
79	Peng Rin	19	Male	27/9/90	Anlong Pouk	Andao Hep
80	Veang Vann	35	Male	12/10/84	Orangkhan	Andao Hep
81	Liam Leap	29	Male	1/2/92	Orangkhan	Andao Hep
82	Lom Yeth	23	Male	13/3/92	Orangkhan	Andao Hep
83	Long Cheth	20	Male	23/8/91	Orangkhan	Andao Hep
84	Cheang Ko	34	Male	8/10/91	Thmar Prous	Andao Hep
85	Dong Samouern	25	Male	25/9/89	Thmar Prous	Andao Hep
86	Cheng Krong	27	Male	4/9/89	Thmar Prous	Andao Hep
87	Chem Savann	35	Male	25/6/89	Thmar Prous	Andao Hep
88	Song Thorm	34	Male	15/6/89	Thmar Prous	Andao Hep
89	Thong Tuern	25	Male	6/9/89	Thmar Prous	Andao Hep
90	Ros Porn	27	Male	17/3/91	Thmar Prous	Andao Hep
91	Bay Mourn	40	Male	5/5/90	Thmar Prous	Andao Hep
92	Bong Bourp	18	Male	26/11/91	Thmar Prous	Andao Hep
93	Din Ngai	19	Male	3/8/91	Thmar Prous	Andao Hep
94	Pron Sarenn	27	Male	22/11/89	Thmar Prous	Andao Hep
95	Prouen Savonn	19	Male	10/10/92	Thmar Prous	Andao Hep
96	Orn Touch	40	Female	17/7/92	Thmar Prous	Andao Hep

Number	Name	Age	Sex	Date of Death	Village	Commune
97	Loy Thea	21	Female	5/5/92	Thmar Pros	Andao Hep
98	Orn Ran	45	Male	17/7/92	Thmar Prous	Andao Hep
99	Yoy Kiv	65	Female	25/8/92	Thmar Prous	Andao Hep
100	Yin Sareth	31	Male	23/1/93	Thmar Prous	Andao Hep
101	Sor Bun Tuern	39	Male	17/2/93	Chipang	Ploumeas
102	Ho Neang	62	Male	19/12/92	Chipang	Ploumeas
103	Nim Seedet	20	Male	6/4/92	Chipang	Ploumeas
104	Fu Kenn	43	Male	11/3/88	Chipang	Ploumeas
105	Heng Yiek	25	Male	15/1/91	Chipang	Ploumeas
106	Chuern Luern	52	Male	7/1/89	Chipang	Ploumeas
107	Hic Soeub	21	Male	16/2/86	Chipang	Ploumeas
108	Ieang Khieu	52	Male	4/3/90	Chipang	Ploumeas
109	Em Bai	22	Male	11/8/87	Chipang	Ploumeas
110	Dol Doeu	30	Male	6/10/89	Chipang	Ploumeas
111	Ong Lout	27	Male	27/6/87	Chipang	Ploumeas
112	Lak Louth	38	Male	20/3/89	Chipang	Ploumeas
113	Cheak Leang	60	Male	16/2/91	Chipang	Ploumeas
114	Tie Kourn	41	Male	4/1/88	Chipang	Ploumeas
115	Na Neab	40	Male	17/6/87	Chipang	Ploumeas
116	Tom Tung	25	Male	6/12/91	Chipang	Ploumeas
117	Phang Tong	15	Male	10/7/92	Chipang	Ploumeas
118	Tourn Noie	12	Male	10/2/93	Chipang	Ploumeas
119	Sa Nay	40	Male	11/4/84	Tropangleang	Ploumeas
120	Ly Bo	35	Male	14/6/87	Tropangleang	Ploumeas
121	Vuern Tom	35	Male	4/7/83	Tropangleang	Ploumeas
122	Pharth Mouern	35	Male	23/2/82	Tropangleang	Ploumeas
123	Duern See	35	Male	27/1/87	Tropangleang	Ploumeas
124	Phu Yin	47	Male	4/5/91	Tropangleang	Ploumeas
125	Phim Phoan	35	Male	19/2/86	Tropangleang	Ploumeas
126	Tuern Ka	18	Male	4/2/88	Tropangleang	Ploumeas
127	Prouen Bo	18	Male	11/6/92	Tropangleang	Ploumeas
128	Gneou Gnim	42	Male	23/8/92	Tropangleang	Ploumeas
129	Che Chuern	59	Male	29/4/87	Tropangleang	Ploumeas
130	Say Sem	45	Male	12/9/85	Tropangleang	Ploumeas
131	Meng Pril	32	Male	16/2/87	Tropangleang	Ploumeas
132	Sen Souern	70	Male	21/4/89	Tropangleang	Ploumeas
133	Yorn Yem	30	Male	3/1/86	Tropangleang	Ploumeas
134	Tie Yun	50	Male	14/9/87	Tropangleang	Ploumeas
135	Loueng Savuth	42	Male	21/9/88	Tropangleang	Ploumeas
136	Chinn Cheang	49	Male	3/6/85	Tropang Leang	Ploumeas
137	Dy Ky	36	Male	6/4/85	Tropangleang	Ploumeas
138	Choy Pem	25	Male	27/12/84	Watt	Ploumeas
139	Ley Thai	29	Male	30/1/85	Watt	Ploumeas
140	Hey Sin	45	Male	13/11/85	Boueng Ktom	Ploumeas
141	Kim Beang	52	Male	17/4/88	Boueng Ktom	Ploumeas
142	Tak Tong	30	Male	27/10/84	Boueng Ktom	Ploumeas
143	Neam Gnem	30	Male	6/2/82	Boueng Ktom	Ploumeas
144	Vann Savine	25	Male	2/3/83	Boueng Ktom	Ploumeas
145	Gnem Ron	21	Male	1/6/89	Boueng Ktom	Ploumeas
146	Tuern Tem	25	Male	1/11/84	Boueng Ktom	Ploumeas
147	Ruern Gneam	56	Male	6/3/84	Ploumeas	Ploumeas
148	Chung Hung How	23	Male	12/9/91	Ploumeas	Ploumeas
149	Ta Tem	29	Male	5/4/85	Ploumeas	Ploumeas
150	Long Louem	23	Male	9/5/92	Ploumeas	Ploumeas
151	Thi Saven	37	Male	6/5/84	Ploumeas	Ploumeas
152	Khiem Sing	26	Male	16/4/86	Ploumeas	Ploumeas
153	Roeung Kec	32	Male	21/8/88	Ploumeas	Ploumeas
154	Hak Chem	45	Male	13/2/86	Chea-Montray	Treng
155	Chum Nuern	29	Male	5/7/91	Chea-Montray	Treng
156	Chhan	21	Male	2/6/89	Chea-Montray	

Number	Name	Age	Sex	Date of Death	Village	Commune
157	Long Touch	37	Male	12/3/91	Chea-Montray	Treng
158	Doeul Porn	30	Male	26/4/86	Chea-Montray	Treng
159	Hueng Phuch	23	Male	29/4/89	Chea-Montray	Treng
160	Veang Hong	39	Male	1/2/88	Chea-Montray	Treng
161	Toy Samen	39	Male	7/1/87	Chea-Montray	Treng
162	Duern Mai	49	Male	8/8/91	Chea-Montray	Treng
163	Trey Tith	50	Male	10/7/91	Chea-Montray	Treng
164	Phum Hang	17	Male	10/7/91	Chea-Montray	Treng
165	Phut Neak	24	Male	15/12/91	Chea-Montray	Treng
166	Cham Peang	38	Male	3/1/89	Chea-Montray	Treng
167	Chan Chenn	24	Male	7/4/92	Chea-Montray	Treng
168	Rann Rinn	26	Male	30/3/92	Chea-Montray	Treng
169	Nak Cham	43	Male	1/6/87	Chea-Montray	Treng
170	Barang	20	Male	6/9/92	Chea-Montray	Treng
171	Heng Chhorm	50	Male	17/11/88	Chea-Montray	Treng
172	Leb Leab	10	Male	23/2/88	Chea-Montray	Treng
173	Loth Chhourn	27	Male	25/12/87	Chisang	Treng
174	Sovan Run	25	Male	15/11/86	Chisang	Treng
175	Uch Choeun	29	Male	5/9/86	Chisang	Treng
176	Horng Phouey	30	Male	10/4/85	Chisang	Treng
177	Morng Seang	26	Male	17/5/86	Chisang	Treng
178	Horn Souen	28	Male	18/4/87	Chisang	Treng
179	Chhuth Teng	27	Male	18/5/86	Chisang	Treng
180	Chhlath	27	Male	14/7/86	Chisang	Treng
181	Thong Rin	28	Male	13/6/87	Chisang	Treng
182	Lign Lang	17	Male	10/2/88	Chisang	Treng
183	Preav Preal	40	Male	10/2/88	Chisang	Treng
184	Terng Chea	7	Male	14/4/87	Chisang	Treng
185	Toeng Yung	5	Female	14/4/87	Chisang	Treng
186	Chheth Chheang	8	Male	14/4/87	Chisang	Treng
187	Chheth Dom	9	Male	14/4/87	Chisang	Treng
188	Nuth Thy	25	Male	14/4/87	Chisang	Treng
189	Chhouen Beth	31	Female	10/1/90	Chisang	Treng
190	Hun Ren	25	Male	15/4/86	Chisang	Treng
191	Koeun Voeun	26	Male	16/6/87	Chisang	Treng
192	Morm Un	43	Male	16/2/86	Chisang	Treng
193	Dung Sarom	40	Female	18/6/90	Chisang	Treng
194	Death Dea	20	Female	10/4/90	Chisang	Treng
195	Svoy Svan	45	Male	10/5/91	Chisang	Treng
196	Bun Sanouen	20	Male	10/8/91	Chisang	Treng
197	Pe Kuch	28	Male	11/8/87	Chisang	Treng
198	Youem Lorm	25	Male	10/9/87	Chisang	Treng
199	Deab Kan	17	Female	8/1/93	Chisang	Treng
200	Hab Heam	22	Male	15/5/92	Chisang	Treng
201	Ngeth Muth	28	Male	14/4/90	Chisang	Treng
202	Sang Kuy	30	Male	1/5/91	Pchaeu	Treng
203	Sang Chhean	20	Male	1/5/91	Pchaeu	Treng
204	Hey Phorn	46	Male	6/10/87	Pchaeu	Treng
205	Koeun Lork	32	Male	6/10/87	Pchaeu	Treng
206	Hey Phar	48	Female	6/10/87	Pchaeu	Treng
207	Phun Men	38	Male	1/5/87	Pchaeu	Treng
208	Yan Yun	30	Male	3/6/91	Pchaeu	Treng
209	Yun Bok	33	Male	6/1/82	Pchaeu	Treng
210	Phun Tho	20	Male	1/11/87	Pchaeu	Treng
211	Tuy Ry	40	Male	5/12/83	Pchaeu	Treng
212	Vey Bum	46	Female	5/12/83	Pchaeu	Treng
213	Seb Chhouen	50	Male	4/6/92	Pchaeu	Treng
214	Deth Louem	60	Female	9/12/83	Pchaeu	Treng
215	Ktung Lean	55	Male	10/9/83	Pchaeu	Treng
216	Sen Hun	21	Male	7/11/87	Pchaeu	Treng

Number	Name	Age	Sex	Date of Death	Village	Commune
217	Som Theng	22	Male	8/12/87	Pchaeu	Treng
218	Tan Chhai	21	Male	10/9/87	Pchaeu	Treng
219	Phun Pheap	20	Male	10/5/84	Pchaeu	Treng
220	Hul Oeun	18	Male	15/2/83	Pchaeu	Treng
221	Brang Roeum	58	Male	8/10/84	Pchaeu	Treng
222	Veay Chorn	27	Male	19/2/89	Pchaeu	Treng
223	Mork Hath	20	Male	10/1/89	Pchaeu	Treng
224	Norn Hor	31	Male	7/5/87	Pchaeu	Treng
225	Phen Nou	29	Male	15/1/90	Pchaeu	Treng
226	Luth Lum	50	Male	5/6/87	Pchaeu	Treng
227	Hul Ky	20	Male	7/11/85	Pchaeu	Treng
228	Var Khun	50	Male	15/10/85	Pchaeu	Treng
229	Sa Muk	20	Male	1/2/91	Pchaeu	Treng
230	Lach Pi	18	Male	2/3/91	Kilo	Treng
231	Parn Kuon	27	Male	5/2/90	Kilo	Treng
232	Vann Pan Poie	19	Male	5/4/91	Kilo	Treng
233	Seng Vouern	19	Male	2/5/90	Kilo	Treng
234	Yath Bouern	33	Male	2/5/90	Kilo	Treng
235	Phai Lom	23	Male	25/2/91	Kilo	Treng
236	Paie Chhourk	30	Male	5/6/89	Kilo	Treng
237	Ly Kae	46	Male	19/1/90	Kilo	Treng
238	Chay Louern	25	Male	2/2/91	Kilo	Treng
239	Vet More	59	Male	7/10/91	Kilo	Treng
240	Youeng Savouern	29	Male	22/2/92	Kilo	Treng
241	Hum Naeng	24	Male	10/2/91	Kilo	Treng
242	Cham Ree	29	Male	2/7/89	Kilo	Treng
243	Chay Say	64	Male	7/10/91	Kilo	Treng
244	Seang Raak	25	Male	13/12/89	Kilo	Treng
245	Huth Cheuv	35	Male	6/7/89	Kilo	Treng
246	Phuch Song	58	Male	12/5/87	Kilo	Treng
247	Sonn Poern	15	Male	12/5/87	Kilo	Treng
24	Norng Seth	29	Male	3/6/87	Kilo	Treng
249	May Phang	36	Male	3/6/89	Kilo	Treng
250	So Seng	30	Male	10/5/89	Kilo	Treng
251	Phart Huong	46	Male	3/8/81	Kilo	Treng
252	Porn Rinn	35	Male	20/6/85	Kilo	Treng
253	Sor Kheang	30	Male	15/2/87	Kilo	Treng
254	Som Moer	35	Male	7/3/87	Kilo	Treng
255	Prom Bram	30	Male	1/8/89	Kilo	Treng
256	Phun Teang	45	Male	4/6/87	Kilo	Treng
257	Sor Sok	22	Male	21/2/89	Kilo	Treng
258	Ros Sophun	23	Male	16/1/86	Kilo	Treng
259	Kann Thin	59	Male	12/3/87	Kilo	Treng
260	Haak Sarong	21	Male	19/4/86	Kilo	Treng
261	Thann Marb	21	Male	5/12/91	Kilo	Treng
262	Thon Thuer	25	Male	11/7/92	Kilo 38	Treng
263	Phuek Venn	24	Male	16/9/84	Kilo 38	Treng
264	Moer Seang	26	Male	9/1/84	Kilo 38	Treng
265	Vern Rom	31	Male	23/2/85	Kilo 38	Treng
266	Chheang Chun	36	Male	27/12/90	Kilo 38	Treng
267	Long Khun	30	Male	10/6/88	Kilo 38	Treng
268	Leo Lim	45	Male	1/6/79	Kilo 38	Treng
269	Chann Suoath	48	Male	4/4/79	Kilo 38	Treng
270	Sok Chem	48	Male	16/3/79	Kilo 38	Treng
271	Suern Hannh	37	Male	11/2/79	Kilo 38	Treng
272	Kok Saroung	40	Female	5/2/79	Kilo 38	Treng
273	Chhouk Cheng	18	Male	2/1/91	Kilo 38	Treng
274	Sok Rett	33	Male	16/3/91	Kilo 38	Treng
275	Po Bung	45	Male	19/5/91	Kilo 38	Treng
276	Cheng Chuert	14	Male	24/6/88	Kilo 38	Treng

Number	Name	Age	Sex	Date of Death	Village	Commune
277	Treng Pingh	30	Male	21/3/92	Kilo 38	Treng
278	Leang Nhib	25	Male	17/2/92	Kilo 38	Treng
279	Thann Youern	30	Male	6/2/93	Kilo 38	Treng
280	Heah Heang	20	Male	2/4/92	Kilo 38	Treng
281	Toy Ouek	24	Male	12/6/92	Kilo 38	Treng

Appendix 3
The Reality of the Present Use of Mines by Military Forces

Rae McGrath, Director, Mines Advisory Group, for the
International Committee of the Red Cross Symposium on Anti-personnel Mines, April 1993

Introduction

Probably the first person to recognise fully the insidious nature of landmines was the British war correspondent Christopher Buckley who, as early as 1943, professed to be worried by mines as a weapon, '… because human qualities were not directly involved … that was the danger of mines, buried and invisible'.[1] Buckley may have become a powerful lobbyist against the proliferation of mines had not his fear been cruelly justified when, in August 1950, he was one of three passengers in a jeep that hit a mine in Korea – all were killed.

Yet what Christopher Buckley identified in 1943 was the crux of the issue that faces more than 20 mine-infested countries today – the persistent and uncontrolled nature of mines. It is also worth recognising that Buckley was making an observation relating to *easily detectable* mines laid in *pre-planned* minefields and, very probably, minefields that were mapped, marked and recorded. As this paper will seek to illustrate, such controlled strategies are an exception in modern military terms, where the mine is neither designed nor disseminated with any thought to its long-term impact or to its eventual removal as a threat to the civilian community in the post-combat period.

This paper will also raise a critical question – are mines designed to meet the planned or stated needs of the military, Or is the development led by manufacturers? References to mine-related strategies in this paper are largely based on practical experience of the situation in Afghanistan, Cambodia, Angola, Mozambique, Iraq and Somalia, from either the author's own observations or those of Mines Advisory Group specialists, or both.

This paper is designed to stimulate debate rather than to present a comprehensive picture of military mines strategy. It should not be seen as limiting the discussion to the issues raised but should be perceived as a starting point. It is deliberately focused on accepted military structures rather than smaller groups involved in mine-laying, since mines are manufactured in the first instance for sale to such financially viable customers.

Targeting Mines

Most military spokesmen would argue that mines have several clearly defined and acceptable roles in combat. They are:

1. to protect military bases and key installations
2. to channel or divert the enemy forces
3. to deny routes and strategic positions to the enemy.

These uses of mines have commonality in that they should allow for the mapping, recording and marking of mined locations but it requires a responsible command structure. In fact, it could be argued that the marking itself would often achieve the desired purpose, thus the common usage of dummy minefields.[2]

However, military strategy demands more of the mine as a weapon in the modern theatre of war than these basic deployment strategies. And here it is necessary to subdivide military use of mines into two categories of deployment philosophy – the *conventional war scenario* and the *counter-insurgency campaign*. This terminology has no bearing on the type, scale or scope of the military operation, rather it relates to the *perception* of the enemy forces. The second Gulf War, for instance, would fall into the former category, as would the Falklands/Malvinas conflict, while the Vietnam War and the Soviet/Afghan War would fall into the latter category of conflict.

In both scenarios mines are deployed using strategies that target enemy forces in such a manner as to ensure that a *long-term humanitarian problem* will exist in the post-combat period.

The Conventional War Scenario

Enemy forces are perceived as an organised army, with rank structure, uniforms, etc.[3] In addition to the three generally accepted and admitted strategies for mine dissemination they are subject to the following, less openly discussed, strategies:

- *Deep strike* deployment of mines into the enemy force's rear areas.[4]

- *Cut-off* deployment of mines behind a retreating, or in front of an advancing, force.

Both of these strategies involve remote[5] dissemination of scatterable mines by fixed-wing aircraft, helicopters, artillery, rocket or mortar. The former strategy would normally be aimed at key junctions on enemy main supply routes (MSRs), supply dumps, loading areas, workshops and headquarter elements. The purpose of the latter usage of scatterable mines, cut-off, is self-explanatory.

What both strategies have in common is the *lack of any reliable methods of recording, mapping or, immediately or subsequently, marking* such concentrations of mines.

The Counter-insurgency Campaign

The terms 'insurgent', 'guerrilla' or 'terrorist' have been usefully employed by conventional military forces to describe an enemy force that does not conform to the *accepted* norms – in many cases this may simply mean that they have fewer resources (although possibly more popular support) than the *real* armies involved in the conflict. It may also, as in the case of the US campaigns against Laos and Cambodia, the Soviet invasion of Afghanistan and the Iraqi campaign against the Kurds, be seen as a more generally accepted way to describe an illegal prosecution of war against an indigenous population.

It is these categories of action that have resulted in the most inhuman and persistent mine dissemination strategies:

1. random and widespread mining of agricultural and community land
2. deliberate use of mines as an anti-morale or terror weapon against civilians
3. mining of villages, water sources, religious shrines, etc.

The military use the fact that the enemy are *hiding in the community* to justify many of these actions, and thus do not feel restricted to any specifically defined military targets since, under such operational definitions, virtually *everywhere* becomes a justifiable target. The use of mines by Soviet forces and by the Kabul regime against the *Mujahideen* in Afghanistan is a classic example of this genocidal tactic – in some areas virtually all mountain grazing land was remotely mined and the whole agricultural infrastructure brought to a halt by the widespread mining of fields, *karez*[6] and surface-irrigation systems.

It is apparent that the mining of agricultural land in order to restrict the supply of food to the enemy (and also, by design or otherwise, to the civilian population

at large) is now accepted by military strategists and field commanders as a *normal* strategy.

In addition it is clear that the use of mines as weapons of terror against the civilian population is also increasingly accepted as a military tactic. It should come as no surprise that the Iraqi government used such strategies against the Kurds and that it is now using the same tactic against the Shia population in the southern marshes of Iraq, nor that the MPLA used a similar strategy in Mozambique, but this strategic thinking is not confined to extremist groups and the armies of dictators. Both Chinese and British training of Khmer forces opposed to the Vietnamese-backed government in Phnom Penh stressed the use of mines (and improvised booby-traps) as an anti-morale weapon targeted against the civilian infrastructure.

To summarise, in modern conflict mines cannot be said to be targeted at military formations in any reasonable definition of the word, since the very design of a great proportion of the mines in use and their method of dissemination is such that civilian casualties and long-term infestation are inevitable rather than coincidental. Military philosophy regarding the use of mines is such that even when devices *are* targeted, their impact on civilian populations is unacceptable by any humanitarian definition.

Design-led Strategy?

There is a strong argument that the military has less to do with the development of mines than the manufacturers – in other words that mine laying strategy has become manufacturer/design led. Obviously such a suggestion may be expected to meet with strong rebuttal from both the military and the manufacturers, but the facts support the hypothesis.

The development of the remotely-delivered scatterable mine should really have little attraction to the military strategist. Rather like the use of chemical and biological weapons, it is a dangerous strategy to embark upon:

1. mines deployed can offer as great a threat to one's own advancing forces as to the enemy in retreat
2. use of unrecorded mines to deny the enemy key areas will inevitably involve the use of valuable manpower, and probably the lives of one's own troops when those area are overrun.

It is inconceivable that the military would themselves call for the design of mines that were virtually undetectable to the enemy and to themselves. But this has been the direction of development over the past 30 years, and the advancement of the low-metallic content mine has far outstripped the development of effective detection technology. Most manufacturers offer metallic detection plates as an *option*, a fact that indicates that there is little or no demand for such an addition from their customers.[7] But why is such an option not popular with the military? *It is the knowledge imparted to the enemy that a minefield has been laid in a particular ares that achieves the main military objective* – there are many more effective methods of killing and maiming enemy troops.

The conclusion must be that:

- *either* the military *aims* to deny land to civilians in the post-combat period, and has a policy of killing and maiming civilians long after the cessation of hostilities, *or*
- international military strategic thinking is so inhuman and short-sighted that it is unaware or uncaring of such considerations, *or*

- it uses what is designed and made available by manufacturers, and develops strategy based on available, and not necessarily desirable, technology.

Conclusions

Acceptance of the factual nature of the points raised in this paper must lead to one frightening conclusion – the military, by perpetuating and refining mine laying strategies which will inevitably kill and maim non-combatants during the period of combat, which continue to kill and maim civilians following a ceasefire, and which lead to long-term denial of land to rural communities, has shown a total disregard for humanitarian law, principles and simple human decency.

Appendix 4
Useful Contact Addresses

As suggested in the introduction and elsewhere in this book, the crisis posed by landmines worldwide is to some extent an avoidable catastrophe. Only by informing and, hopefully, motivating public opinion can future pollution by these weapons be avoided and appropriate levels of commitment be generated to ensure that where mines already pose humanitarian problems appropriate levels of resources will be released to tackle their legacies, i.e. to demine. This book is part of an international campaign seeking to achieve both these ends – a ban on the manufacture, distribution and deployment of mines, and appropriate response from the international community to ensure that existing problems are addressed. Einstein wrote, 'I believe the world to be in greater danger from those who passively tolerate evil than from those who actively commit it.' So many of the problems facing the world today are so big, their causes so hard to discern, that the informed observer often feels powerless to act. Fortunately, the threat posed to the global community by landmines is not like this. Its causes and prevention are obvious, and action can and does have results. For this reason contact addresses are given below for those readers who feel they would like to know more about the international campaign, and perhaps feel a desire to participate in it.

UK

Rae McGrath
Mines Advisory Group
54a Main Street
Cockermouth
Cumbria CA13 9LU
Tel: 0900 828580/688   Fax: 0900 827088

John Sprange
Greenpeace International
5 Baker's Row
London EC1A 3DB
Tel: 071 833 0600   Fax: 071 837 6606

(Greenpeace is mounting a large campaign focusing on the manufacturers of landmines)

France

Tim Carstairs
Handicap International
ERAC 14, Ave. Berthelot
69361 Lyon CEDEX 07
Tel: 78 69 79 79   Fax: 78 69 79 94

USA

Jody Williams
Vietnam Veterans of America Foundation
2001 'S' Street, NW
Suite 740
Washington DC 20009
Tel: 202 483 9222   Fax: 202 483 9312

United Nations

Paddy Blagdon
UN Mines Expert
Department of Humanitarian Affairs
The United Nations
New York
Tel: 212 963 2627   Fax: 212 963 6460

Notes and References

Foreword

1. William Shawcross, *Sideshow: Kissinger, Nixon and the Destruction of Cambodia* (London, 1979), pp. 65, 24: and Seymour M. Hersh, *The Prince of Power: Henry Kissinger in the Nixon White House* (New York, 1983), pp. 177–78.
2. Pol Pot, 'Report of Activities of the Party Center According to the General Political Tasks of 1976', 20 December 1979, in Chanthou Boua, David P. Chandler, and Ben Kiernan, (eds.), *Pol Pot Plans the Future: Confidential Leadership Documents from Democratic Kampuchea, 1976–1977* (New Haven: Yale Council on Southeast Asia Studies, 1988) p. 190.
3. See John Pilger, 'Black Farce in Cambodia', *New Statesman and Society*, 11 December 1992, p. 10, and the resulting exchange with Derek Tonkin, 15 January 1993, p. 26.
4. General John Sanderson, in John Pilger and David Munro's film, *Return to Year Zero*, 1993. See also 'One Limb at a Time', *New Statesman and Society*, 20 October 1993.

Introduction

1. *Hidden Killers: the Global Problem With Uncleared Landmines – A Report on International Demining* (US Department of State, Bureau of Political-Military Affairs).
2. *Afghanistan, Angola,* Armenia, Azerbaijan, Bosnia, Burma, *Cambodia,* Colombia, Chad, Croatia, Cuba, El Salvador, Eritrea, Ethiopia, Falklands-Malvinas Islands, Guatemala, Honduras, Iran, *Iraq,* Kuwait, *Laos,* Libya, *Mozambique,* Myanmar, Nicaragua, Peru, Russia, Rwanda, *Somalia,* Sri Lanka, Sudan, Tajikistan, Uganda, Uzbekistan, Vietnam, Zimbabwe (Mines Advisory Group Statistics, May 1993). Those countries italicised should be considered as acute problems due to the scale of existing casualty rates.
3. For a fuller discussion of the definition of anti-personnel landmines see Chapter 1 of Rae McGrath's *Landmines in Rural Communities: a Guide for Fieldworkers* (MAG/Oxfam, forthcoming).
4. *Cambodian Mine Reference Manual* (prepared by the Cambodian Mine Action Centre, August 1993).
5. C.Foss and T. Gander, (eds.) *Jane's Military Vehicles and Logistics 1991–92* (Jane's Information Group, Twelfth Edition, 1991).

Chapter 1

1. David Chandler, 'Cambodia before the French: Politics in a Tributary Kingdom 1794–1848' (dissertation, University of Michigan, 1973).
2. Nayan Chanda, *Brother Enemy: The War After the War* (Macmillan, 1986), p. 251.

3. Ibid, pp. 377–78.
4. Eva Mysliwec, *Punishing the Poor: The International Isolation of Cambodia* (Oxford: Oxfam 1988).

Chapter 2

1. Rae McGrath and Eric Stover, *Landmines in Cambodia: The Cowards' War* (Asia Watch and Physicians for Human Rights Report, September.1991) p. 21. Known hereafter as *The Cowards' War*.
2. In a study conducted for CMAC by David Gould, *Cambodian Landmine Victim Survey* (7 August 1993, Phnom Penh – known hereafter as Gould's survey), it is revealed that during the period January 1992 to June 1993 Rattanak Mondul had the second highest incidence of recorded landmine injuries (166) out of the 171 districts which make up the country.
3. Cambodia is divided into 272 1:50,000 scale maps. As at 24 March 1993 CMAC's minefield mapping database had information on minefields on 145 of these maps. A staff sergeant working with the database pointed out that this was by no means the 'whole picture'. Large areas of Cambodia occupied by the Khmer Rouge which are known to contain mines do not appear in the database due to the group's refusal to release the information.
4. Lt. Col. George Focsaneanu speaking at CMAC, Phnom Penh, 24 March 1993
5. For a comprehensive study of these raids see William Shawcross's *Sideshow: Kissinger, Nixon and the Destruction of Cambodia* (The Hogarth Press,1986). Known hereafter as *Sideshow*.
6. Such a delivery method is clearly defined as 'indiscriminate' in the Land Mines Protocol. See Chapter 8.
7. Shawcross, *Sideshow*, p. 65.
8. Haing Ngor, *A Cambodian Odyssey* (New York: Warner Books, 1987) p. 70.
9. Elizabeth Becker, *When the War Was Over: Cambodia's Revolution and the Voices of Its People* (New York: Simon and Schuster, 1986) p. 164.
10. *The Cowards' War*, p. 21.
11. H.Ngor, *Cambodian Odyssey*, p. 378.
12. *Cambodia: Human Rights Before and After the Elections* (Asia Watch vol. 5. no. 10, May 1993).
13. For example, the camp of Sa Keo, in Prachinburi Province in eastern Thailand, was one of the sites to which the Khmer Rouge and its supporters and captive populations were taken by the Thai authorities when they were first forced over the border in 1979–80. Sa Keo is 50 km inside Thailand. For further details see William Shawcross, *The Quality of Mercy: Cambodia, Holocaust and Modern Conscience* (New York: Simon and Schuster, 1984) pp. 176–77.
14. The CGDK was in reality a fraud, as noted in Chapter 2, despite the fact that it held the UN seat for Cambodia throughout the 1980s. The coalition was dominated both

politically and militarily by the Khmer Rouge, and operationally the forces of the NCR operated under the direction and co-ordination of the Khmer Rouge.

15. *The Cowards' War*, pp. 28 and 30.
16. Just over 9 per cent of the amputee mine victims identified in a comprehensive random survey of the disabled in Battambang in 1992 (organised by Kevin Malone a consultant working for a local NGO) had their accidents while working as *Kor Bram* labourers. They constitute nearly 7.5 per cent of Battambang's disabled population.
17. During the mounting tension in late 1992 and 1993 in Battambang many villagers were conscripted to do *Kor Bram*, but this referred to forced labour on defensive positions in and around their local districts, not in the border region.
18. Interview at CMAC, 24 March 1993.
19. *The Cowards' War*, p. 35.
20. A response to the repeated incursions from both non-communist and Khmer Rouge resistance fighters operating from bases along the north western border section.
21. Peter Newman, Project Manager Banteay-Meanchay, the HALO Trust, Mongkol Berei, 28 April 1993.
22. *The Cowards' War*, p. 42.
23. Ibid, p. 43.
24. Ibid, p. 35.
25. Ibid.
26. Ibid, pp. 37–8.
27. Ibid, p. 39.
28. Interview with author, March 1993.
29. Peter Newman, the Halo Trust, 28 April 1993.
30. Ibid.
31. A driver who works for the British Aid agency the Cambodia Trust in Phnom Penh said how saddened he was by the use of automatic weapons instead of fireworks (as in the past) to celebrate the Cambodian New Year in 1993. In Battambang aid workers were also shocked on the various eclipses of the moon and during particularly heavy thunderstorms to discover just how many of their Cambodian neighbours have AK-47s and have incorporated their use into contemporary culture. When it rains heavily half the town erupts, firing wildly into the sky to 'drive off' the rain. Similarly, during lunar eclipses, which Cambodians believe are caused by an enormous frog eating the moon, the frog is now driven off not with fireworks but with AK-47 fire.
32. *Cambodia: Human Rights Before and After the Elections* (Asia Watch) p. 27.
33. John Pilger, *Distant Voices* (London: Vintage, 1992) p. 183.
34. Personal comments made by an aid worker to the author, Phnom Penh, April 1993.
35. *The Cowards' War*, p. 40.
36. Ibid, p. 41.
37. In October 1990 Margaret Thatcher, then UK Prime Minister, said, 'There is no British Government training, equipping or co-operating with the Khmer Rouge forces or those allied with them'. Then, on 27 June in a written parliamentary answer the Armed Forces Minister, Archie Hamilton, admitted that British forces 'provided training to the armed forces of the Cambodian non-communist resistance from 1983 to 1989'.

38. In other words, a usage which can be limited to acceptable military purposes, avoiding long-term risks for civilians, within the laws of war. See Chapter 8.
39. CMAC, Phnom Penh, 5 May 1993.
40. *The Cowards' War*, p. 42.
41. Reported to Warrant Officer McCracken, CMAC, concerning a unilateral demining attempt by the royalist faction. It should be noted that this demining fiasco was conducted entirely by the Sihanoukist faction and was in no way connected with the UN demining operation in Cambodia. Told to the author May 1993.
42. Sgt Jansen, CMAC, 24 March 1993.
43. Fiona King 'Landmine Injury in Cambodia: A Case Study' (London School of Hygiene and Tropical Medicine, MSc Thesis, 1992), p. 97. Based on a case study of both Battambang and Mongkol Berei (ICRC-assisted) hospitals, the study found that 34 per cent of mine injuries were 'Pattern A' – resulting from standing on a mine – the most common injury type resulting in amputation. Statistics from military hospitals in Battambang and Phnom Penh suggest that over the past few years on average mine accidents have resulted in amputations in 43 per cent and 38 per cent of the cases respectively. Figures for Battambang provincial hospital in 1992 suggest that 58 per cent of mine cases resulted in leg amputations. Known hereafter as King's thesis.
44. For example, Gould's survey (1993) revealed that of 1,200 mine victims only 7.4 per cent were female. David Appleton, Director of the Cambodia Trust Limb Project 1992–93, operating out of the Calmette hospital, Phnom Penh, estimated that females constituted only 5 per cent (approx.) of patients receiving prostheses.
45. Suggested by Benoit Denise, Director, Handicap International, Phnom Penh, 21 April 1993.
46. UNICEF *Cambodia: The Situation of Children and Women* (Phnom Penh, Cambodia: UNICEF, 1990).
47. Considered the two most heavily affected provinces in Gould's survey.
48. The fourth highest in the country according to Gould's survey.
49. Battambang's population in 1993, with the addition of several tens of thousands of returnees, is estimated at around the 600,000 mark.
50. King's thesis, p. 53 (6.1.5), reveals that 60 per cent of the ICRC database cases knew that others had been injured in the area they entered before having their mine accident. Other studies suggest that 60–70 per cent of mine victims knew they were entering mined areas. These finding have been confirmed in Gould's survey.
51. Benoit Denise, Director, Handicap International, Phnom Penh, Cambodia, April 1993.
52. From information gathered across the western and south eastern provinces, 1991–93. Of 572 individuals for whom military or civilian status was recorded, some 263 were military personnel (46 per cent) and 309 were civilians (54.2 per cent).
53. See, for example, Ches Sary's story in Chapter 4. She was injured while cutting bamboo shoots near the Sangke river.
54. *Phnom Penh Post*, vol. 2, no. 3, 29 January to 11 February 1993, p. 3.

55. King's thesis, p. 46.
56. Ibid, p. 88. There may have been some seasonal bias in the ICRC database when King was using it. At that stage it had been running for only 9 months and was geographically more restricted. Spread now over a wider range of provinces, the database will present a truer picture of the cyclical risks of agricultural life in mine-affected areas (see Chapter 3).
57. Ibid, p. 88.
58. Gould's survey, p. 10.
59. King's thesis, p. 96.
60. Ibid, p. 101.
61. Ibid, p. 32.
62. See, for example, the graphic description of experiences in Battambang Hospital by the mother of Sdeng Phal, one of the mine victims whose story is told in Chapter 4.
63. King's thesis, p. 14.
64. Statistics received from Battambang Provincial Hospital Authorities, March 1993.
65. Suggested by their predecessors – German Army medics serving with UNAMIC.
66. Soldiers will go fishing and seek natural fruits and vegetables from the forests in these areas to supplement the extreme paucity of army rations. Medical statistics from the Battambang Military Hospital reflect these poor dietary conditions – some 30 per cent of medical admissions had Beri-Beri, a product of vitamin deficiency caused by inadequate diet.

Chapter 3

1. Literally 'good place of the bright shining things'.
2. Operation Samaki was designed to demonstrate Cambodian military independence and its ability to deal with the Vietminh and Khmer Issarak bands that operated out of the inaccessible forests in the north west of the country.
3. David Chandler, *The Tragedy of Cambodian History* (Yale University Press, 1991), p. 164.
4. Term used by Kev Sophal, Rattanak Mondul's district leader, February 1993, and typical of local prejudice towards the tribal 'black Khmer'.
5. The original Samlaut village, in today's Treng Commune, was raised to the ground by Sihanouk, and several hundreds of peasants were hunted down and executed. A militia was recruited in Battambang town to supplement the army and was sent to the area to hunt down the 'Red Khmer' who, Sihanouk charged, were behind this revolt, an uprising he could only see in personal terms as being an insult to his personal authority as father of the nation. In fact, the uprising had nothing to do with the CPK who had felt Cambodia was not yet ready for class struggle. The severity of the government's crackdown following the uprising indicated to the CPK that armed struggle was not yet a viable option. However the alienation produced among the peasantry helped to swell communist ranks. The people from Samlaut are still living in Treng Commune, now relocated to Beng Ampil displaced persons' camp (see below).
6. Chandler, *The Tragedy of Cambodian History*, p. 166.

7. Interview with author, February 1993.
8. UNHCR had provided a grant for the restoration of the main hospital building, and local officials had started repair work on the district office. In December 1991 an unexploded mortar could still be seen protruding from the wall of the main meeting room in the district office. Until it was made safe, a wood and thatch makeshift office on the other side of the market square served the district leader and his staff.
9. In the spring of 1993 at the end of a much feted CPAF 'offensive' on Pailin the author drove past three ancient T-54 tanks parked just off the roadside in the military zone south of Treng. These represented the CPAF's entire strength, in terms of tanks, in the district.
10. This is something of a classic example of 'overkill' usage of mines by Cambodians (see reference to the extraordinary density of mine-laying mentioned in Chapter 2). While Chinese training manuals, found by the authors of *The Cowards' War* to have been used with Cambodian resistance fighters in the 1980s, emphasise the use of excessive amounts of explosives in booby-traps and etc for 'demoralisation' purposes, the stacking of mines, common to all four Cambodian factions, is perhaps a more home-grown peculiarity. Since Cambodian soldiers seemed to believe that more of something is bound to be better, mines have often been found stacked in such a fashion. However, the military efficacy of such techniques is limited, even when mines are primed properly (often they are not).
11. These 'stayers' were usually already refugees who had earlier been driven from their homes in the western areas of Ploumeas and Treng, and refused to move any further away – often because they had no relatives or means of supporting themselves in the sanctuaries around Battambang town.
12. At least seven men were killed in one week during the attempt.
13. Nearly two years after the camp was established and a year after the multi-million dollar arrival of UNTAC.
14. One of the myths of Cambodia in the 1980s was that the refugees in Thailand and those Cambodians who had remained under State of Cambodia (SOC) control were two dramatically different groups of people. For some, the border people (excluding those with the misfortune of ending up in Khmer Rouge controlled camps) were a convenient 'non-communist' constituency, while those inside the country were portrayed as 'pro-Vietnamese' at worst, or 'communist' at best. These distinctions were to serve other people's needs and did not reflect Cambodian realities. A great deal of effort was made during the repatriation to ensure the successful reintegration of these two supposedly divergent communities. While the returnees did suffer at the hands of SOC officials, among ordinary Cambodians there were very few reintegration difficulties. In reality, even in pressure points like Rattanak Mondul, or neighbouring Phnom Tippidae in Moung Russey district there was little friction between the returnee and local community in part because repatriation involved family reunification. Even Tes Heanh, the vigorous and sometimes anti-returnee SOC first Vice Governor in Battambang, had himself relatives and friends who had

fled to the border in 1979 and had succeeded in being granted asylum in a third country.

15. Clearly the best of a series of 'options' provided for the returnees by UNHCR. Option A consisted of a package for returnees which involved a housing kit, some equipment, and more importantly a theoretical commitment to 2 hectares of prime agricultural land for each family. In Battambang hardly any families received a genuine Option A package.

16. During the study period when research on this book was being carried out (January–May 1993). Even given the vast expansion in organised demining in the district as noted below, such stark realities will endure for many years not least because of the continuing pressure placed upon the demined land by newly arrived returnees, who continued to relocate to Rattanak Mondul months after the repatriation finished.

17. Burning off minefields does lead to some mines exploding. Others, however, become intensely unstable and even harder to deal with than in their undisturbed state. Repeated burnings of mined areas marked off and left fallow for several years *is* regarded by some demining experts as a good method of tackling a heavy mine problem in low priority areas, because the mines will gradually degrade as they become exposed to the elements.

18. The only mines with a significant metal content found in large numbers in Rattanak Mondul.

19. Throughout 1993 there was much debate in UN and NGO demining circles in Cambodia about the future possible role of such 'village deminers'. On the one hand there was the desire to recognise, and if possible enhance, the existing ongoing efforts of these impromptu local deminers operating outside the 'official' demining structures established both by the UN and the demining NGOs . It was argued that since they were doing it anyway out of necessity, without training, equipment, etc, and as a result dying and getting injured, any help we could give them would inevitably make things better. On the other hand it was felt that either you do demining properly, or you don't do it at all. By 'doing it properly' experts mean adhering to the training and operating standards necessary to provide minimum safety during and after demining, for both deminers and future users of demined land. Without the management discipline of the team structure and its strict operating and reporting procedures chaos was likely to ensue, and a systematic prioritised response to the nationwide mine problem could be put in jeopardy. For example, if standards slip during the demining phase accidents are bound to occur on 'cleared land', rendering the investment in demining useless, since local confidence in cleared land will disappear. (See Chapter 5 for a fuller discussion of the politics of demining.)

20. The WFP was the UN agency tasked to co-ordinate relief efforts for Cambodia's internally displaced people. WFP was directly responsible for providing food inputs.

21. In 1992 UNDP and WFP commissioned a 'Needs Assessment Survey' of Cambodia's internally displaced people in order to calculate the amount and nature of relief assistance most appropriate for their programmes in 1993.

22. This is believed to be the first time ever that official SOC local government records of these injury and death rates have been published.

23. Given 225 named survivors of mine accidents and 281 fatalities in the official statistics for the 1979–92 period, a district population of around 20,000 people and an average family size of five. The statistics for both the survivors of landmine accidents, and those who have died from them in Rattanak Mondul reveal that only 9.33 per cent (21 of 225 survivors) are women (and 4.44 per cent children under the age of 18, of whom 80 per cent were boys). Only 4.98 per cent (14 of 281) of those who died were women (6.76 per cent were children under the age of 18, of whom 90 per cent were boys). This reveals very clearly that mine accidents are sex specific, and that this is related to a gender-based breakdown in occupational roles in areas such as Rattanak Mondul. In other words, it is the men who venture into the distant forests who are most likely to have mine accidents. For an in-depth discussion of these issues see Chapter 2.

24. Calculated on the assumption that typically two-thirds of Cambodia's population are women, and that at least half of the population are under 15. Such characteristics of the Cambodian population are in reality likely to be more pronounced in a community like Rattanak Mondul due to the fact that the war, in general terms, has had a very high impact in this district, making this calculation a conservative estimate based on conservative data. The true figure may be far higher.

Chapter 4

1. Given a population of 8.5 million and an estimated 25,000 amputees, the rough 'national figure' is one in 340.

2. He was lucky. If the mines had been the Type-72B their removal by this method might have set them off – the 72B has a 'tilt device' controlled by a printed circuit which uses a Motorola designed chip. A 72B is virtually indistinguishable from a 72A, and Sophal could not tell them apart. Such a dense concentration of mines is a classic example of the unnecessarily dense mine-laying practised in Cambodia, as noted in Chapter 2. Such practices are not restricted to the CPAF alone, since the minefield in question was subsequently found to have been laid during the Khmer Rouge occupation of the area in 1990–91 to protect an outpost on the forest edge.

3. 'Moto-taxis' as they are known are ubiquitous in Cambodia, providing local people with a cheap means of transport for short- to medium-range journeys. They consist of a small motorbike – sometimes the standard Honda 90 which seems to have dominated the private-sector transport in Cambodia for the last 30 years – which has been adapted to pull a long trailer in which up to ten people can squeeze. They allow an adult to lie at full stretch, and thus provide a very basic vehicle on which to evacuate patients to hospital. Fortunately, Rattanak Mondul district was in possession of an ambulance during the time of this study, thus the longer 35 km trip to the provincial hospital in Battambang was usually done in a good deal more comfort.

4. The ancient language of Cambodian Buddhism, originally of Indian descent, used in religious and court (until very recently) ceremonial occasions.

5. Some, for example those injured in remote logging areas, may have been cremated in such remote camps rather than carried back to their home villages.

6. However, just as areas thought by locals to be safe may not in fact be so, areas thought to be 'unsafe' because one person has been injured there may contain no more mines. One of the tragedies of landmine warfare is that the perceived presence of mines denies vast tracts of land to people as they gradually build up mental maps, passed down in local knowledge, of which places are mined and which are mine free. This is a very important consideration when appraising the work of demining NGOs (see Chapter 5). As Mike Croll of the HALO Trust commented, the work of deminers should not be evaluated in terms of the numbers of mines removed but in terms of the amount of land returned to the community from the stranglehold of fear which the *de facto* presence of mines and the fear of them create. Thus at one site in Pursat province HALO had worked for several weeks clearing the area around an old Vietnamese fort. Although they had found no mines here, this task had not been a waste of time since locals had believed the area to be mined and had not been using it.

7. Her late completion of primary school bears witness not only to the total destruction of education services under the Khmer Rouge but also to the weaknesses of the system under both Sihanouk and Lon Nol in rural areas like Rattanak Mondul. Primary education was extended to such places under the Vietnamese, often for the first time.

8. Undoubtedly hospital staff in Cambodia are corrupt, charging for services and supplies which are technically 'free'. However, if they did not charge they too would be unable to feed their families on the irregularly-paid state salaries of as little as $8 per month. The 'corruption' of staff is hardly providing them with opulence at the expense of the poor. Corruption stems from the economic embargo extended to Cambodia throughout the 1980s which had the effect of punishing the poor (as mentioned in Chapter 1), coming on top of the almost total destruction of human and material resources achieved by the Khmer Rouge.

9. See Chapter 2 for a more detailed discussion of medical provisions and mine injuries.

10. The use of the Thai currency is, perhaps significantly, commonplace in western Cambodia.

11. As at the end of 1992. The figure, sadly, continues to grow.

12. A rate of one in 43, twice the district average, which as noted above is four times the national average.

13. Delayed primary closure of an amputated limb is the correct surgical procedure; it allows damaged and swollen tissue a chance to recover before the wound is closed, and results in a satisfactory amount of muscle and skin to cover the bone end and produce a stump that which can support a prostheseis. Unfortunately without an adequate infection-control regime in the surgical recovery wards such correct surgical procedures can result in increased infection risks. Landmine injuries produce a high incidence of infection problems: during such injuries, large amounts of soil and other particles are commonly blasted into the tissue, and unless these are all removed during surgery they are potential causes of infection. In Mongkol Berei Hospital, in neighbouring Banteay-Meanchay province, ICRC found that it was not good enough merely to take over surgical facilities in the hospital, only to watch an unacceptable number of patients fail to make satisfactory recoveries, or die, on the surgical wards where they were supposed to be recovering. In the end ICRC took the unusual step of taking over medical care on the surgical ward to provide a holistic package for mine victims and other surgical cases in their care. Such infection problems are common in Cambodian hospitals, especially in the military hospitals where resources are even sparser and patients even poorer; they result in some patients having several amputations as a result of one mine accident, sometimes leaving very small stumps on which it is almost impossible to fit a prosthesis.

14. Such interventions and close supervision of patients in the Cambodian-run provincial hospital had to be handled with tact. Not only were the NGOs working in Battambang hospital 'partners', mandated only to assist and advise the existing Cambodian health structure, but for World Vision, working in a rural district, involvements in the provincial hospital had to be carefully co-ordinated with other NGOs such as Medecin Sans Frontieres (MSF, France), whose 'turf' the provincial hospital was at this time.

15. The top of the hill harboured an infantry unit and a couple of heavy machine guns, anti-aircraft guns originally, trained on the Khmer Rouge zone of influence south of the river. The base, sides and approaches to the mountain have been heavily mined.

16. Attendance at 'meetings' was a common Khmer Rouge euphemism for execution.

17. It usually takes at least a year for a stump to stabilise, the muscles shrinking back to reach a new status quo.

18. For a fuller discussion of the complexities surrounding the provision of prostheses in a Cambodian environment see Chapter 6.

Chapter 5

1. The bilateral aid agency of the British government.
2. Benoit Denise, Director of Handicap International (HI), Phnom Penh 21 April 1993.
3. 'UNTAC Blasted by Top Minesweeper: Clearing Techniques Wasteful', *Nation*, 8 February 1993.
4. Col. Neal Bradley, speaking at a meeting at CMAC on Friday 7 May 1993.
5. Lt General Sanderson, interviewed by John Pilger for his programme *Return to Year Zero*, (Central TV, April 1993).
6. For a fuller discussion of the complexities surrounding the provision of prostheses in a Cambodian environment see Chapter 6.
7. Lt. Col. Mulliner, CO MCTU, Phnom Penh, 20 April 1993.
8. Handicap International briefing paper for the NGO Forum on Cambodia, 7 December 1992.
9. The under-employment of trained deminers was one of the most serious problems during the UN-sponsored demining initiative (1992–93), and will be addressed below.

10. Benoit Denise, as above.
11. Lt. Col. Mulliner, as above.
12. Lt. General Sanderson, as above.
13. Handicap International Statement 'Action on Landmines' for the NGO Forum on Cambodia, December 1992.
14. *Agreements on a Comprehensive Political Settlement of the Cambodia Conflict*, Paris, 23 October 1991. Annex 1: UNTAC Mandate: Section C 'Military Functions', Para 1.e., which reads, 'Assisting with clearing mines and undertaking training programmes in mine clearance and a mine awareness programme among the Cambodian people.'
15. The idea was first put to the SNC in April 1992.
16. *Financing of the United Nations Transitional Authority in Cambodia*, Report of the Secretary General, 7 May 1992, A/46/903, p. 55, para 106.
17. Cambodian Mine Action Centre, 27 November 1992, Phnom Penh.
18. MCTU Weekly Sitrep as at 060500Z MAR 93: Week 01 MAR till 06 MAR/MCTU09.SIT.
19. 'UNTAC Blasted by Top Minesweeper', *Nation*, 8 February 1993.
20. MCTU Weekly Sitrep as at 270500z FEB 93: Week 22 Feb till 27 Feb 93/Deploy08.SIT.
21. Major Vishw Ambhar Singh, Indian Engineers, CO of MCTU, Battambang, 5 March 1993.
22. They had been designed for use in the Gulf War, 1991: the war had finished before they were ready.
23. Focsaneanu, when interviewed (24 March 1993), was genuinely under the impression that the machines had been donated. His junior officer, Capt. Jim Vince, informed him, 'I saw a UN purchase order, sir.'
24. MCTU in Cambodia had also trialed a mechanical flail, the 'Mine Master', again the property of a private company. A detailed report was prepared by MCTU recommending changes to the machine that would be necessary if the UN were to consider purchasing and endorsing it. MCTU's commanding officer even met with company representatives and potential investors, actively persuading them that the machine was worth 'putting a bit of investment money into'. He said that if the adaptations were made, as per the report, he would be willing to conduct further trials – at the UN's expense. MCTU also admitted that if the D7s were adapted in ways recommended in the report they would consider retrialing them as well.
25. I write nominally non-communist because at the UNHCR-hosted inter-agency meeting held in Aranyaprathet (Thailand), October 1992, an NGO worker involved in implementing the repatriation process in these non-communist resistance areas reported the 'total breakdown of the non-communist administrative and police and military structures', their high officials almost ubiquitously non-resident – living the good life in Phnom Penh in expectation of electoral invincibility, while on the ground the parallel administrative, police and military components of the NADK (aka the Khmer Rouge) had the real power. The official cited several examples of the 'olive branch' approach of local Khmer Rouge officials among these nominally non-communist controlled populations. In September 1993 the newly constituted Cambodian Armed Forces (CAF) launched a major offensive against Khmer Rouge enclaves in these non-communist areas, driving them across the Thai border. They were (once again) given free access and allowed to transit through Thailand to rejoin Khmer Rouge units further to the south.
26. John Pilger, in his documentary *Return to Year Zero*, interviews a British serviceman who claims the Khmer Rouge specifically requested British deminers because they had been so impressed with the training they had given them in the past.
27. The Bangladeshis had lost a man in an assault on their positions in Angkor Chum the previous week, and had been engaged in a series of increasingly hostile actions with the Khmer Rouge. 'We didn't come here to fight,' said one of the Bangladeshi majors at the sector HQ, 'but to establish a peace'. Later in April the Khmer Rouge took over the town itself for a few hours and, true to form, sought out Vietnamese residents of Cambodia for execution.
28. The data that has been collated in a computerised system capable of producing minefield information in the form of a map overlay at the touch of a button, as referred to in Chapter 2.
29. By October 1993 CMAC was to have 40 demining teams, ten minefield marking teams, ten war-dog teams and five EOD teams. The demining teams were deployed in a still not ideal, but far more rational, distribution with some 16 teams allocated in Banteay-Meanchay province, 14 in Battambang (all in Rattanak Mondul), eight working out of Phnom Penh and two allocated to the Angkor Wat area in Siem Reap.
30. For example, the new Cambodian government was adamant about its refusal to allow foreign military personnel to operate on its soil, given its commitment to a policy of strictly non-aligned status and neutrality.
31. John Pilger, 'A Washing of Hands in Cambodia', *New Statesman and Society*, 29 October 1993.
32. Which also established a $100 million trust fund for demining worldwide.
33. Pilger, 'A Washing of Hands', p. 14.
34. Most notably the Canadian, Australian, New Zealand and Dutch governments.
35. Quoted in Shawcross, *Sideshow*.

Chapter 6

1. Estimates suggest that one in 236 Cambodians are amputees, a higher proportion than in other heavily mine-affected nations such as Angola, where the number of amputees *per se* is far higher.
2. Heinz Trebbin, ortho-prosthetist, ICRC Factory, Phnom Penh, 23 March 1993.
3. The MLSA was the ministry charged with responsibility for rehabilitation services, including prosthetics. Following the 1993 election, prosthetics passed to the control of the Ministry of Veteran's Affairs.
4. Dr Peter Carey, *Cambodia Trust Limb Project: An Overview 1989–93* (January 93). In the course of use such limbs often have to be replaced through wear and tear, or, in the case of adolescents, because new limbs have to be periodically replaced to allow for normal bodily growth.

5. Heinz Trebbin, ortho-prosthetist, ICRC Components Factory, Phnom Penh, March 1993.

6. Ibid.

7. As told to David Appleton, Field Director, Cambodia Trust, Phnom Penh, 1993.

8. While a prosthesis replaces a missing part of the body, an ortheses attempts to make up for a missing function. A pair of glasses are an orthotic device. Ortheses are required for many polio cases, for example. Heinz Trebbin of ICRC Phnom Penh noted that in every Third World country the numbers needing ortheses is usually greater than those requiring prostheses, and he expected this to be the case in Cambodia, despite its high incidence of amputee mine victims. To plan a prosthetic workshop without giving equal space to orthotics – given the considerable overlap of materials required, technology, etc – seemed illogical to Heinz, and yet donors seem consistently more keen to give for prosthetics than orthotics. Perhaps it is the visibility and immediacy of 'replacing a leg' that attracts them, or the traumatic way in which the injury occurred. Either way, Trebbin believed, agencies that are starting to meet the orthotics need (such as ICRC and the Cambodia Trust) should prioritise such activities and launch donor education programmes.

9. Throughout the 1980s and early 1990s this had been the Ministry of Labour and Social Affairs. After the elections in 1993 responsibility passed to the Ministry of Veterans' Affairs.

10. Based on estimates given in a paper, *Summary of Prosthetics Programming in Cambodia* (AFSC, December 1992).

11. *Barang*, 'foreigner' in Khmer.

12. Benoit Denise, Director of Handicap International, Phnom Penh, April 1993.

13. As noted in the Sdeng Phal case history in Chapter 4, children generally do not survive mine accidents due to the disproportionate impact of the injuries on their smaller bodies and their inability to cope with the extended lead times between the injury occurring and treatment being received in Cambodia's weak health system.

14. In other words employees of the Ministry of Social Action seconded to work with the agencies and receiving a 'top-up' salary from the agencies to complement the $ 8–10 a month official 'salary'. Nevertheless, some workshops have reported losing skilled personnel to the excessive salaries paid by the UN.

15. Peter Carey, *Cambodia Trust Newsletter*, 25 May 1993.

16. Becky Jordan, who now works with HI, interviewed in Battambang, 11 March 1993.

17. Hinduism prevailed in Cambodia before Buddhism but even as late as 1965 Brahiminist priests resided in the royal court in Phnom Penh.

18. Ven. Maha Ghosananda speaking in Wat Lanka, Phnom Penh, 22 April 1993.

19. Benoit Denise, HI Office, Phnom Penh, 21 April 1993.

20. Kevin Malone, Battambang, 30 April 1993.

21. In 1993 the members of the 'Rehabilitation Sector of the Cambodia Cooperation Committee' (a forum of NGOs working in Cambodia) presented to leading figures in UNTAC and the SNC a series of proposals for 'Promotion of the Rights of Disabled and Handicapped Cambodians,' including suggestions for a 'Disabled Bill of Rights' for the new constitution. To date (June 1993) they have had a disappointing response.

22. Several key hospital staff from Rattanak Mondul left to join the election staff on 20 times their Cambodian hospital wages.

23. Tony Banbury, UNTAC Human Rights Officer for Battambang to Becky Jordan, HI. As told to the author by Jordan in Battambang, 11 March 1993.

24. In fact one of the terms of admission to the school is the designation of family members who will take on the duties of the handicapped person while they are attending the school.

25. Opinion of Cambodian Red Cross official in informal conversation with the author.

26. Conversations with patients waiting to be measured for first-time prostheses in Battambang revealed that for the men the primary motivation in seeking an artificial leg was to improve their chances of employment. Secondary to this was the hope that the increased level of 'wholeness' about their appearance would help them to be accepted and free them from being seen as 'just another amputee'. Unfortunately, improved personal mobility does not, of itself, equate with improved job opportunities, as the beggars testify.

27. Discussions with Kevin Malone in Battambang (30 April 1993) revealed that the hostel had indeed been sold, and about half of the amputees given land. The remainder have built themselves small shacks next to the building, which remains bolted, awaiting its new private-sector owners.

28. Malone and others note that while state pensions paid by the SOC regime to the war wounded, and those disabled as a result of injuries sustained during periods of forced labour (K5), are small and sometimes irregular; the SOC's treatment of such individuals is far better than the KPNLF administration of Site 2 which left its amputees 'to rot', according to Malone.

Chapter 7

1. It should be noted that even where maps and records existed they were not made available to UN-sponsored mine clearance teams by either the Soviets or the, then, Afghan government following the Soviet withdrawal.

2. In fact many of the PFM-1s *were* live – the six-month lifespan was not reliable and the mine often remained active for two years or more.

3. The VP12 and VP13 initiators employed printed circuitry and remote sensors to Fire OZM bounding mines and MON series directional mines when a 'suitable' target came within range. The devices were designed to analyse target movement and not respond to grazing animals.

4. *Report of the Mines Survey of Afghanisan* (Mines Advisory Group, Peshawar, February 1991).

5. There are certainly no credible arguments to counter the obvious concerns regarding the use of humanitarian aid money to fund arms manufactures:

    1. that profits from such funding increase the company's ability to produce weapons- specifically, in this case, landmines

2. that the involvement of mine manufactures in such programmes is a vital asset to their research and development, and increases their capacity to produce more 'effective' mines.

6. David Sogge, *Sustainable Peace - Angola's Recovery* (Southern African Research and Documentation Centre, Harare, 1992, ISBN 0–7974–1113–5). This source recorded direct attacks (5,899), ambush (4,683) and multiple ambush (4,708) as the next most common reason for war deaths.

7. 'Operation Reindeer' was mounted on Kassinga by more than 700 soldiers and reportedly left nearly 1,500 dead and wounded, mostly civilians.

8. Landmines in Angola (Human Rights Watch, New York, January 1993, ISBN 1–56432–091–X).

9. This was actually an extreme case of understatement – the social needs of victims were simply not dealt with at all.

10. The elections were held under UN supervision on 29 and 30 September 1992. MPLA, under Jose Eduardo dos Santos, won 129 seats in the National Assembly, UNITA, under Jonas Savimbi, won only 70. In the Presidential elections dos Santos polled 49.6 per cent against Savimbi's 40.1 per cent which, since there was no outright majority, should have led to a run-off between dos Santos and Savimbi. This was never held, Savimbi declared the election to have been rigged and UNITA forces withdrew from the new united army leading to a resurgence of the civil war. (It is probable that Savimbi would not have taken such a step if the US had immediately recognised the election result - their failure to do so and their ambiguous stance prior to the elections undoubtedly convinced Savimbi that the US would continue to support and arm UNITA in a renewed civil war.)

11. It is probable that the mine in this incident was a US-manufactured M18A1 Claymore or a derivative of that mine, probably South African. The use of such mines as randomly deployed trip wire devices rather than ambush weapons (normally removed if the ambush is not 'sprung') appears to be peculiar to Southern Africa and Central America.

12. Source: Mines Advisory Group Field Assessment.

Chapter 8

1. This chapter should be read in conjunction with Appendix 3.

2. It will be argued here that in several parts of Cambodia, Rattanak Mondul included, specific provisions of international law have been ignored and broken.

3. Adam Roberts, Montague Burton Professor of International Relations and joint editor of *Documents on the Laws of War* (Oxford: Clarendon Press, 1989) p. 14.

4. See, for example, the comments of both the New Zealand and Federal Republic of Germany delegates during the negotiations of Protocol II Additional to the Geneva Conventions of 1949 during the Diplomatic Conference 1974–77 (CDDH/I/SR.23 at paras 19 and 30 respectively). The former stated that '... realism demanded certain steps by States involved in the law making process.

One essential was the protection of of the individual, a matter of paramount importance.'

5. Kende, 'Twenty Five Years of Local Wars', *Journal of Peace Research*, 5, 1971.

6. This avoids the need to ascertain whether or not war has been declared.

7. Judith Gardam, *Non-Combatant Immunity as a Norm of International Humanitarian Law,* (Martinus Nijhoff, 1993), pp. 6–7.

8. 'The World's Wars', *The Economist*, March 1988.

9. Customary humanitarian principles in armed conflicts were observed by the Greeks and the Romans, many of which have survived to this day to inspire and shape the codification of international humanitarian law in various bilateral and multilateral treaties.

10. Roberts, *Documents*, p. 2.

11. No disrespect is intended to the valuable efforts of the 'peace movement', but the point needs to be made that the desire to see an improvement in the effectiveness of regulation of modern armed conflicts is not a struggle of aspirational nature but of reaffirmation of ancient principles which have been constituted in the attempt to bring a measure of civilisation and decency to the public relations of armed parties and/or states.

12. Roberts, *Documents*, p. 14.

13. Professor Adam Roberts, letter to author, 6 September 1993.

14. Definition offered to the author during a briefing in Phnom Penh by Doris Pfister, ICRC Delegate, March 1993.

15. Gardam referring to the ICJ's judgment in the *Nicaragua Case; Non-Combatant Immunity*, p. 166.

16. The virtually unprecedented multilateral actions of the international community in forming an entirely new UN humanitarian aid agency (the United Nations Border Relief Organisation – UNBRO) to channel aid to the domestic populations of the resistance factions who collectively represented Cambodian sovereignty throughout the majority of the 1980s, indicates a tacit acceptance in practice of the way these sovereign representatives themselves viewed the struggle. Furthermore, the bilateral and oftentimes covert, assistance of the Thais, the Chinese, the Americans and even the British also indicates an acceptance of the fundamental legitimacy of the CGDK and their international struggle against Vietnam and the cold war significance and international ramifications of the Vietnamese invasion and occupation of Cambodia.

17. Such statements continued to be issued, with increasing ferocity, by the non-participating Khmer Rouge throughout the UN-sponsored peace process 1991–93.

18. Frits Kalshoven, 'Applicability of Customary International Law in Non-International Armed Conflicts', in A. Cassese (ed.), *Current Problems of International Law* (Milan: Dott. A. Giuffre, 1975).

19. Gardam, *Non Combatant Immunity*, p. 175.

20. Neither Cambodia nor Vietnam have ratified it.

21. Roberts, p. 388.

22. Ibid, p. 85.

23. See the ruling of the ICJ in the *Nicaragua Case* (1986) that the mere existence of 'contrari-state practice' does not invalidate customary norms *per se*.

24. Roberts, *Documents*, p. 4.
25. Francoise Hampson, Department of Law and Centre for Human Rights, University of Essex, in a paper 'Anti-Personnel Mines and the Law: The Legal Background', presented originally to the NGO Conference on Anti-Personnel Mines, London, 24–26 May 1993.
26. C. Greenwood, 'Customary Law Status of the 1977 Geneva Protocols', in Delissen and Tanja (eds.), *Humanitarian Law of Armed Conflict: Challenges Ahead*, (Martinus Nijhoff, 1991, 93.), p. 108.
27. Ibid, p. 109.
28. *The Cowards' War*, pp. 40–42, notes:

    Khmer Rouge mine strategy tends to mirror Chinese doctrine, while the strategy of the KPNLF and ANS – the two non-communist resistance forces – reflects British special forces training … our informants said that the overall objective of the course was to produce effective field commanders who could operate independently in enemy territory, with emphasis on the destruction of military and civilian infrastructure … Our delegation obtained a Chinese military manual used in the training of both KPNLF and Khmer Rouge fighters. The manual emphasises the use of improvised booby- traps, often employing 'over-kill' quantities of explosives for maximum physical and anti-morale effect.

29. Article 1 reads: 'The High Contracting Parties undertake to respect and to ensure respect for the present Convention *in all circumstances* '. Article 3 (1). reads: 'Persons taking no active part in the hostilities … *shall in all circumstances be treated humanely* …' [emphasis added].
30. Roberts, *Documents*, PP85/6 and personal comments to the author, 1 July 1993.
31. Greenwood, *the 1977 Geneva Protocols*, p. 95.
32. McGrath, 'The Reality of the Present Use of Mines By Military Forces' (April 1993, reproduced here as Appendix 3).
33. Many would argue that their 'unofficial purpose' is to wound and injure with a view to creating a profoundly disabled population, and hence to demoralise, impoverish and terrorise whole populations regardless of combatant or non-combatant status in a strategy which amounts to a declaration of total war.
34. Some lobbyists are opposed to self-neutralisation devices, arguing that even though the mines in a field may have become benign, unless they self-destruct there is no knowing that this essential deactivation has taken place. Therefore the field would have to be demined – as if it were still a live field – for civilians to use it again with any confidence.
35. Also found in Article 51 (4) (b) of Protocol I.
36. 1. To protect military bases and key installations. 2. To channel or divert the enemy forces. 3. To deny routes and strategic positions to the enemy – simple 'area denial' tasks.
37. See, for example, the comments of Lt. Col. Mulliner cited in Chapter 5. Other deminers strongly expressed the opinion that mines should not be supplied without the manufacturers being obliged to supply fencing, signs and other materials necessary for those deploying them to distinguish mined land from clear areas.
38. *The Cowards' War*, p. 42. On 27 June 1991 in a written parliamentary answer the Armed Forces Minister, Archie Hamilton, admitted that British forces 'provided training to the armed forces of the Cambodian non-communist resistance from 1983 to 1989'.
39. ICRC, *Mines: A Perverse Use of Technology*, (ICRC) p. 14.
40. Greenwood, *The 1977 Geneva Protocols*, p. 105.
41. Roberts, *Documents*, p. 377.
42. Ibid, p. 378.
43. Greenwood, *The 1977 Geneva Protocols*, p. 109.
44. Frits Kalshoven, *Constraints on the Waging of War*, (ICRC and Martinus Nijhoff, 1987), p. 94.
45. Greenwood, *The 1977 Geneva Protocols*, p. 111.
46. Kalshoven, *Constraints*, pp. 29–30.
47. David Appleton, then Field Director of the Cambodia Trust.
48. Greenwood, *The 1977 Geneva Protocols*, p. 110.
49. M. Bothe, K. Partsch and W. Solf *New Rules for Victims of Armed Conflicts: Commentary on the two 1977 Protocols Additional to the Geneva Convention of 1949* (Geneva, 1982), p. 339.
50. Gardam, *Non Combatant Immunity*, pp. 176–77.
51. Ibid, pp. 178–79.
52. Ibid, p. 179.
53. Kalshoven quoted from, 'A Tentative Appraisal of the Old and New Humanitarian Law of Armed Conflict', in Cassesse (ed.), *The New Humanitarian Law of Armed Conflict* (Naples: Editori Scientifica, 1979), p. 492.
54. Gardam, *Non-Combatant Immunity*, p. 182.
55. Louise Doswald-Beck, Legal Advisor to the ICRC, speaking at a seminar in London (17 February 1993).
56. Statement issued by the ICRC for the UN General Assembly First Committee reviewing the 1981 Weapons Convention (27 October 1992).
57. *Indiscriminate Weapons – Landmines* (the Medical Educational Trust – Background Papers no.12, February 1993, revised).
58. Rae McGrath, Mines Advisory Group, 'Undeclared War', (a lecture given in Brussels, 2 November 1992).
59. Due to their 'non-detectability' once embedded in human flesh, plastic mines are also theoretically proscribed under Protocol I (Protocol on Non-Detectable Fragments) additional to the 1981 Weapons Convention.
60. Interesting in the light of Professor Roberts' comments cited at the beginning of this chapter about the norms of the international law of armed conflict arising from an ancient and customary tradition of soldiers and statesmen themselves to regulate armed conflict, such that the laws can be seen as a direct outgrowth of the international system rather than as an imposition upon it.

Appendix 3

1. Alan Moorehead, *Tom Pollock* (London: Bodley Head, 1990).
2. Dummy minefields are areas marked with mine warning signs but which do not actually contain mines. The purpose is to achieve land denial without actually laying mines.

3. It should be noted that acceptance of this kind does not carry with it any guarantee of popular support. The Iraqi Army, for instance, was reviled by a large part of the population and had a high percentage of unwilling conscripts, nonetheless it was treated by the coalition force as a *real* army and strategy was designed accordingly.

4. 'Deep strike' and similar terms are not necessarily accept military terms but are employed by the author for their clarity of meaning to non-military readers.

5. 'Remote' as distinct from manually laid.

6. Karez – stone-lined underwater irrigation tunnels which tap the water table and provide a complex supply of irrigation and drinking water in many areas of Afghanistan.

7. Mines lifted by Mines Advisory Group teams and other organisations in Iraq, Cambodia, Afghanistan, Kuwait and other countries bear testimony to the fact that few military customers pay for the detection insert option.

Index